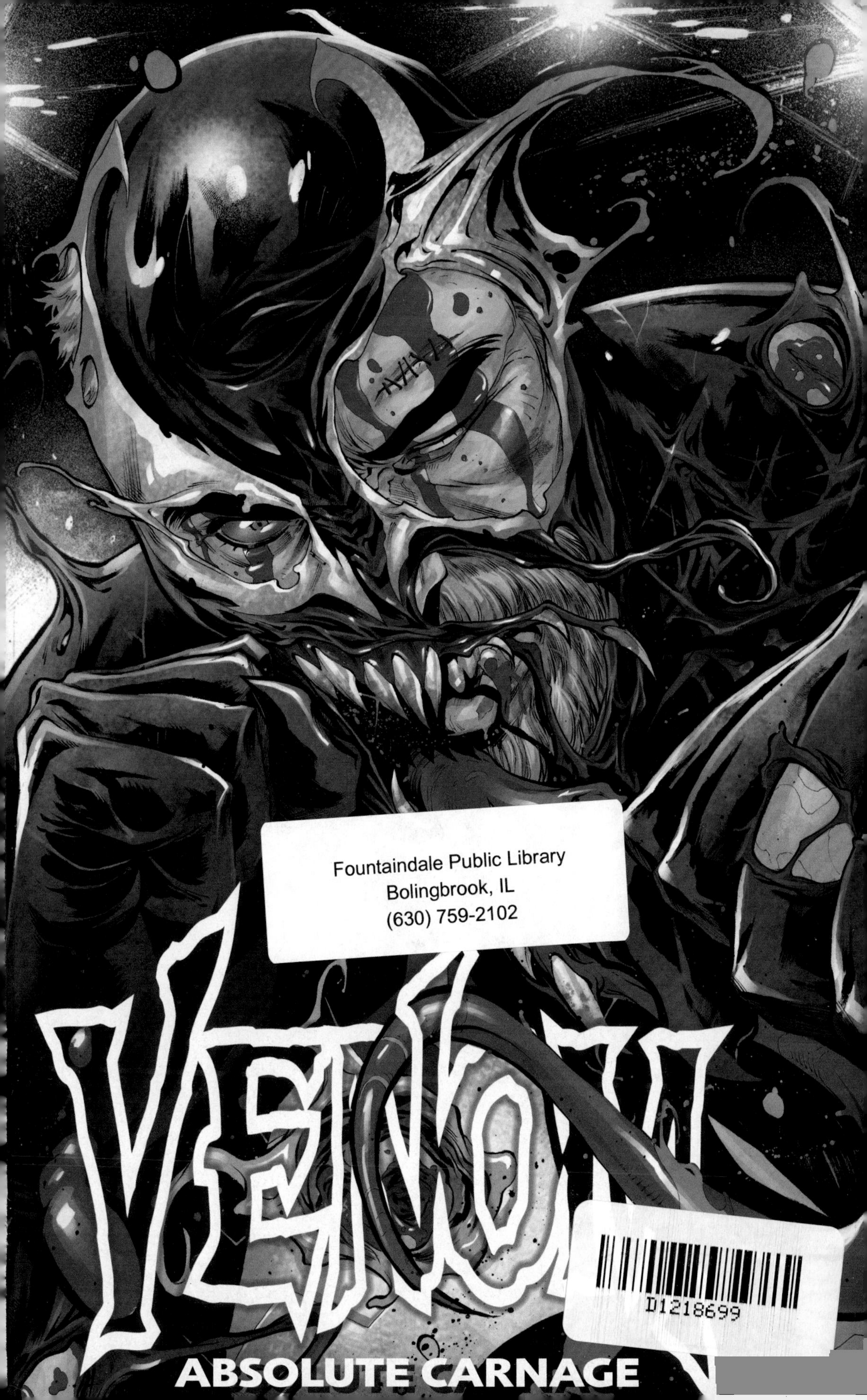
VENOM
ABSOLUTE CARNAGE

VENOM BY DONNY CATES VOL. 3: ABSOLUTE CARNAGE. Contains material originally published in magazine form as VENOM (2018) #16-20. First printing 2019. ISBN 978-1-302-91997-9. Published by MARVEL WORLDWIDE, INC., a subsidiary of MARVEL ENTERTAINMENT, LLC. OFFICE OF PUBLICATION: 1290 Avenue of the Americas, New York, NY 10104. © 2019 MARVEL No similarity between any of the names, characters, persons, and/or institutions in this magazine with those of any living or dead person or institution is intended, and any such similarity which may exist is purely coincidental. **Printed in Canada.** KEVIN FEIGE, Chief Creative Officer; DAN BUCKLEY, President, Marvel Entertainment; JOHN NEE, Publisher; JOE QUESADA, EVP & Creative Director; TOM BREVOORT, SVP of Publishing; DAVID BOGART, Associate Publisher & SVP of Talent Affairs; Publishing & Partnership; DAVID GABRIEL, VP of Print & Digital Publishing; JEFF YOUNGQUIST, VP of Production & Special Projects; DAN CARR, Executive Director of Publishing Technology; ALEX MORALES, Director of Publishing Operations; DAN EDINGTON, Managing Editor; SUSAN CRESPI, Production Manager; STAN LEE, Chairman Emeritus. For information regarding advertising in Marvel Comics or on Marvel.com, please contact Vit DeBellis, Custom Solutions & Integrated Advertising Manager, at vdebellis@marvel.com. For Marvel subscription inquiries, please call 888-511-5480. **Manufactured between 12/13/2019 and 1/14/2020 by SOLISCO PRINTERS, SCOTT, QC, CANADA.**

DISGRACED REPORTER EDDIE BROCK STUMBLED UPON AN AGGRESSIVE ALIEN ORGANISM, CALLED A SYMBIOTE, DURING ONE OF THE LOWEST POINTS OF HIS LIFE. THE TWO WERE JOINED AND USED THEIR COMBINED LUST FOR VIOLENCE TO MAKE THEIR CITY SAFER. BUT AFTER RECENTLY BEING SEPARATED AGAIN, BROCK HAS BEEN UNABLE TO RESIST USING BRUTALITY TO SOLVE HIS PROBLEMS. AS DIFFICULT AS IT MAY BE TO ADMIT, EVEN WITHOUT THE SYMBIOTE, EDDIE BROCK IS...

VENOM

ABSOLUTE CARNAGE

WRITER

DONNY CATES

JUAN GEDEON (#16)
& IBAN COELLO (#17-20)
WITH **ZÉ CARLOS** (#20)

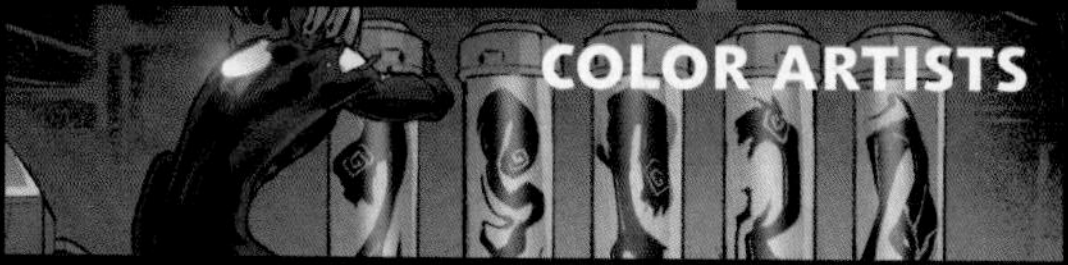

ARTISTS

COLOR ARTISTS

JESUS ABURTOV (#16)
RAIN BEREDO (#17-20)

VC's CLAYTON COWLES

JOSHUA **CASSARA** & RAIN **BEREDO** (#16);
KYLE **HOTZ** & DAN **BROWN** (#17-20)

LETTERER

COVER ARTISTS

ASSISTANT EDITOR

EDITOR

EXECUTIVE EDITOR

DANNY KHAZEM
DEVIN LEWIS
NICK LOWE

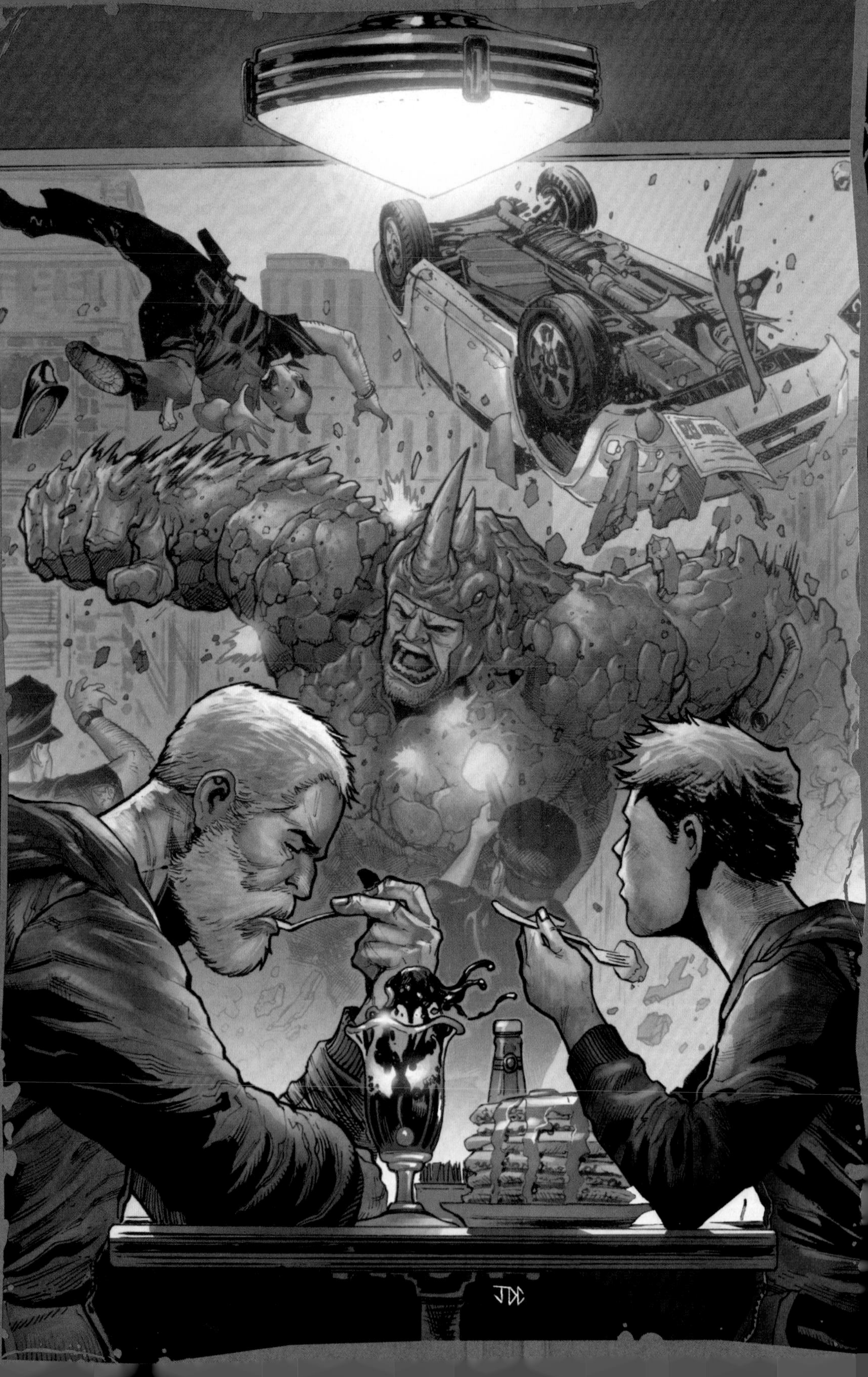

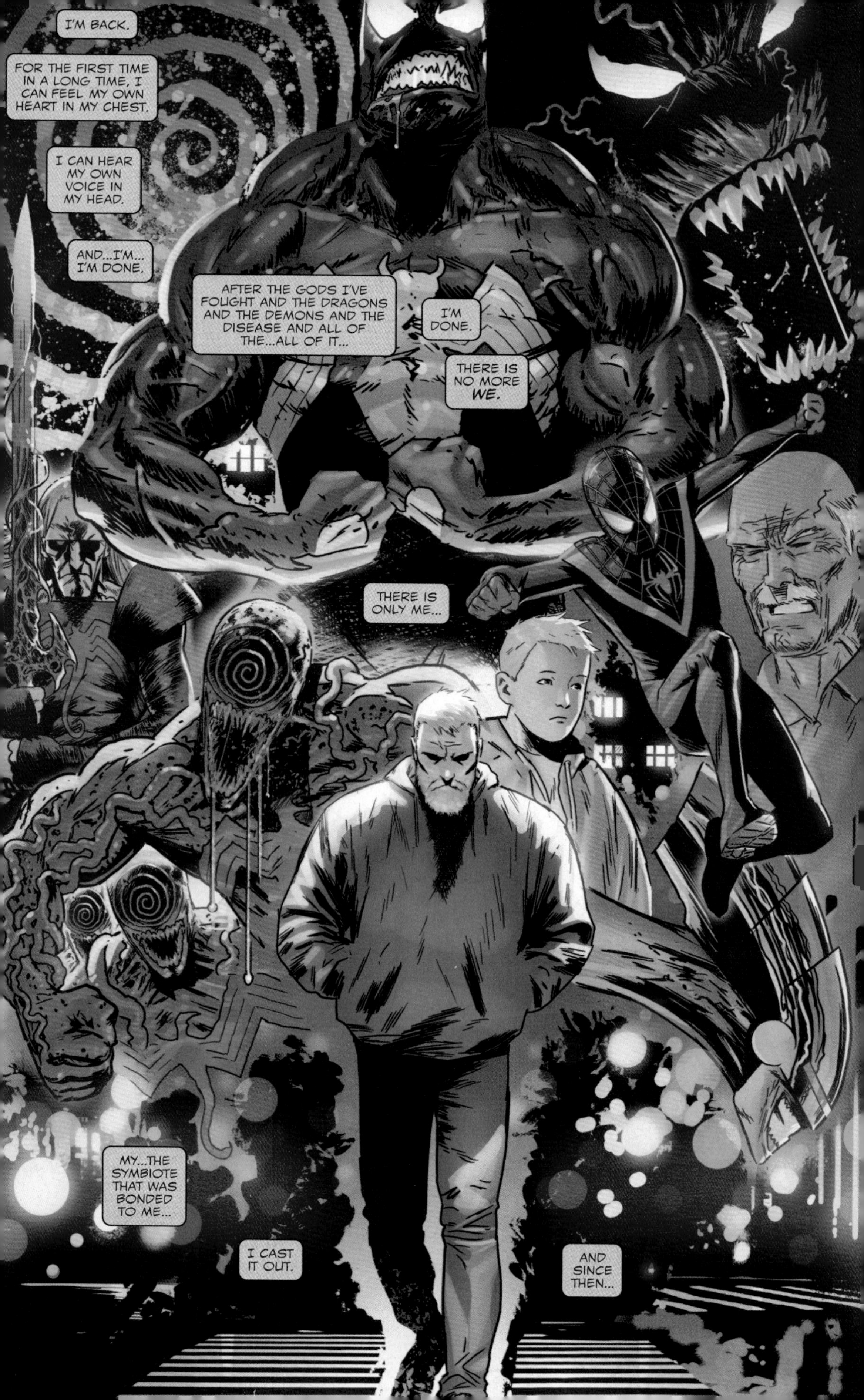
I'M BACK.
FOR THE FIRST TIME IN A LONG TIME, I CAN FEEL MY OWN HEART IN MY CHEST.
I CAN HEAR MY OWN VOICE IN MY HEAD.
AND...I'M... I'M DONE.
AFTER THE GODS I'VE FOUGHT AND THE DRAGONS AND THE DEMONS AND THE DISEASE AND ALL OF THE...ALL OF IT...
I'M DONE.
THERE IS NO MORE WE.
THERE IS ONLY ME...
MY...THE SYMBIOTE THAT WAS BONDED TO ME...
I CAST IT OUT.
AND SINCE THEN...

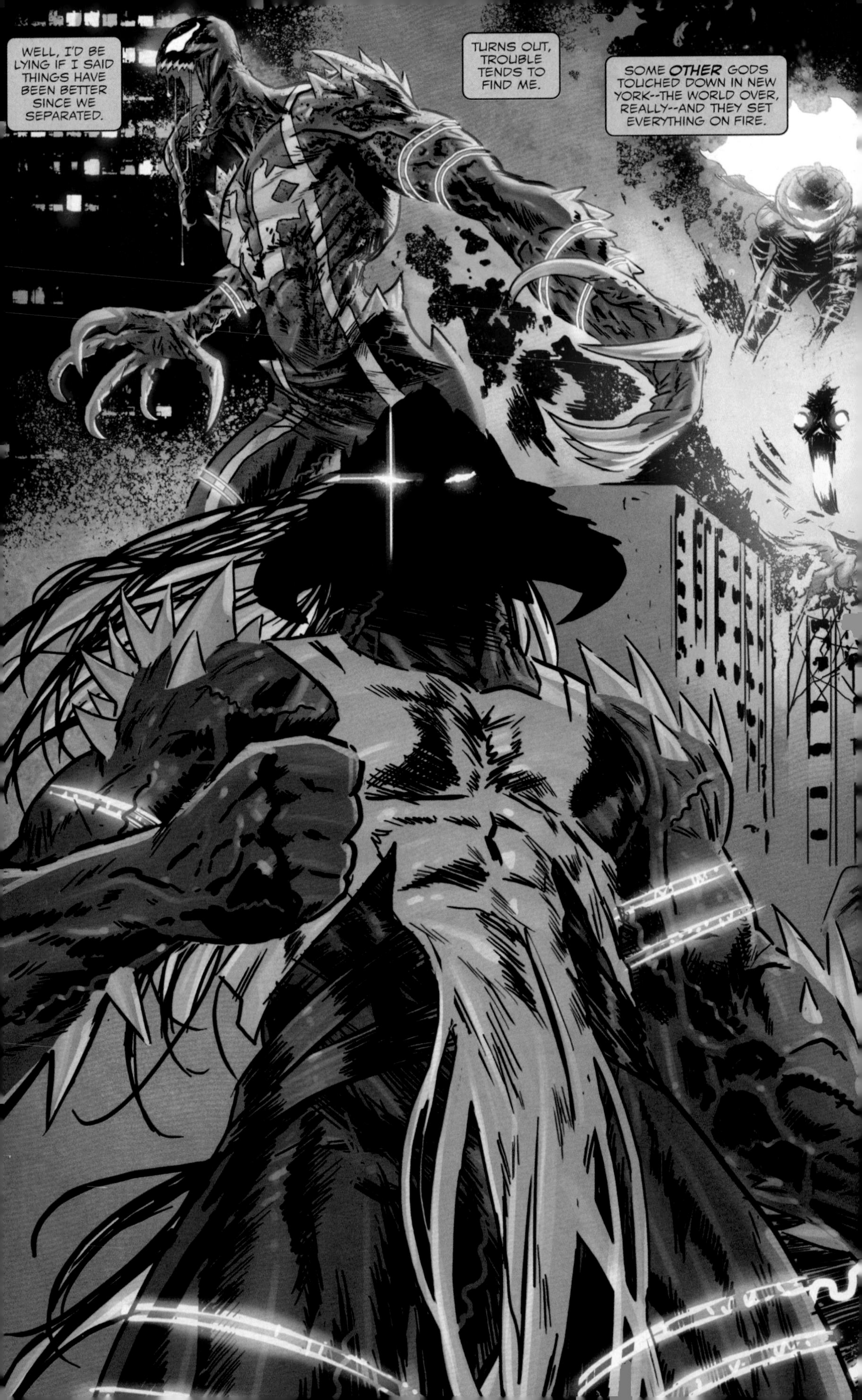
WELL, I'D BE LYING IF I SAID THINGS HAVE BEEN BETTER SINCE WE SEPARATED.
TURNS OUT, TROUBLE TENDS TO FIND ME.
SOME OTHER GODS TOUCHED DOWN IN NEW YORK--THE WORLD OVER, REALLY--AND THEY SET EVERYTHING ON FIRE.

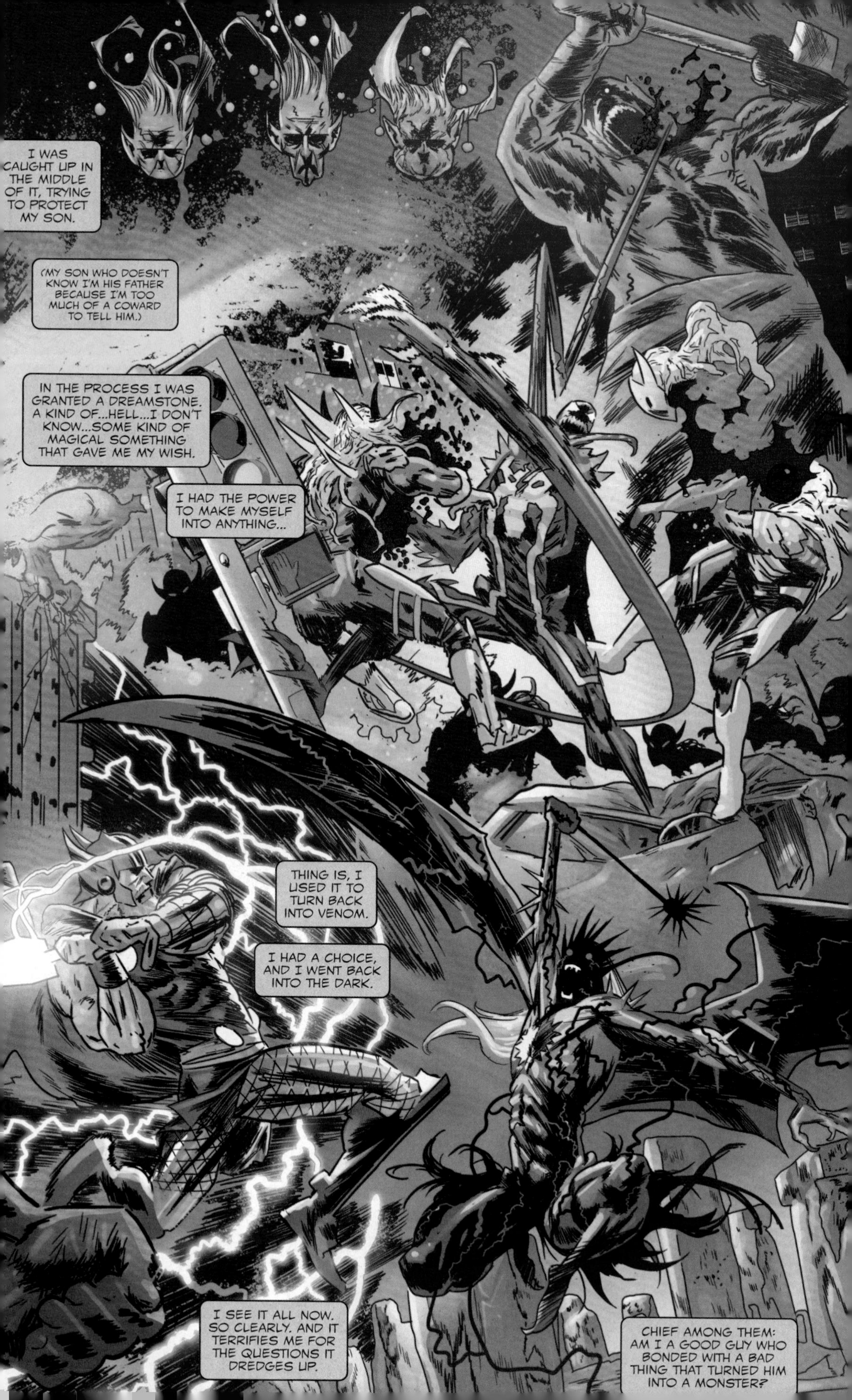
I WAS CAUGHT UP IN THE MIDDLE OF IT, TRYING TO PROTECT MY SON.
(MY SON WHO DOESN'T KNOW I'M HIS FATHER BECAUSE I'M TOO MUCH OF A COWARD TO TELL HIM.)
IN THE PROCESS I WAS GRANTED A DREAMSTONE. A KIND OF...HELL...I DON'T KNOW...SOME KIND OF MAGICAL SOMETHING THAT GAVE ME MY WISH.
I HAD THE POWER TO MAKE MYSELF INTO ANYTHING...
THING IS, I USED IT TO TURN BACK INTO VENOM.
I HAD A CHOICE, AND I WENT BACK INTO THE DARK.
I SEE IT ALL NOW. SO CLEARLY. AND IT TERRIFIES ME FOR THE QUESTIONS IT DREDGES UP.
CHIEF AMONG THEM: AM I A GOOD GUY WHO BONDED WITH A BAD THING THAT TURNED HIM INTO A MONSTER?

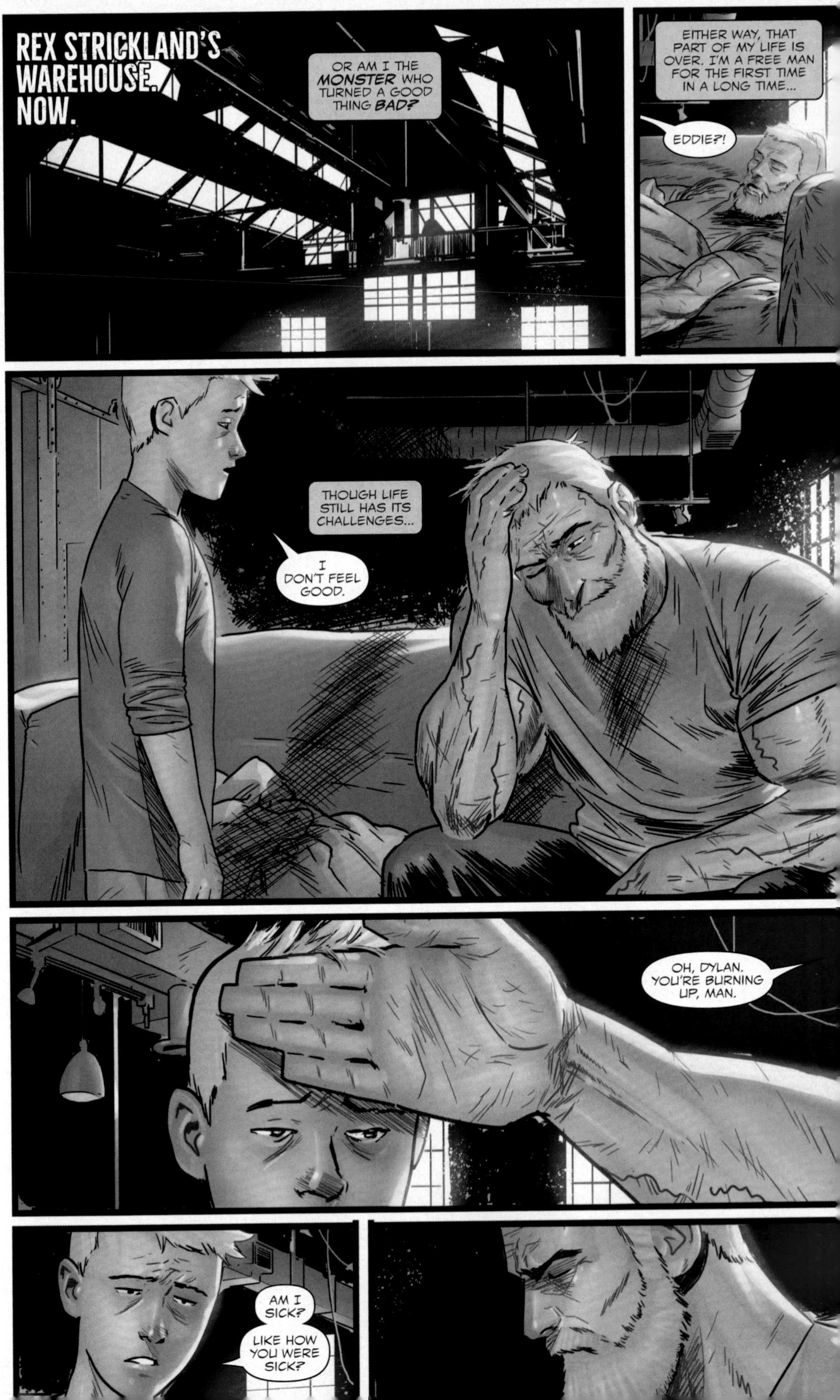
REX STRICKLAND'S WAREHOUSE. NOW.
OR AM I THE MONSTER WHO TURNED A GOOD THING BAD?
EITHER WAY, THAT PART OF MY LIFE IS OVER. I'M A FREE MAN FOR THE FIRST TIME IN A LONG TIME...
EDDIE?!
THOUGH LIFE STILL HAS ITS CHALLENGES...
I DON'T FEEL GOOD.
OH, DYLAN. YOU'RE BURNING UP, MAN.
AM I SICK?
LIKE HOW YOU WERE SICK?

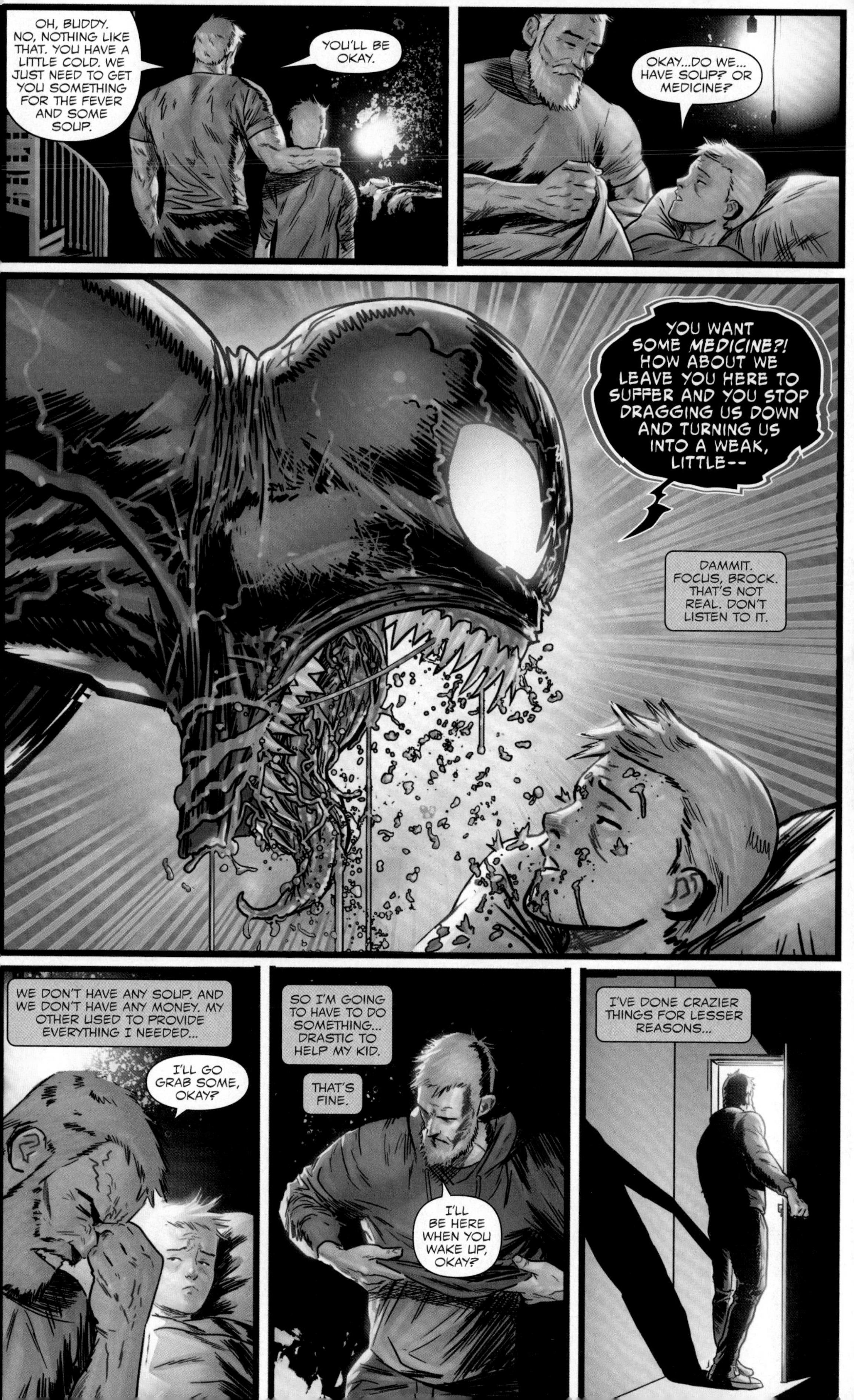
OH, BUDDY. NO, NOTHING LIKE THAT. YOU HAVE A LITTLE COLD. WE JUST NEED TO GET YOU SOMETHING FOR THE FEVER AND SOME SOUP.
YOU'LL BE OKAY.
OKAY...DO WE... HAVE SOUP? OR MEDICINE?
YOU WANT SOME MEDICINE?! HOW ABOUT WE LEAVE YOU HERE TO SUFFER AND YOU STOP DRAGGING US DOWN AND TURNING US INTO A WEAK, LITTLE--
DAMMIT. FOCUS, BROCK. THAT'S NOT REAL. DON'T LISTEN TO IT.
WE DON'T HAVE ANY SOUP. AND WE DON'T HAVE ANY MONEY. MY OTHER USED TO PROVIDE EVERYTHING I NEEDED...
I'LL GO GRAB SOME, OKAY?
SO I'M GOING TO HAVE TO DO SOMETHING... DRASTIC TO HELP MY KID.
THAT'S FINE.
I'LL BE HERE WHEN YOU WAKE UP, OKAY?
I'VE DONE CRAZIER THINGS FOR LESSER REASONS...

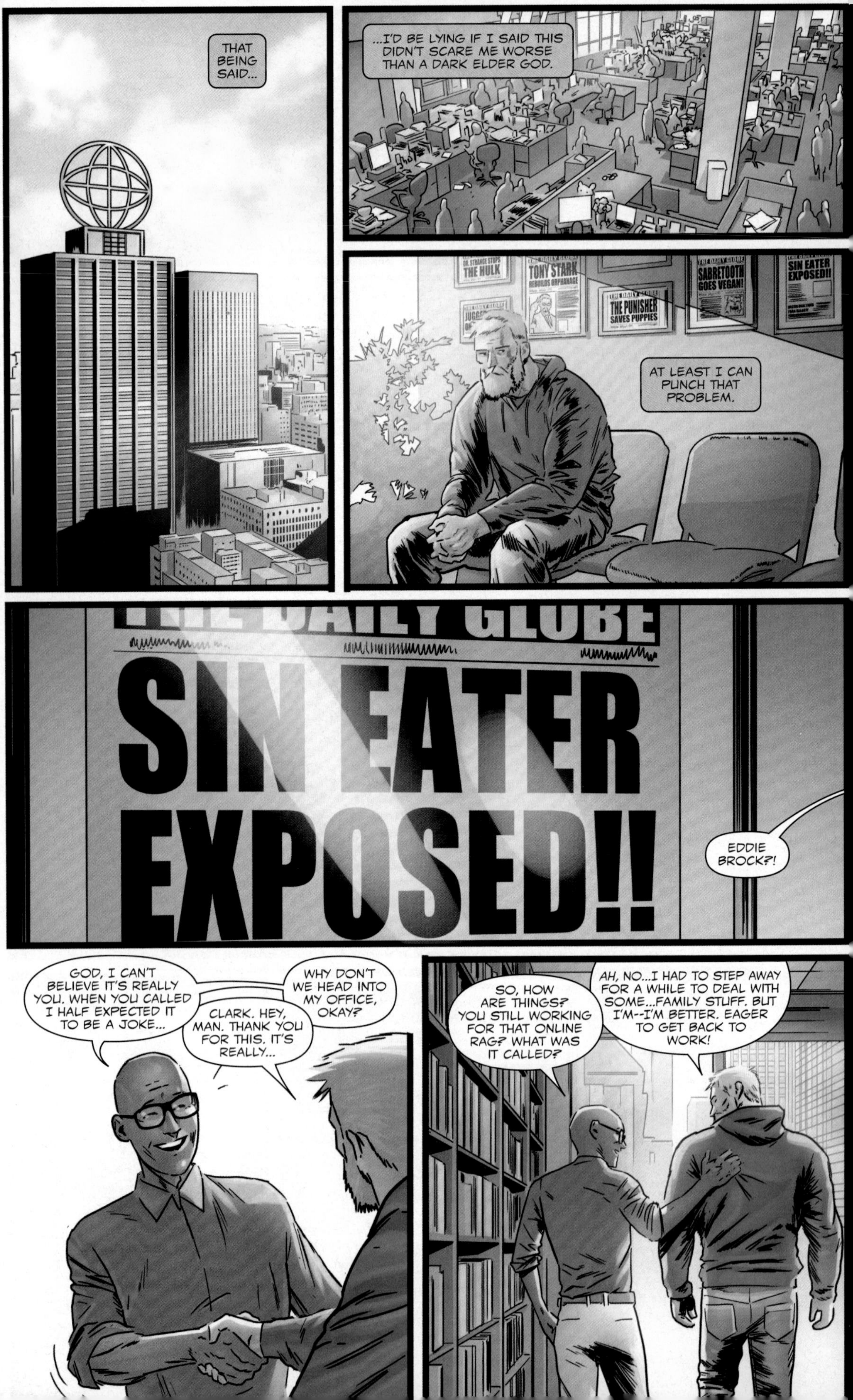
THAT BEING SAID...
...I'D BE LYING IF I SAID THIS DIDN'T SCARE ME WORSE THAN A DARK ELDER GOD.
DR. STRANGE STOPS THE HULK
TONY STARK REBUILDS ORPHANAGE
THE PUNISHER SAVES PUPPIES
SABRETOOTH GOES VEGAN!
SIN EATER EXPOSED!!
AT LEAST I CAN PUNCH THAT PROBLEM.
SIN EATER EXPOSED!!
EDDIE BROCK?!
GOD, I CAN'T BELIEVE IT'S REALLY YOU. WHEN YOU CALLED I HALF EXPECTED IT TO BE A JOKE...
CLARK. HEY, MAN. THANK YOU FOR THIS. IT'S REALLY...
WHY DON'T WE HEAD INTO MY OFFICE, OKAY?
SO, HOW ARE THINGS? YOU STILL WORKING FOR THAT ONLINE RAG? WHAT WAS IT CALLED?
AH, NO...I HAD TO STEP AWAY FOR A WHILE TO DEAL WITH SOME...FAMILY STUFF. BUT I'M--I'M BETTER. EAGER TO GET BACK TO WORK!

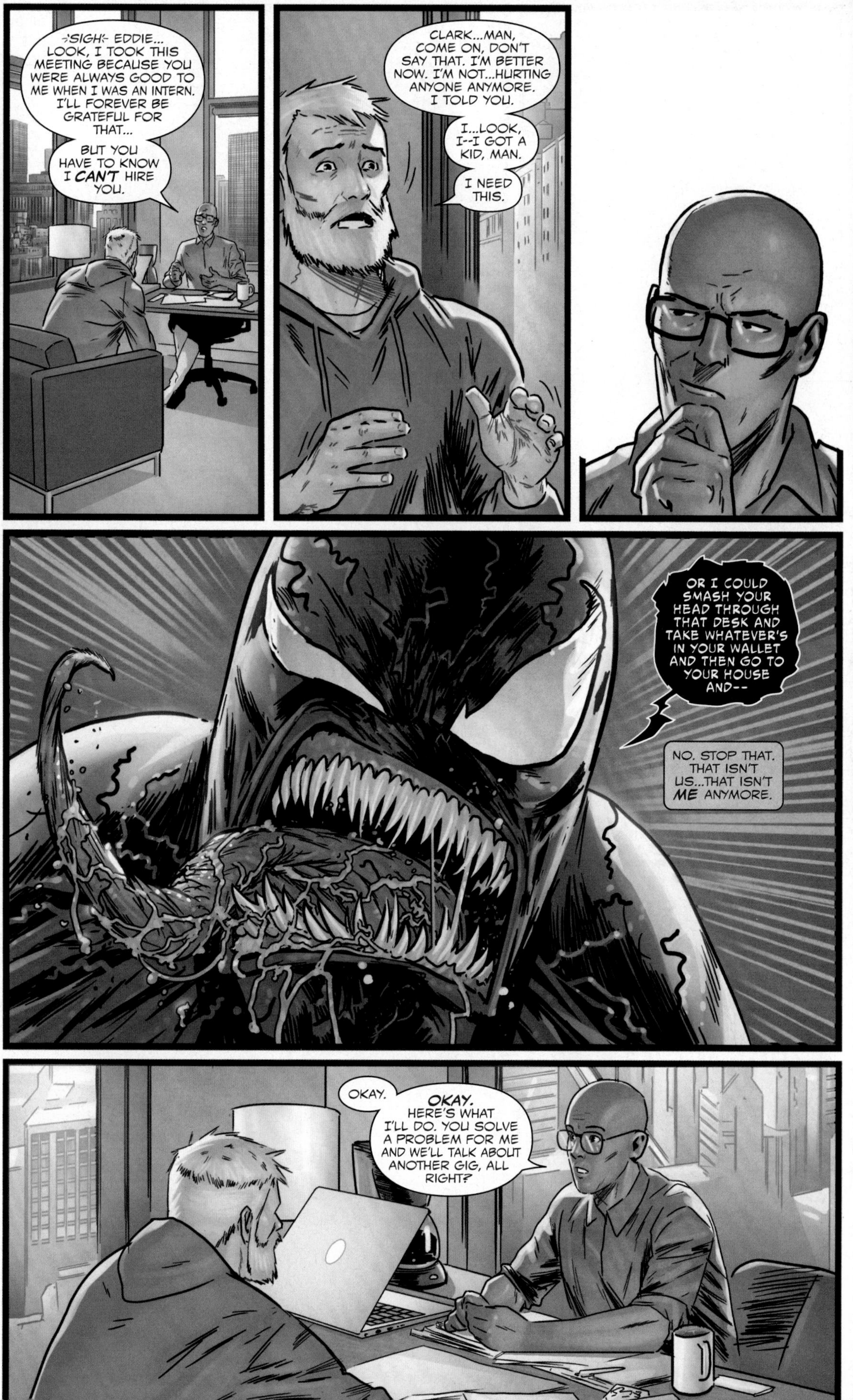

SIGH EDDIE... LOOK, I TOOK THIS MEETING BECAUSE YOU WERE ALWAYS GOOD TO ME WHEN I WAS AN INTERN. I'LL FOREVER BE GRATEFUL FOR THAT...
BUT YOU HAVE TO KNOW I CAN'T HIRE YOU.
CLARK...MAN, COME ON, DON'T SAY THAT. I'M BETTER NOW. I'M NOT...HURTING ANYONE ANYMORE. I TOLD YOU.
I...LOOK, I--I GOT A KID, MAN.
I NEED THIS.
OR I COULD SMASH YOUR HEAD THROUGH THAT DESK AND TAKE WHATEVER'S IN YOUR WALLET AND THEN GO TO YOUR HOUSE AND--
NO. STOP THAT. THAT ISN'T US...THAT ISN'T ME ANYMORE.
OKAY.
OKAY. HERE'S WHAT I'LL DO. YOU SOLVE A PROBLEM FOR ME AND WE'LL TALK ABOUT ANOTHER GIG, ALL RIGHT?

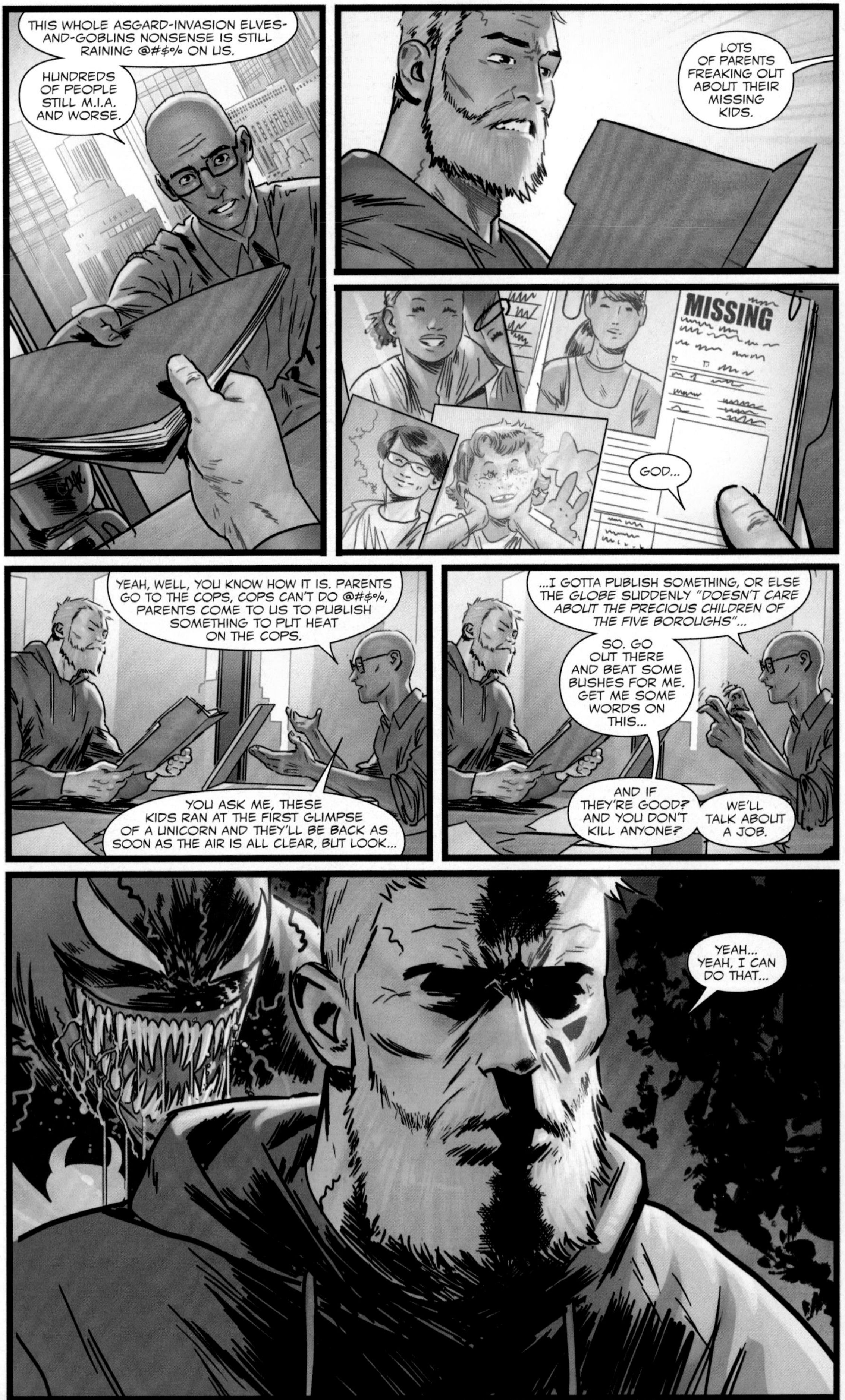
THIS WHOLE ASGARD-INVASION ELVES-AND-GOBLINS NONSENSE IS STILL RAINING @#$% ON US.
HUNDREDS OF PEOPLE STILL M.I.A. AND WORSE.
LOTS OF PARENTS FREAKING OUT ABOUT THEIR MISSING KIDS.
MISSING
GOD...
YEAH, WELL, YOU KNOW HOW IT IS. PARENTS GO TO THE COPS, COPS CAN'T DO @#$%, PARENTS COME TO US TO PUBLISH SOMETHING TO PUT HEAT ON THE COPS.
YOU ASK ME, THESE KIDS RAN AT THE FIRST GLIMPSE OF A UNICORN AND THEY'LL BE BACK AS SOON AS THE AIR IS ALL CLEAR, BUT LOOK...
...I GOTTA PUBLISH SOMETHING, OR ELSE THE GLOBE SUDDENLY "DOESN'T CARE ABOUT THE PRECIOUS CHILDREN OF THE FIVE BOROUGHS"...
SO. GO OUT THERE AND BEAT SOME BUSHES FOR ME. GET ME SOME WORDS ON THIS...
AND IF THEY'RE GOOD? AND YOU DON'T KILL ANYONE?
WE'LL TALK ABOUT A JOB.
YEAH... YEAH, I CAN DO THAT...

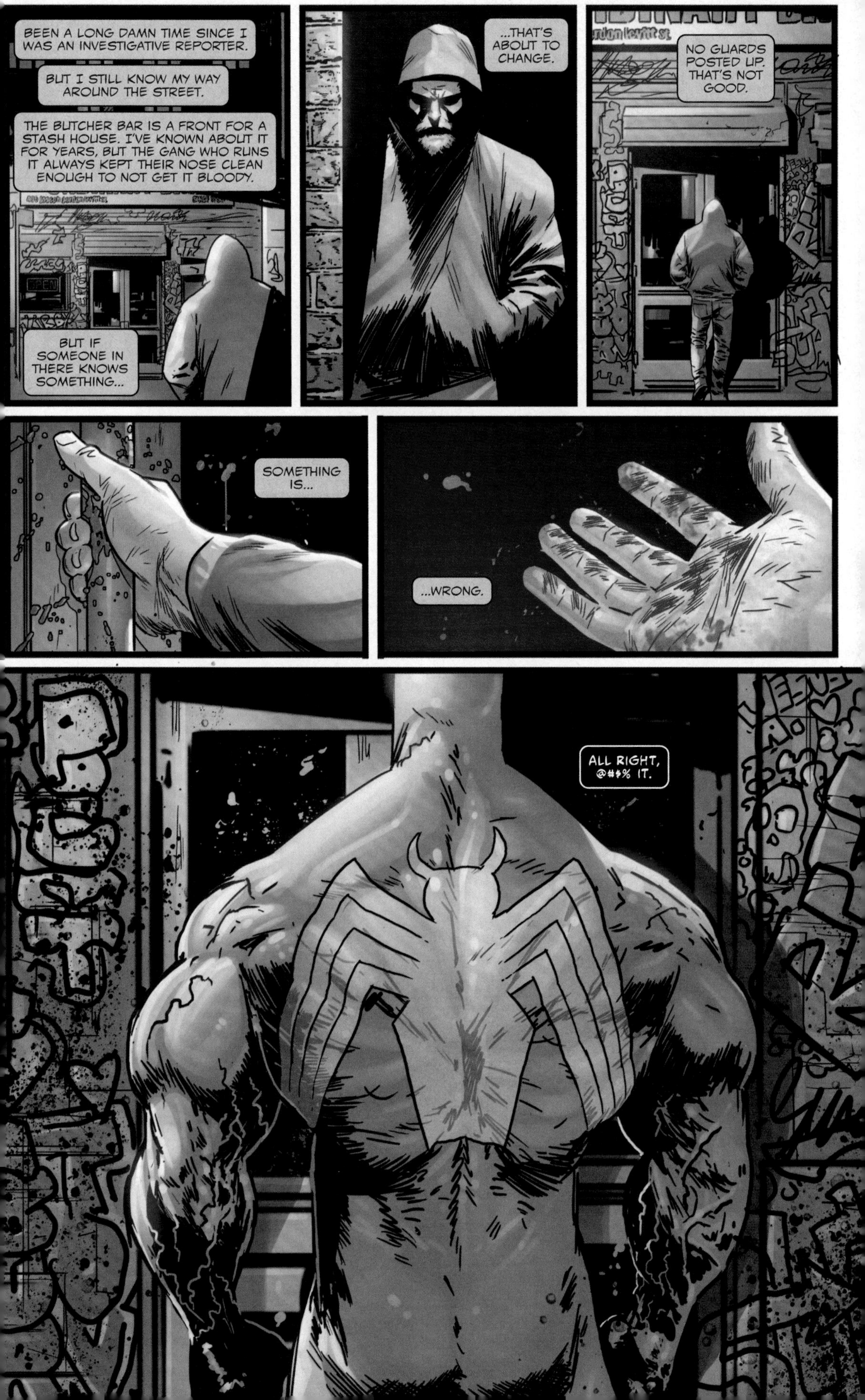
BEEN A LONG DAMN TIME SINCE I WAS AN INVESTIGATIVE REPORTER.
BUT I STILL KNOW MY WAY AROUND THE STREET.
THE BUTCHER BAR IS A FRONT FOR A STASH HOUSE. I'VE KNOWN ABOUT IT FOR YEARS, BUT THE GANG WHO RUNS IT ALWAYS KEPT THEIR NOSE CLEAN ENOUGH TO NOT GET IT BLOODY.
BUT IF SOMEONE IN THERE KNOWS SOMETHING...
...THAT'S ABOUT TO CHANGE.
NO GUARDS POSTED UP. THAT'S NOT GOOD.
SOMETHING IS...
...WRONG.
ALL RIGHT, @#$% IT.

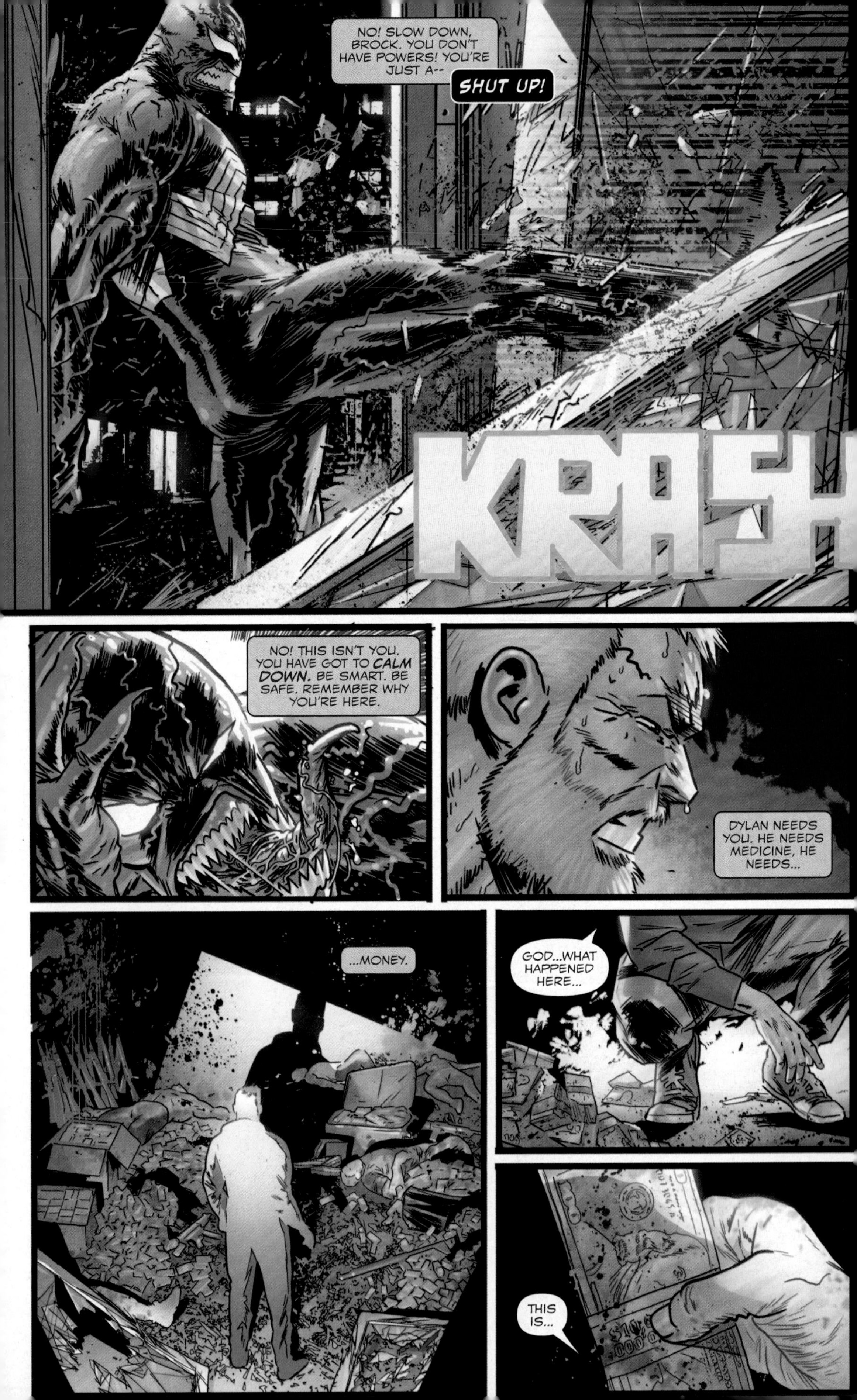
NO! SLOW DOWN, BROCK. YOU DON'T HAVE POWERS! YOU'RE JUST A--
SHUT UP!
KRASH
NO! THIS ISN'T YOU. YOU HAVE GOT TO CALM DOWN. BE SMART. BE SAFE. REMEMBER WHY YOU'RE HERE.
DYLAN NEEDS YOU. HE NEEDS MEDICINE, HE NEEDS...
...MONEY.
GOD...WHAT HAPPENED HERE...
THIS IS...

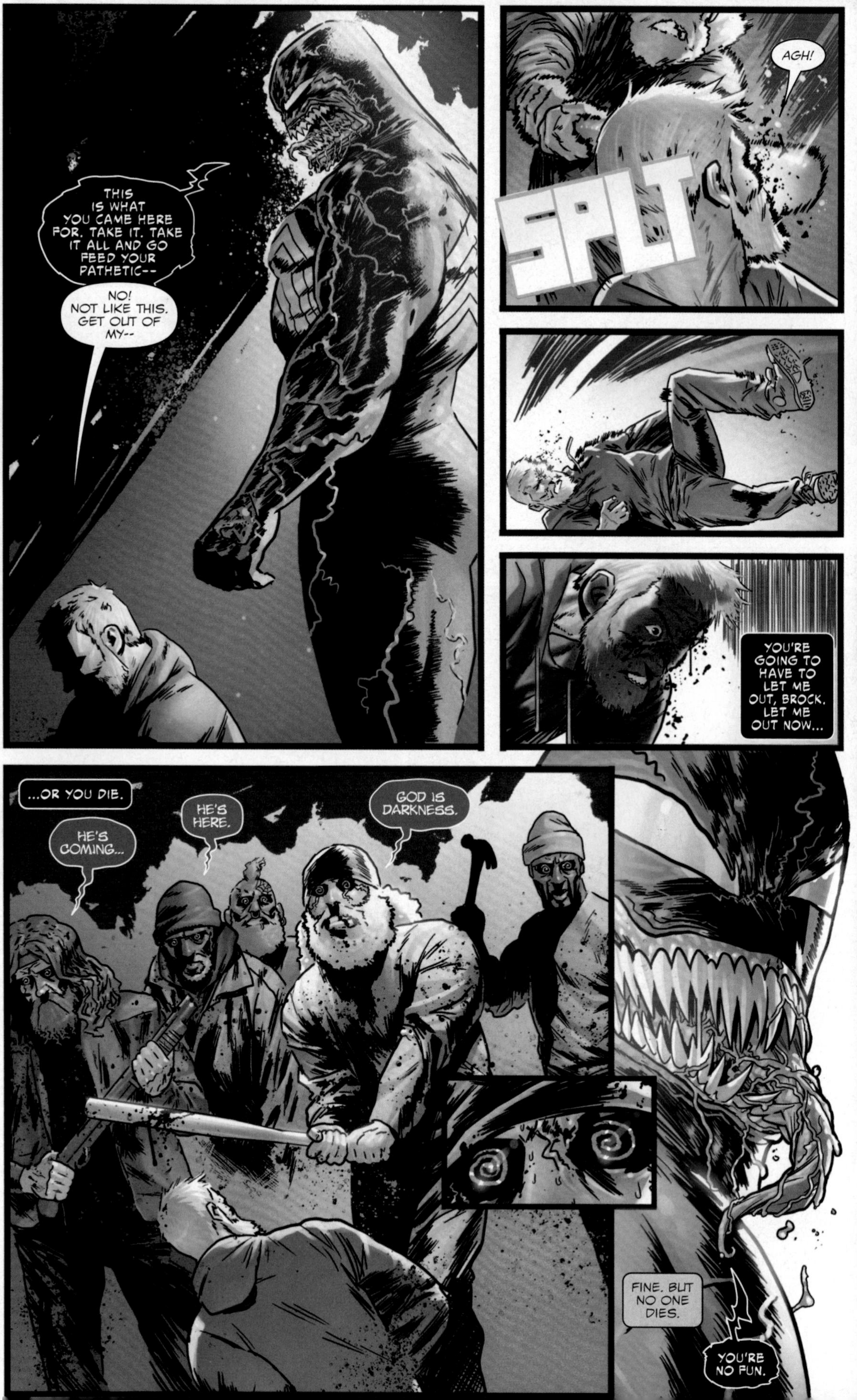
THIS IS WHAT YOU CAME HERE FOR. TAKE IT. TAKE IT ALL AND GO FEED YOUR PATHETIC--
NO! NOT LIKE THIS. GET OUT OF MY--
AGH!
SPLT
YOU'RE GOING TO HAVE TO LET ME OUT, BROCK. LET ME OUT NOW...
...OR YOU DIE.
HE'S COMING...
HE'S HERE.
GOD IS DARKNESS.
FINE. BUT NO ONE DIES.
YOU'RE NO FUN.

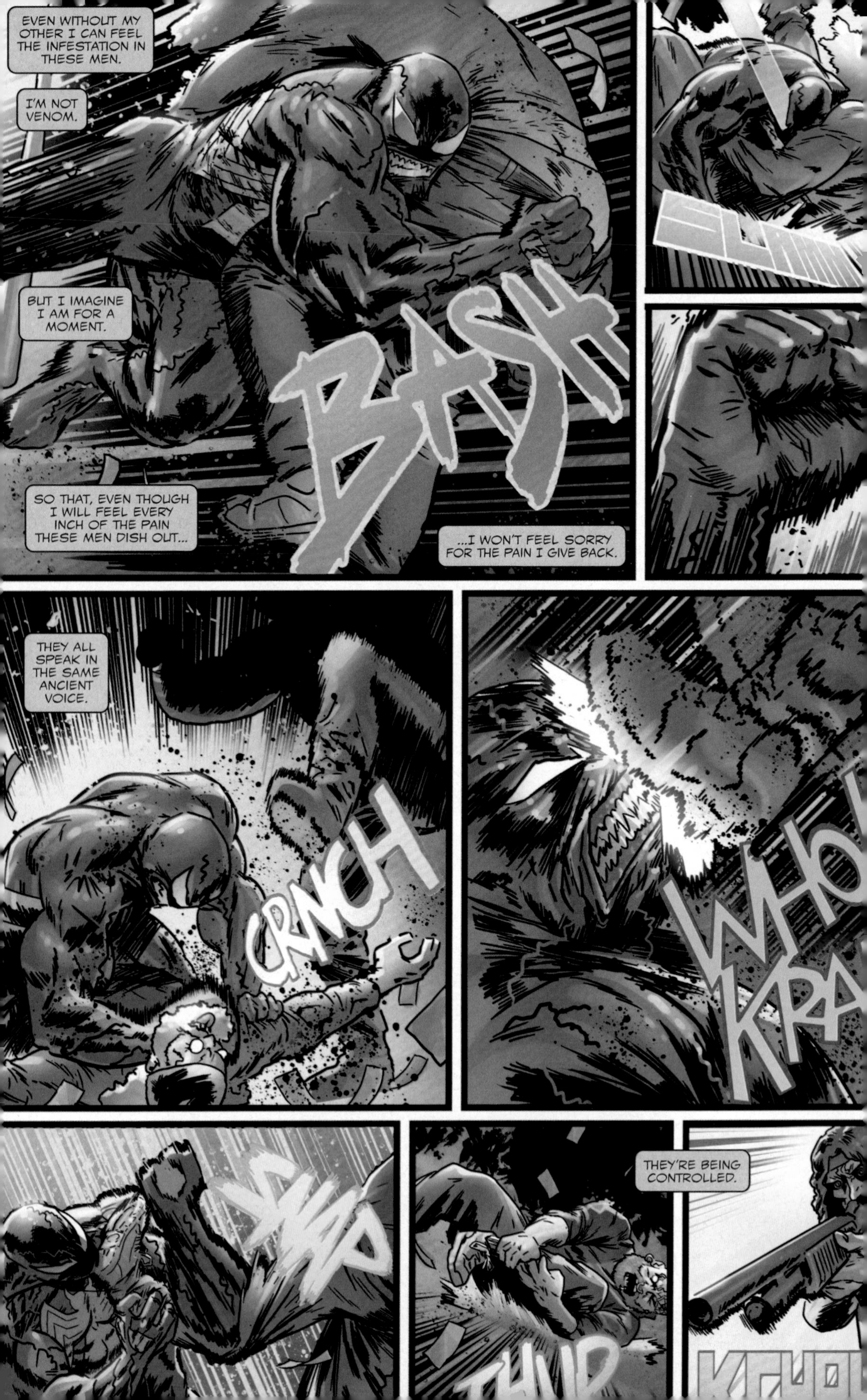
EVEN WITHOUT MY OTHER I CAN FEEL THE INFESTATION IN THESE MEN.
I'M NOT VENOM.
BUT I IMAGINE I AM FOR A MOMENT.
SO THAT, EVEN THOUGH I WILL FEEL EVERY INCH OF THE PAIN THESE MEN DISH OUT...
BASH
...I WON'T FEEL SORRY FOR THE PAIN I GIVE BACK.
THEY ALL SPEAK IN THE SAME ANCIENT VOICE.
CRNCH
THEY'RE BEING CONTROLLED.

CRUNCH

BY SOMETHING DARK...

SLICE

...AND RED...

KRACK KRACK KRACK

...AND FAMILIAR.

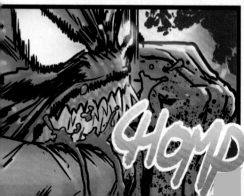

CHOMP

WHOK

THEY'RE STRONG, AND INSANE.

SPLAT

CRACK'K

LUCKY FOR ME...

WHO

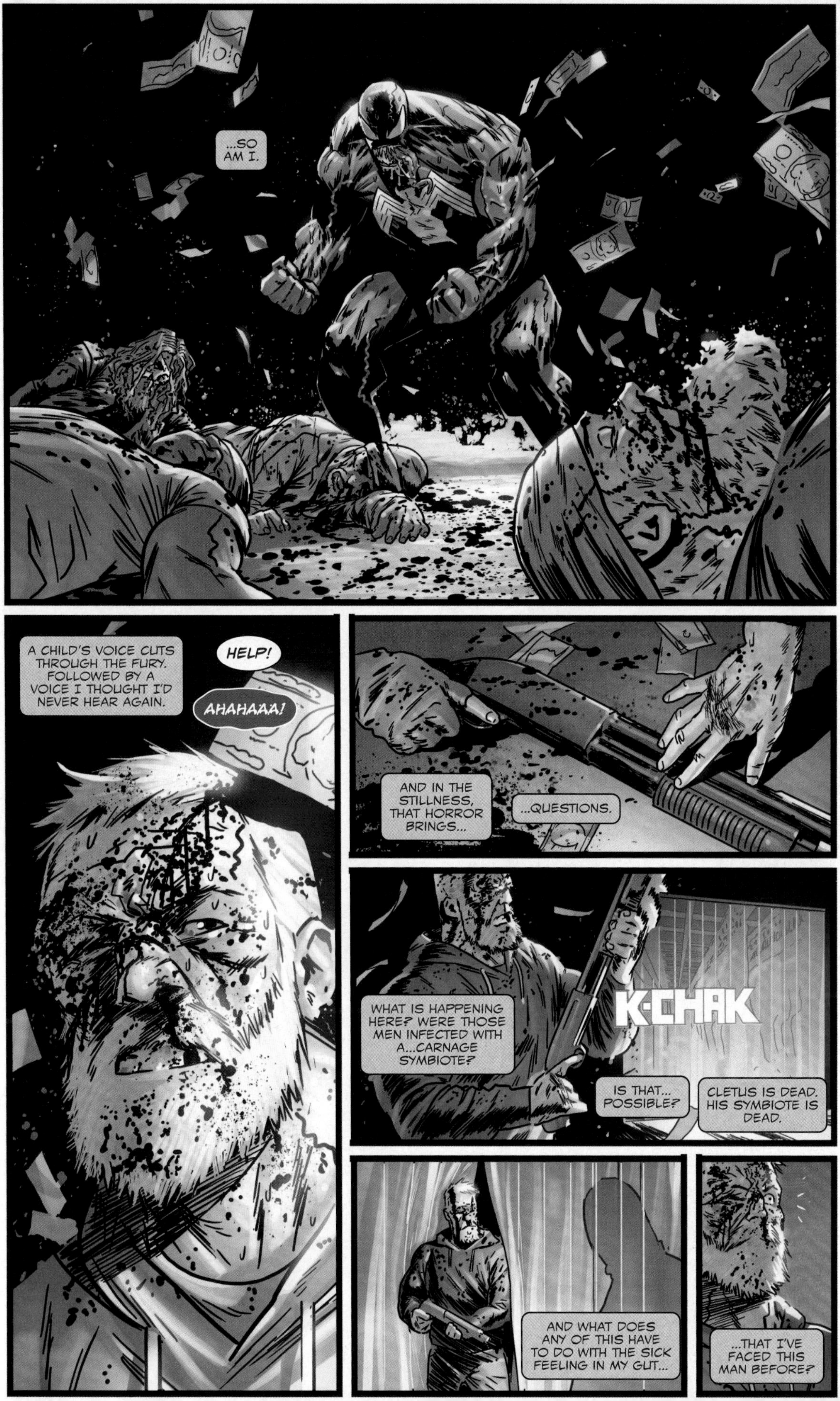
...SO AM I.
A CHILD'S VOICE CUTS THROUGH THE FURY. FOLLOWED BY A VOICE I THOUGHT I'D NEVER HEAR AGAIN.
HELP!
AHAHAAA!
AND IN THE STILLNESS, THAT HORROR BRINGS...
...QUESTIONS.
K-CHAK
WHAT IS HAPPENING HERE? WERE THOSE MEN INFECTED WITH A...CARNAGE SYMBIOTE?
IS THAT... POSSIBLE?
CLETUS IS DEAD. HIS SYMBIOTE IS DEAD.
AND WHAT DOES ANY OF THIS HAVE TO DO WITH THE SICK FEELING IN MY GUT...
...THAT I'VE FACED THIS MAN BEFORE?

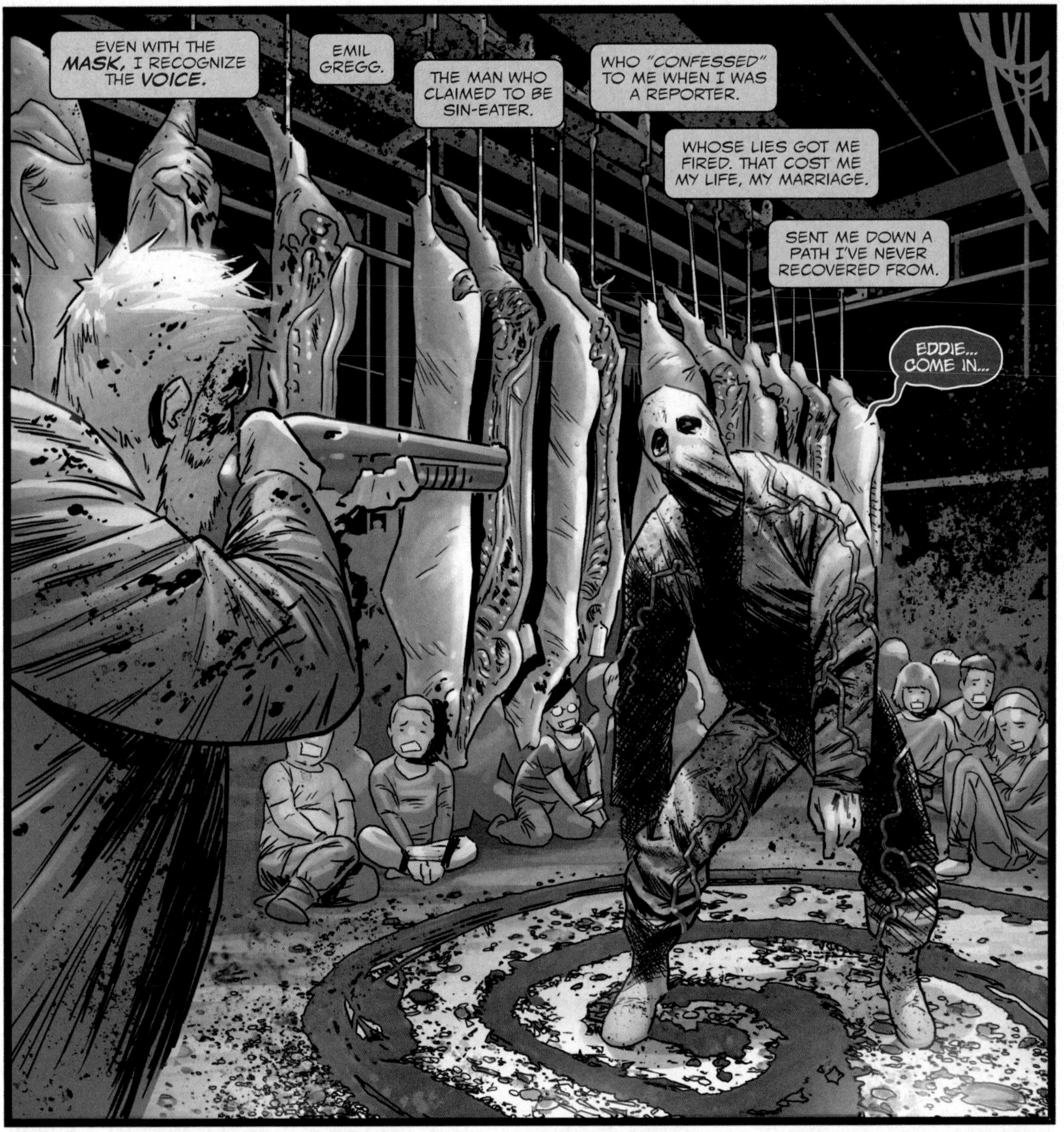
EVEN WITH THE MASK, I RECOGNIZE THE VOICE.
EMIL GREGG.
THE MAN WHO CLAIMED TO BE SIN-EATER.
WHO "CONFESSED" TO ME WHEN I WAS A REPORTER.
WHOSE LIES GOT ME FIRED. THAT COST ME MY LIFE, MY MARRIAGE.
SENT ME DOWN A PATH I'VE NEVER RECOVERED FROM.
EDDIE... COME IN...
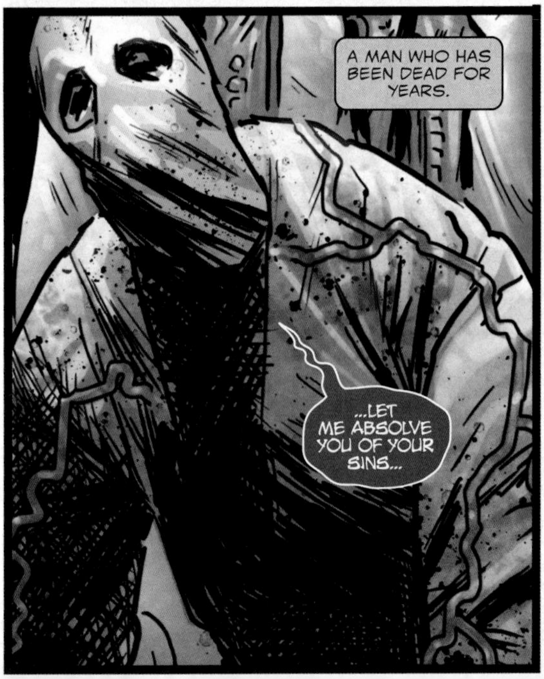
A MAN WHO HAS BEEN DEAD FOR YEARS.
...LET ME ABSOLVE YOU OF YOUR SINS...
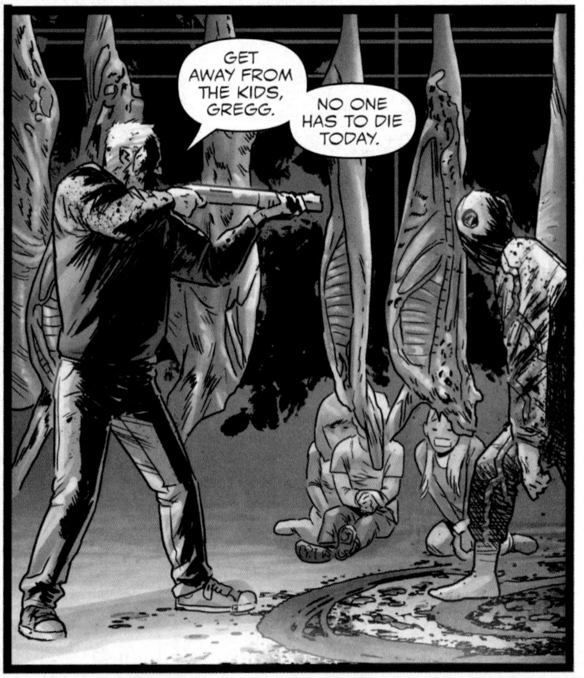
GET AWAY FROM THE KIDS, GREGG.
NO ONE HAS TO DIE TODAY.

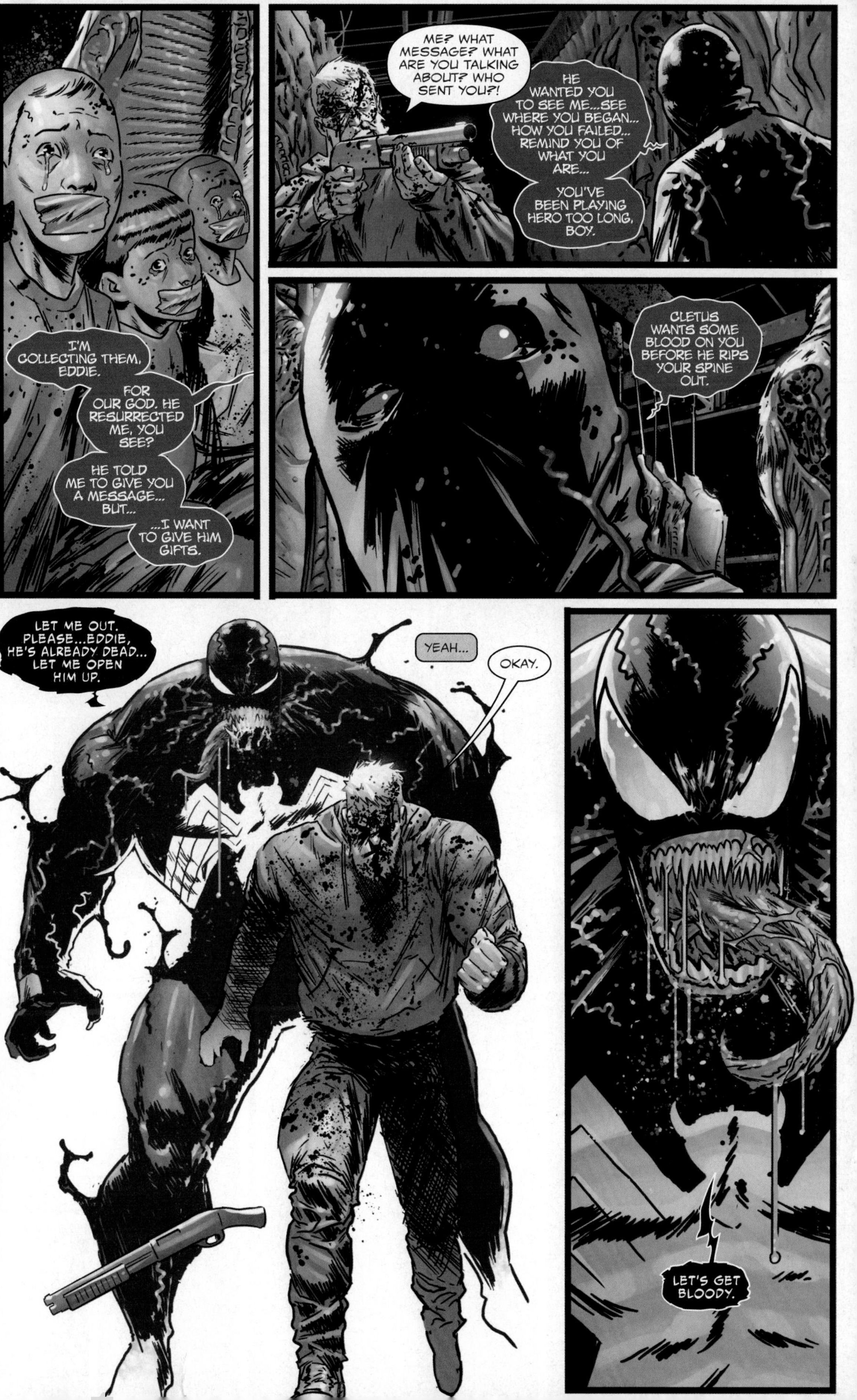
I'M COLLECTING THEM, EDDIE.
FOR OUR GOD. HE RESURRECTED ME, YOU SEE?
HE TOLD ME TO GIVE YOU A MESSAGE... BUT...
...I WANT TO GIVE HIM GIFTS.
ME? WHAT MESSAGE? WHAT ARE YOU TALKING ABOUT? WHO SENT YOU?!
HE WANTED YOU TO SEE ME...SEE WHERE YOU BEGAN... HOW YOU FAILED... REMIND YOU OF WHAT YOU ARE...
YOU'VE BEEN PLAYING HERO TOO LONG, BOY.
CLETUS WANTS SOME BLOOD ON YOU BEFORE HE RIPS YOUR SPINE OUT.
LET ME OUT. PLEASE...EDDIE, HE'S ALREADY DEAD... LET ME OPEN HIM UP.
YEAH...
OKAY.
LET'S GET BLOODY.

WAM

THUD

CARNAGE IS BACK.

BEFORE HIS BODY TURNED BACK INTO DUST, EMIL GAVE ME HIS MESSAGE...

RAAVAVA

RESURRECTED BY SOME INSANE CULT THAT WORSHIPS KNULL, THE GOD OF THE SYMBIOTES.

THEY GAVE HIM A PIECE OF THE GRENDEL. THE BIG-ASS SYMBIOTE DRAGON I FOUGHT AND THOUGHT I KILLED.

CRUNCH

WHICH MAKES HIM DAMN NEAR UNKILLABLE, AND MORE POWERFUL THAN EVER.

KRK

BASH BAM CRNCH KRAK SNIP

AND HE'S COMING FOR ME. AND EVERYONE ELSE WHO'S EVER WORN A SYMBIOTE.

I SHOULD BE TERRIFIED. BUT HONESTLY...

SPLOT

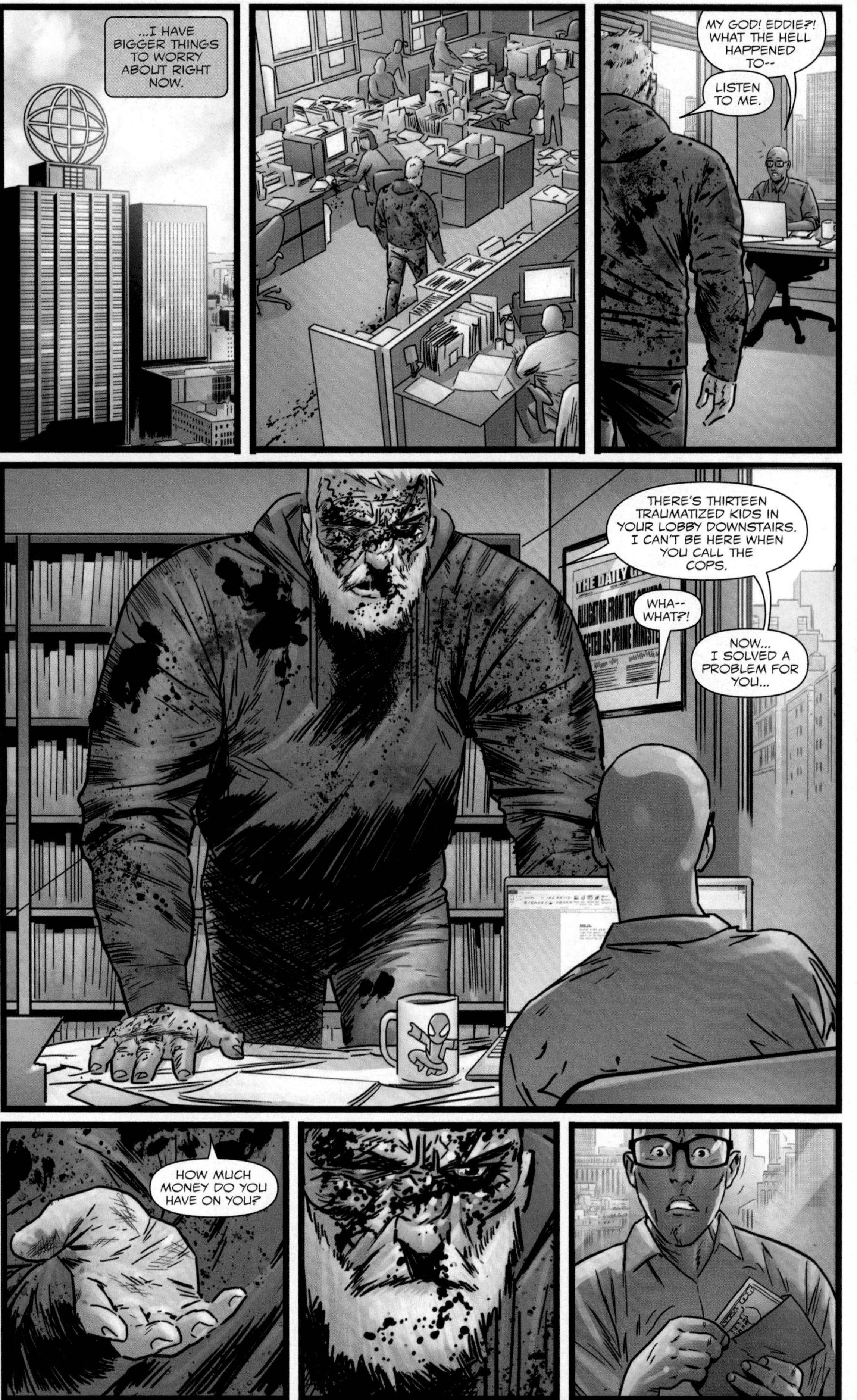
...I HAVE BIGGER THINGS TO WORRY ABOUT RIGHT NOW.
MY GOD! EDDIE?! WHAT THE HELL HAPPENED TO--
LISTEN TO ME.
THERE'S THIRTEEN TRAUMATIZED KIDS IN YOUR LOBBY DOWNSTAIRS. I CAN'T BE HERE WHEN YOU CALL THE COPS.
WHA-- WHAT?!
NOW... I SOLVED A PROBLEM FOR YOU...
HOW MUCH MONEY DO YOU HAVE ON YOU?

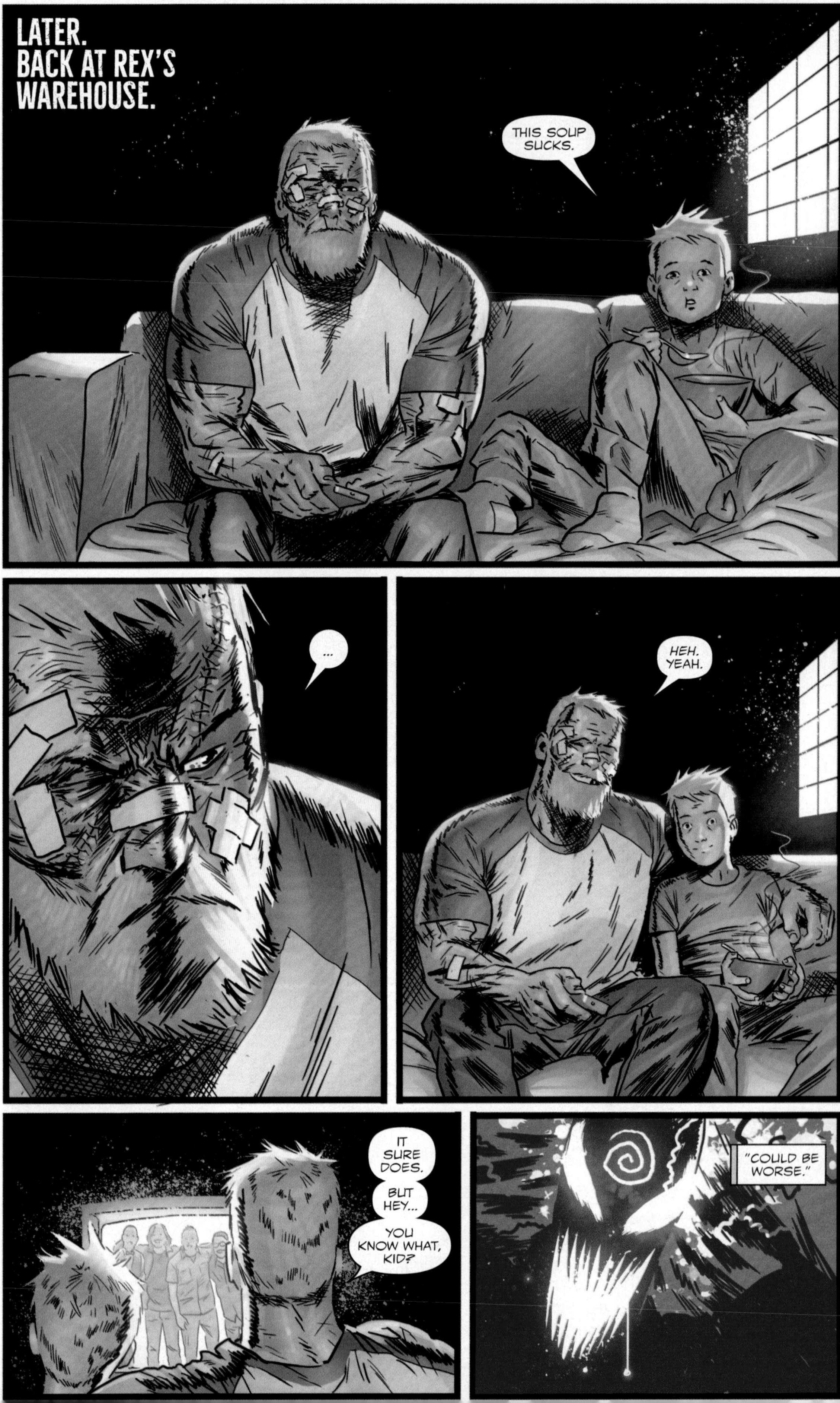
LATER.
BACK AT REX'S
WAREHOUSE.
THIS SOUP SUCKS.
...
HEH. YEAH.
IT SURE DOES.
BUT HEY...
YOU KNOW WHAT, KID?
"COULD BE WORSE."

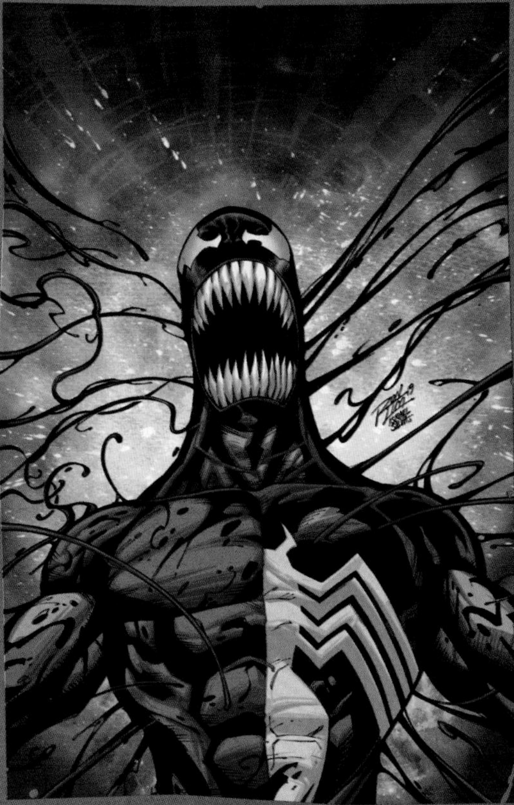

#16 CARNAGE-IZED VARIANT
BY **RON LIM** & **ISRAEL SILVA**

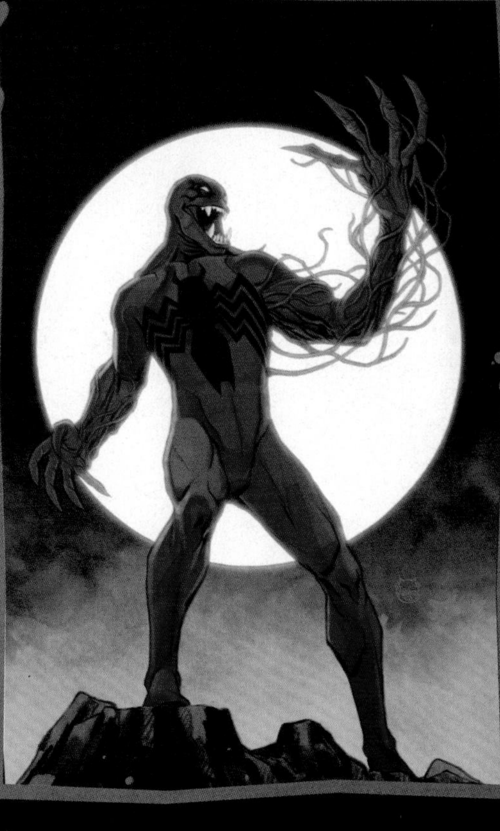

#17 VARIANT
BY **DAVE JOHNSON**

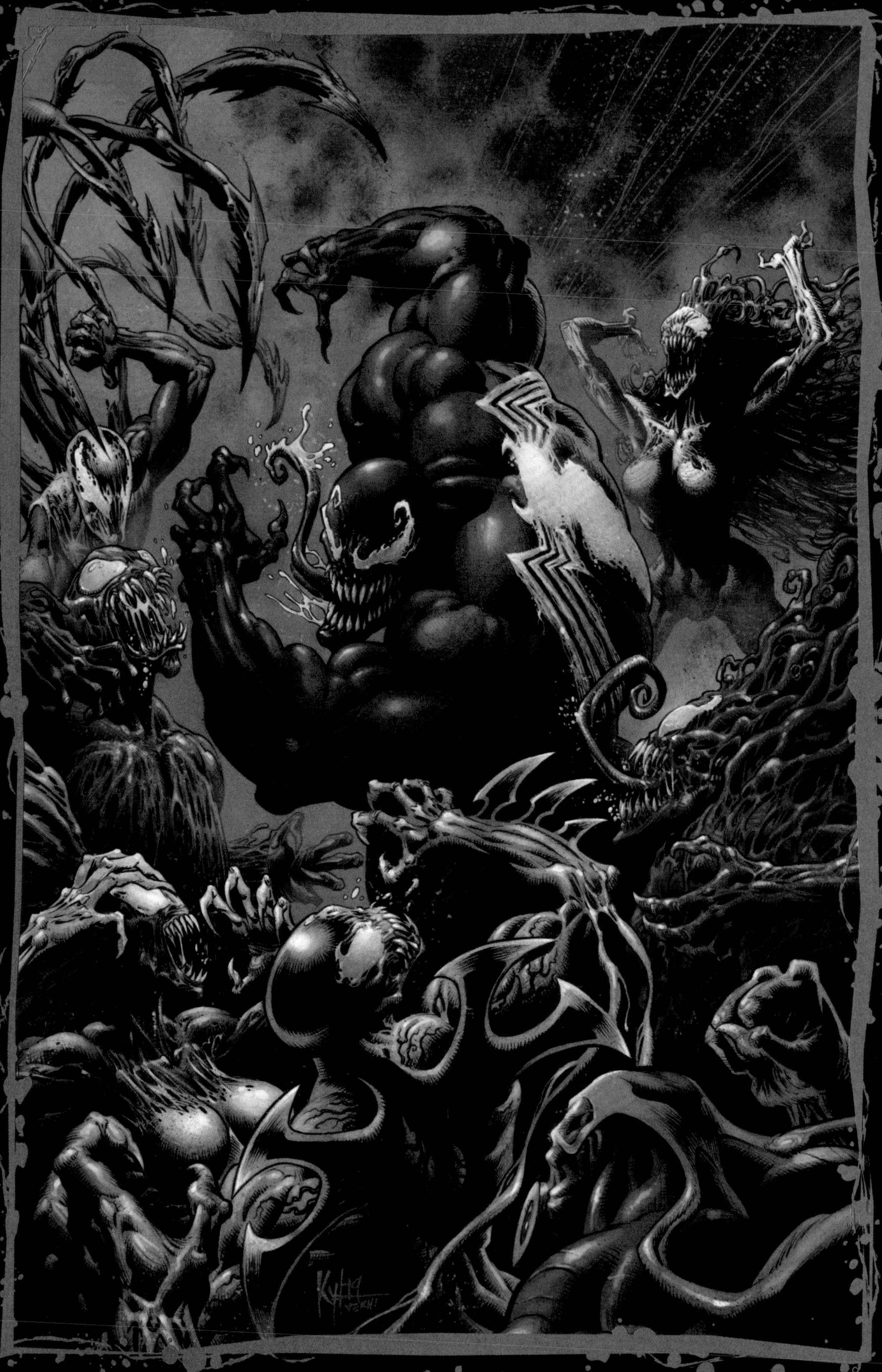

17

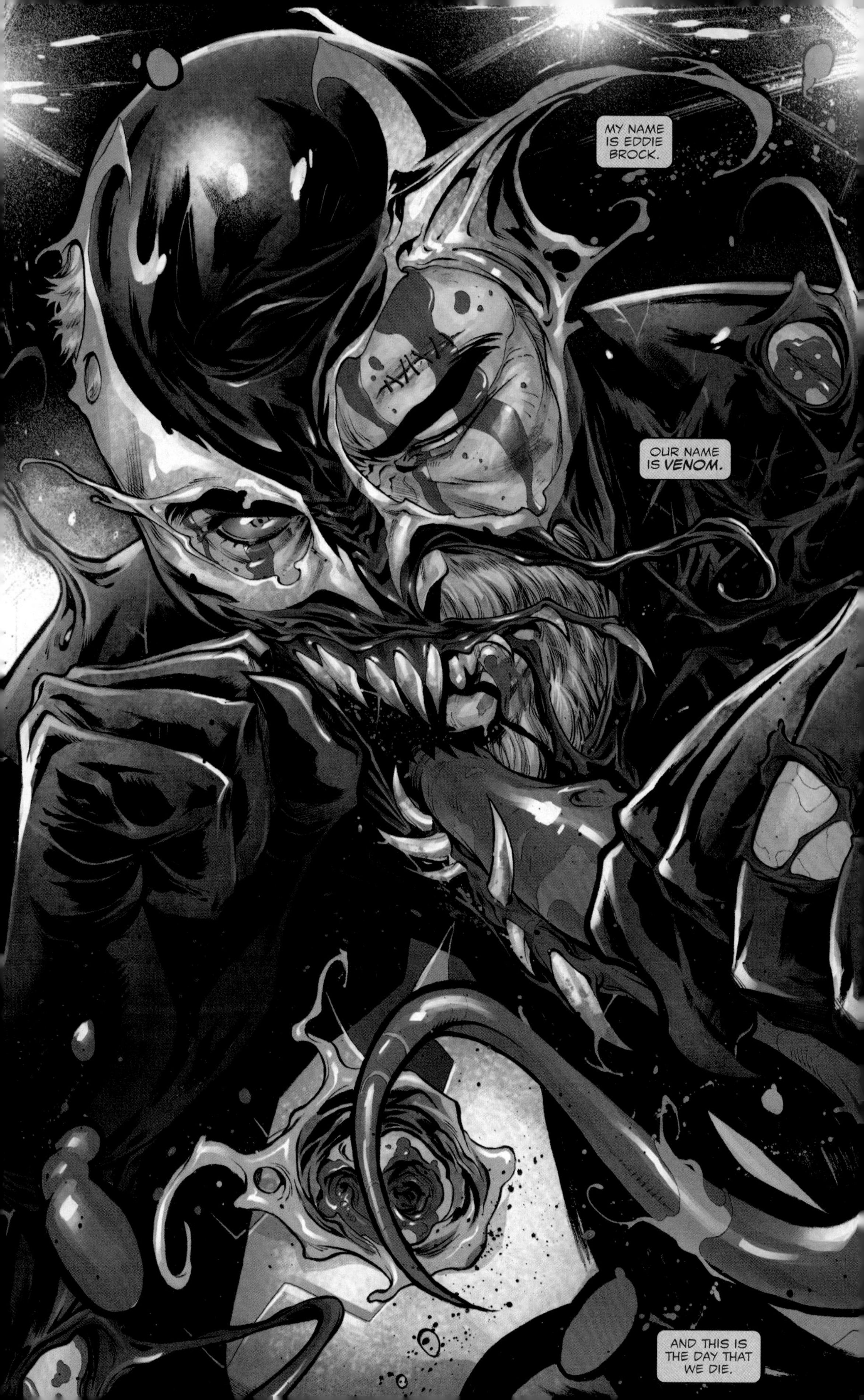
MY NAME IS EDDIE BROCK.
OUR NAME IS *VENOM.*
AND THIS IS THE DAY THAT WE DIE.

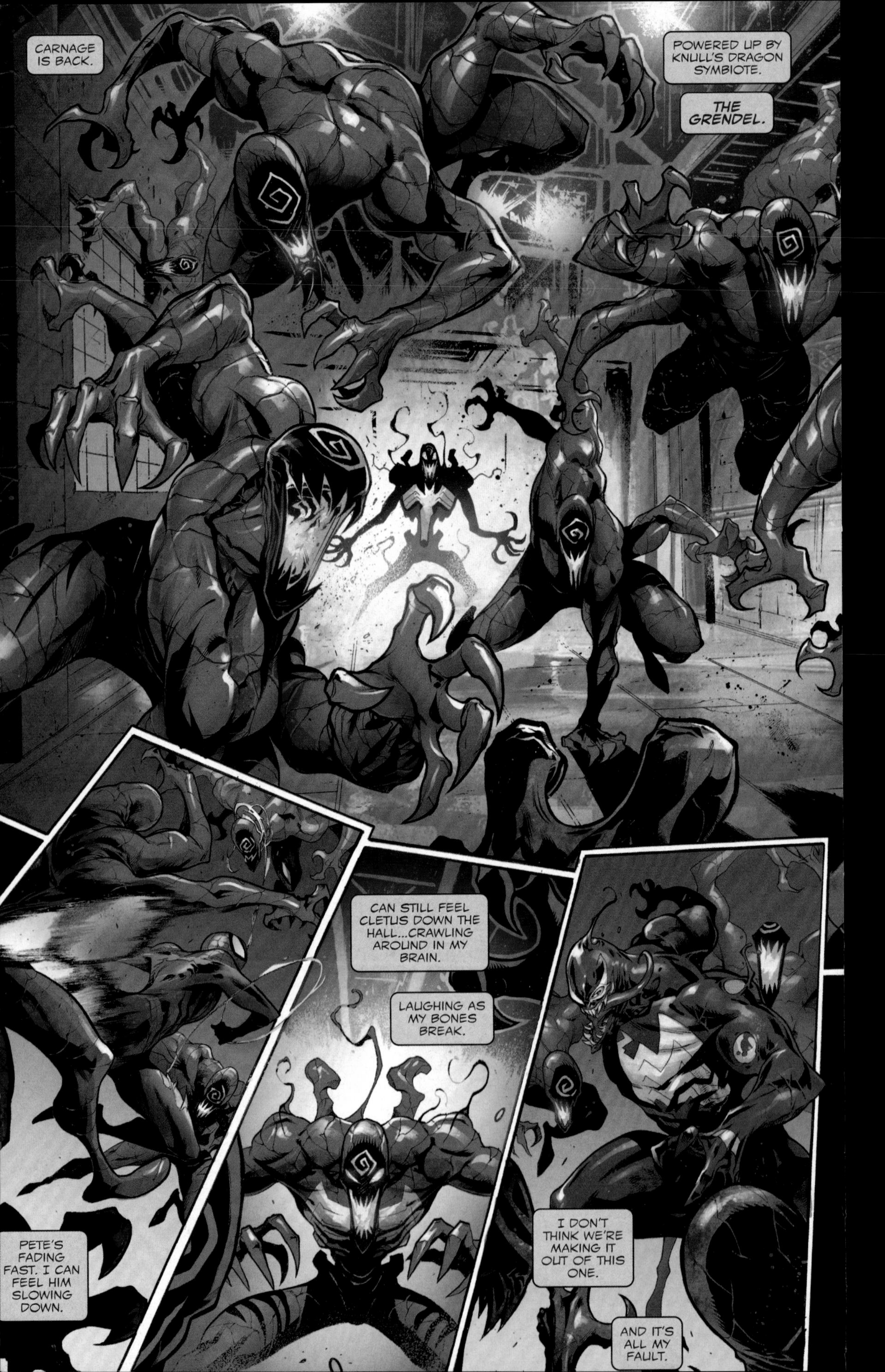
CARNAGE IS BACK.
POWERED UP BY KNULL'S DRAGON SYMBIOTE.
THE GRENDEL.
PETE'S FADING FAST. I CAN FEEL HIM SLOWING DOWN.
CAN STILL FEEL CLETUS DOWN THE HALL...CRAWLING AROUND IN MY BRAIN.
LAUGHING AS MY BONES BREAK.
I DON'T THINK WE'RE MAKING IT OUT OF THIS ONE.
AND IT'S ALL MY FAULT.

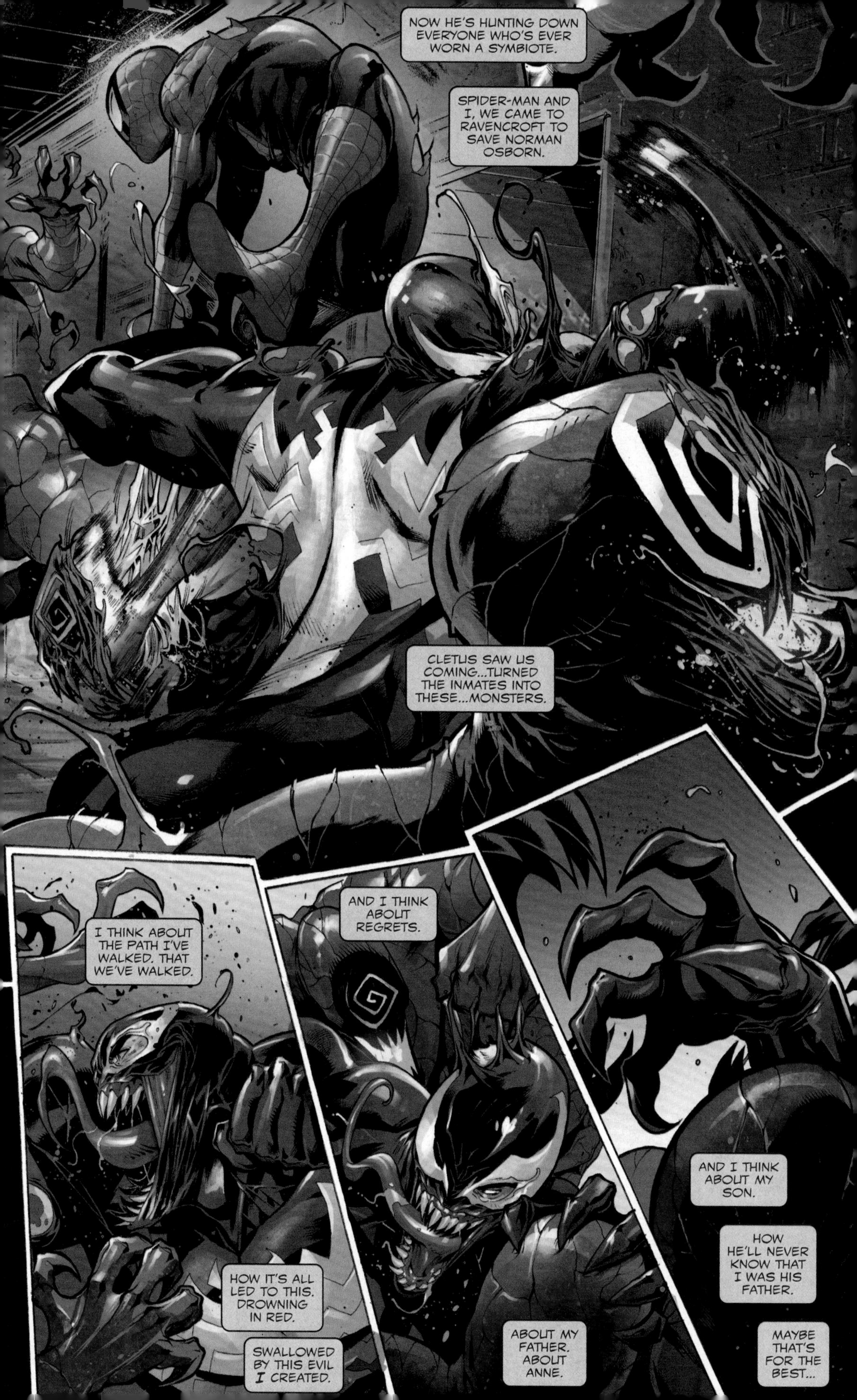
NOW HE'S HUNTING DOWN EVERYONE WHO'S EVER WORN A SYMBIOTE.
SPIDER-MAN AND I, WE CAME TO RAVENCROFT TO SAVE NORMAN OSBORN.
CLETUS SAW US COMING...TURNED THE INMATES INTO THESE...MONSTERS.
I THINK ABOUT THE PATH I'VE WALKED. THAT WE'VE WALKED.
HOW IT'S ALL LED TO THIS. DROWNING IN RED.
SWALLOWED BY THIS EVIL I CREATED.
AND I THINK ABOUT REGRETS.
ABOUT MY FATHER. ABOUT ANNE.
AND I THINK ABOUT MY SON.
HOW HE'LL NEVER KNOW THAT I WAS HIS FATHER.
MAYBE THAT'S FOR THE BEST...

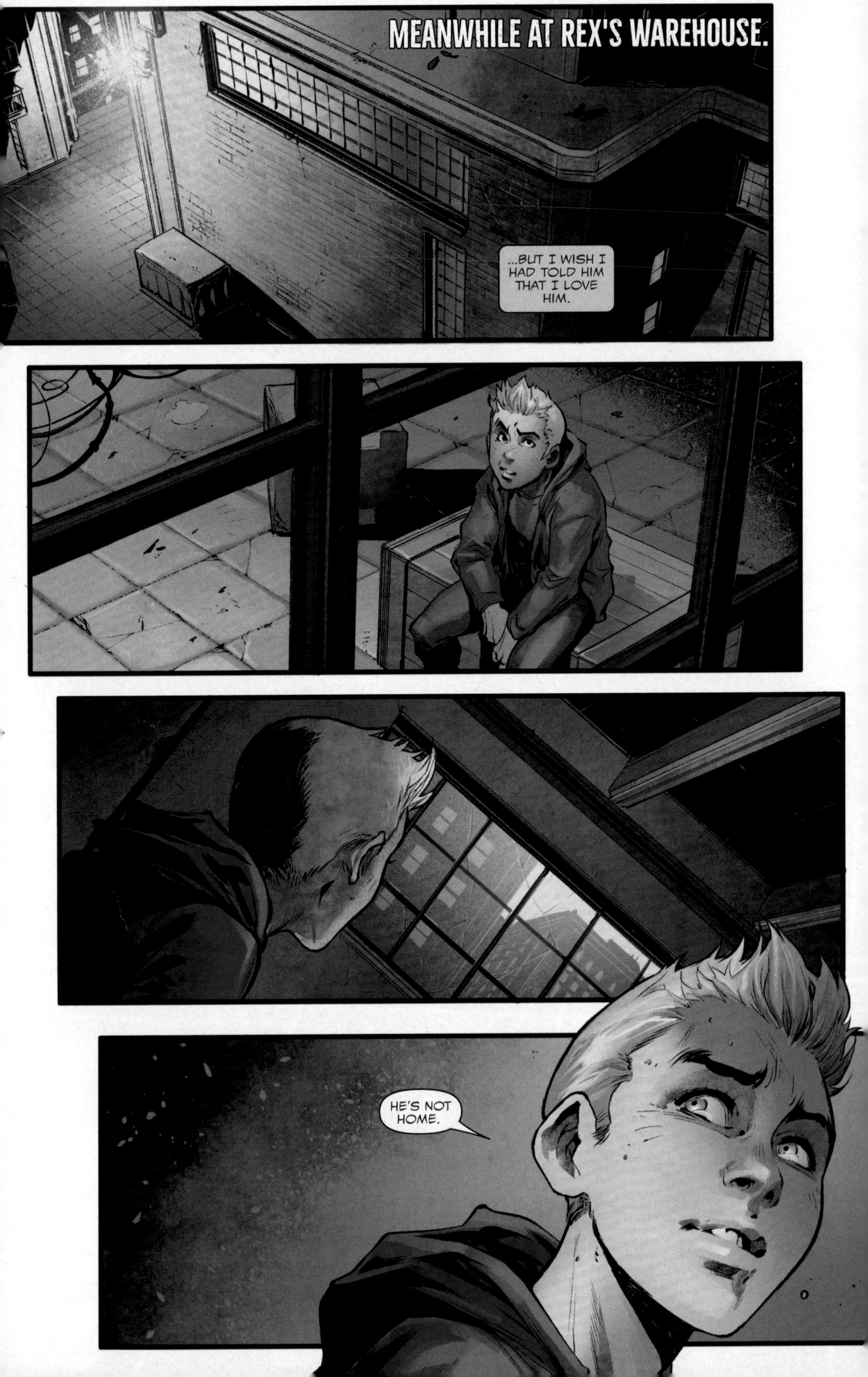
MEANWHILE AT REX'S WAREHOUSE.
...BUT I WISH I HAD TOLD HIM THAT I LOVE HIM.
HE'S NOT HOME.

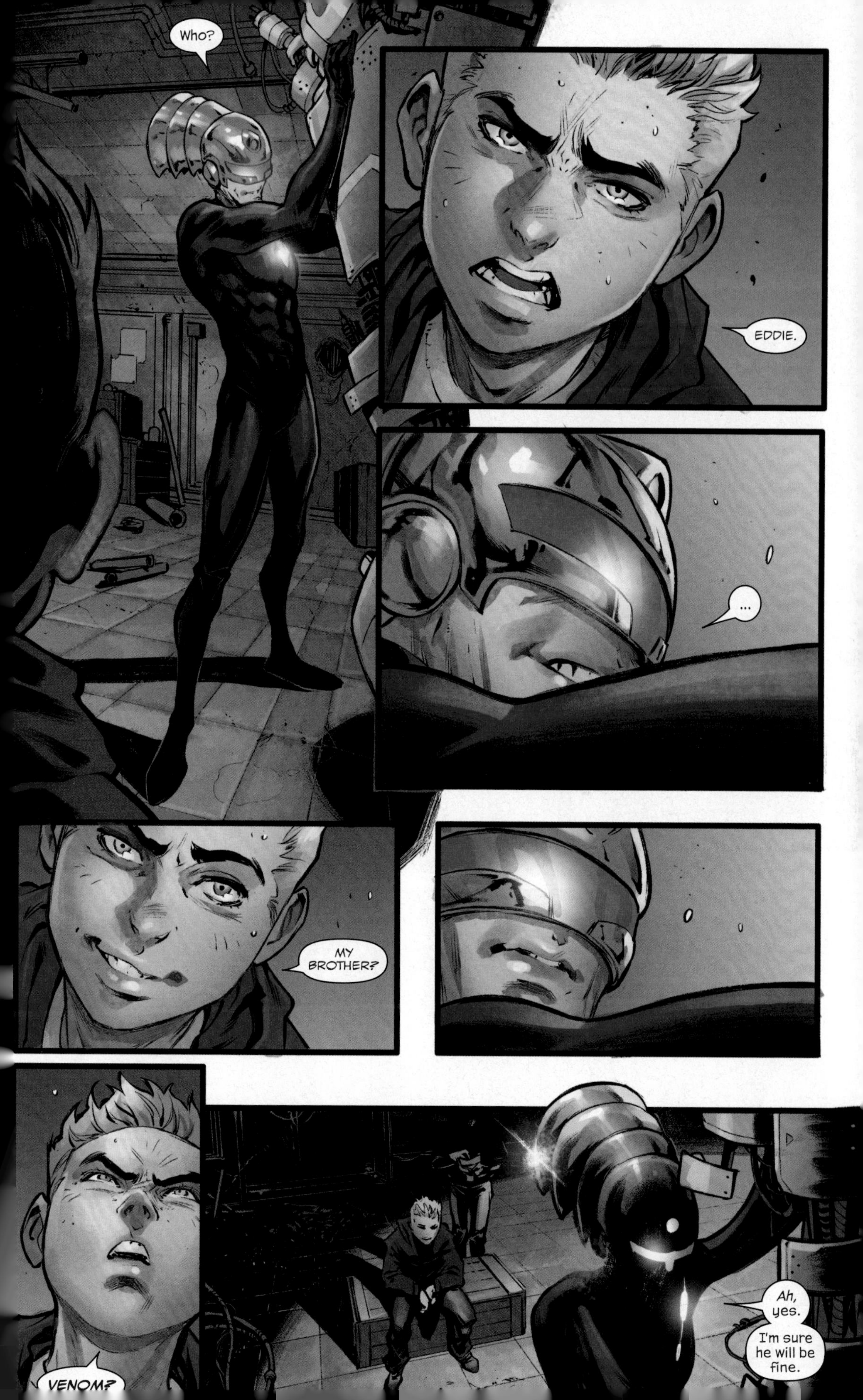
Who?
EDDIE.
...
MY BROTHER?
VENOM?
Ah, yes.
I'm sure he will be fine.

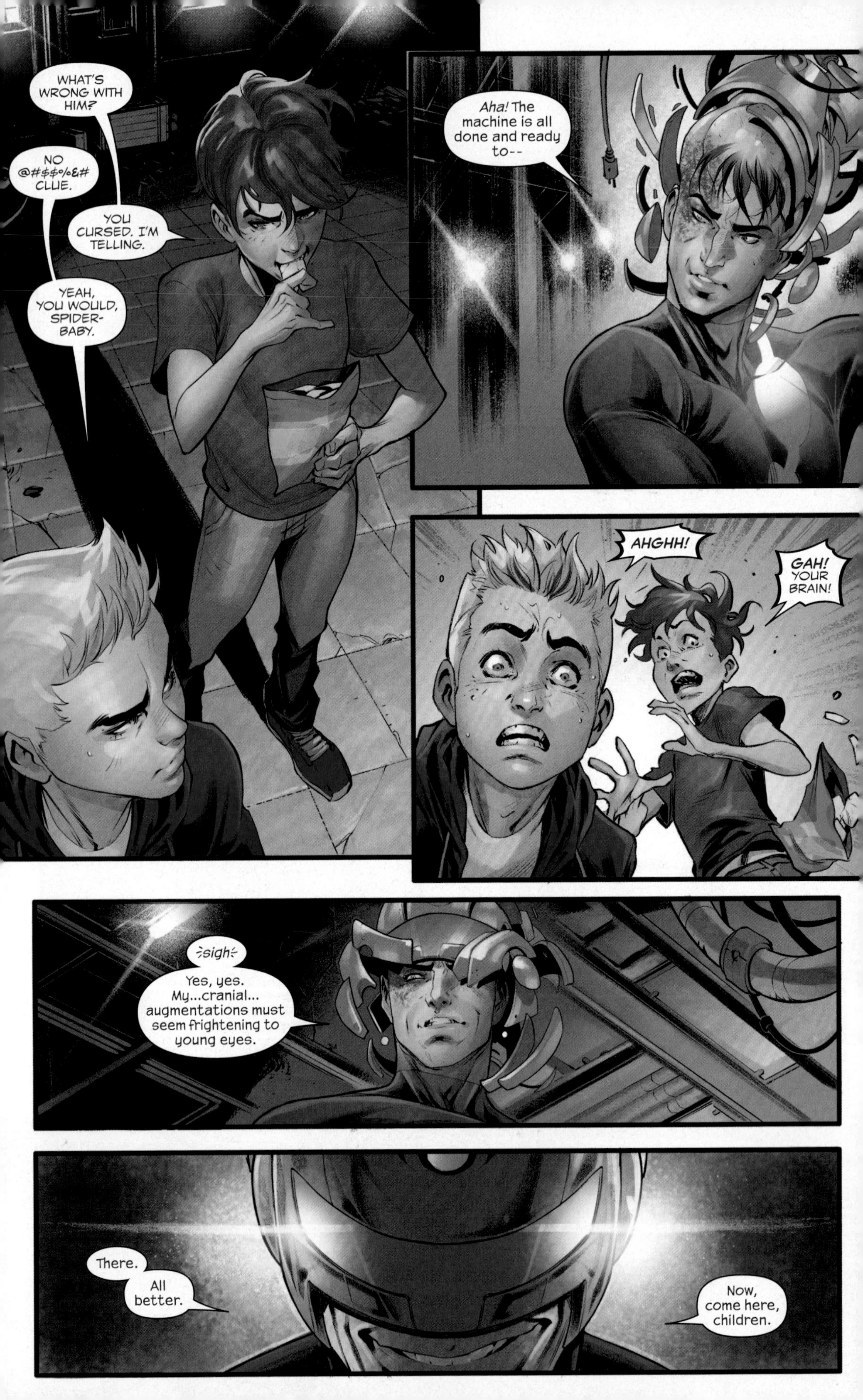
WHAT'S WRONG WITH HIM?
NO @#$$%&# CLUE.
YOU CURSED. I'M TELLING.
YEAH, YOU WOULD, SPIDER-BABY.
Aha! The machine is all done and ready to--
AHGHH!
GAH! YOUR BRAIN!
sigh
Yes, yes. My...cranial... augmentations must seem frightening to young eyes.
There.
All better.
Now, come here, children.

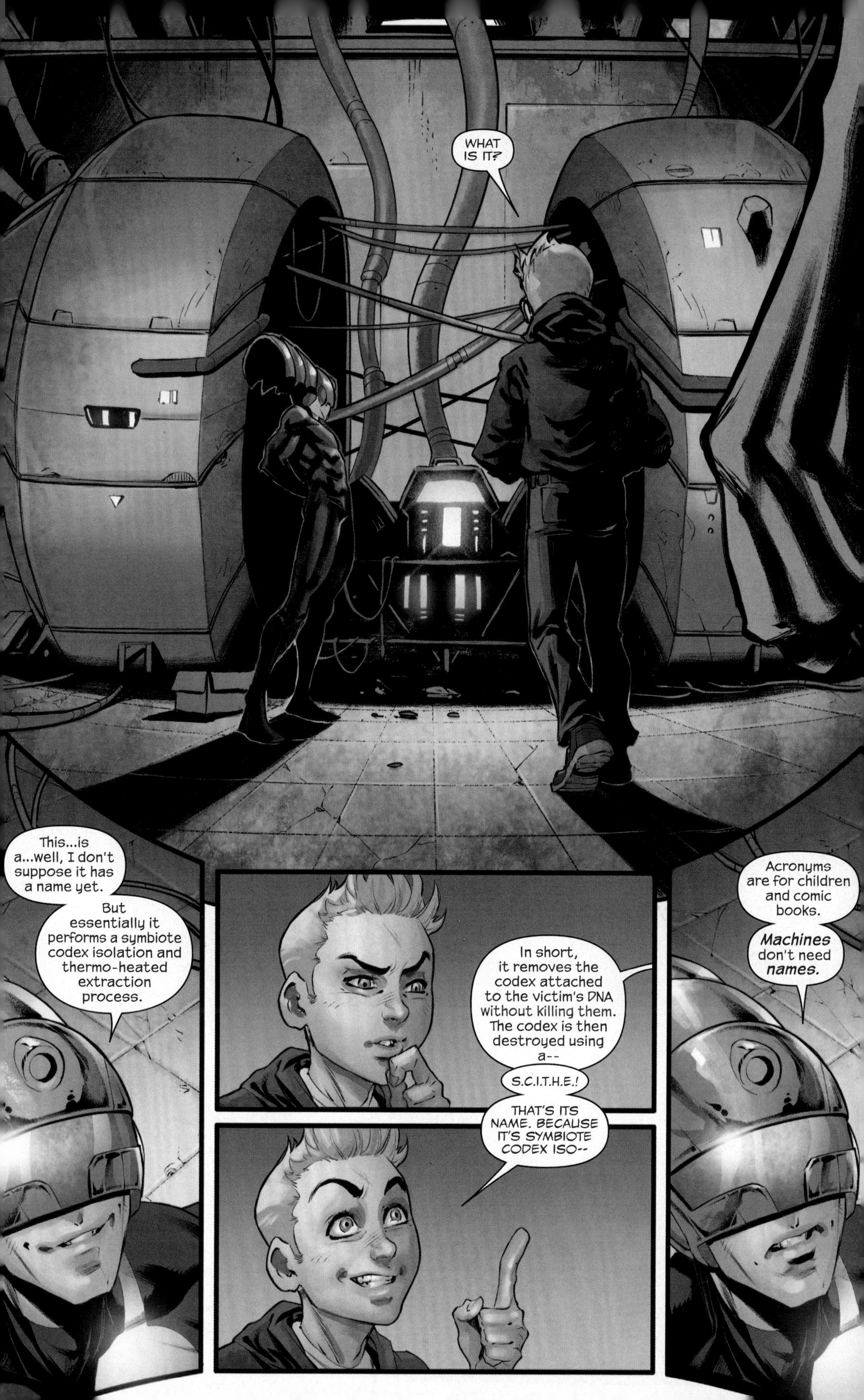
WHAT IS IT?
This...is a...well, I don't suppose it has a name yet.
But essentially it performs a symbiote codex isolation and thermo-heated extraction process.
In short, it removes the codex attached to the victim's DNA without killing them. The codex is then destroyed using a--
S.C.I.T.H.E.!
THAT'S ITS NAME. BECAUSE IT'S SYMBIOTE CODEX ISO--
Acronyms are for children and comic books.
Machines don't need *names.*

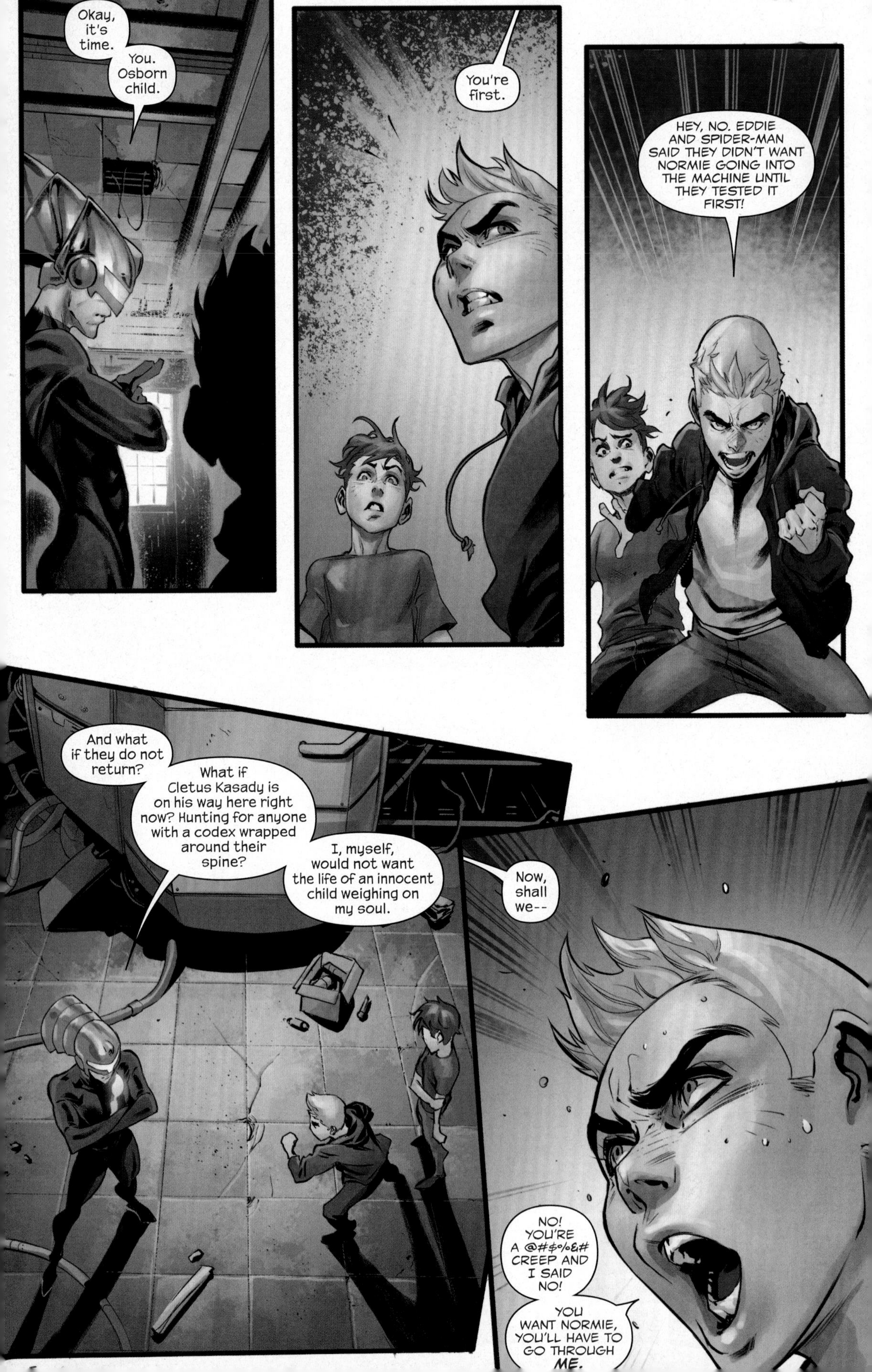

Okay, it's time.
You. Osborn child.
You're first.
HEY, NO. EDDIE AND SPIDER-MAN SAID THEY DIDN'T WANT NORMIE GOING INTO THE MACHINE UNTIL THEY TESTED IT FIRST!
And what if they do not return?
What if Cletus Kasady is on his way here right now? Hunting for anyone with a codex wrapped around their spine?
I, myself, would not want the life of an innocent child weighing on my soul.
Now, shall we--
NO! YOU'RE A @#$%&# CREEP AND I SAID NO!
YOU WANT NORMIE, YOU'LL HAVE TO GO THROUGH ME.

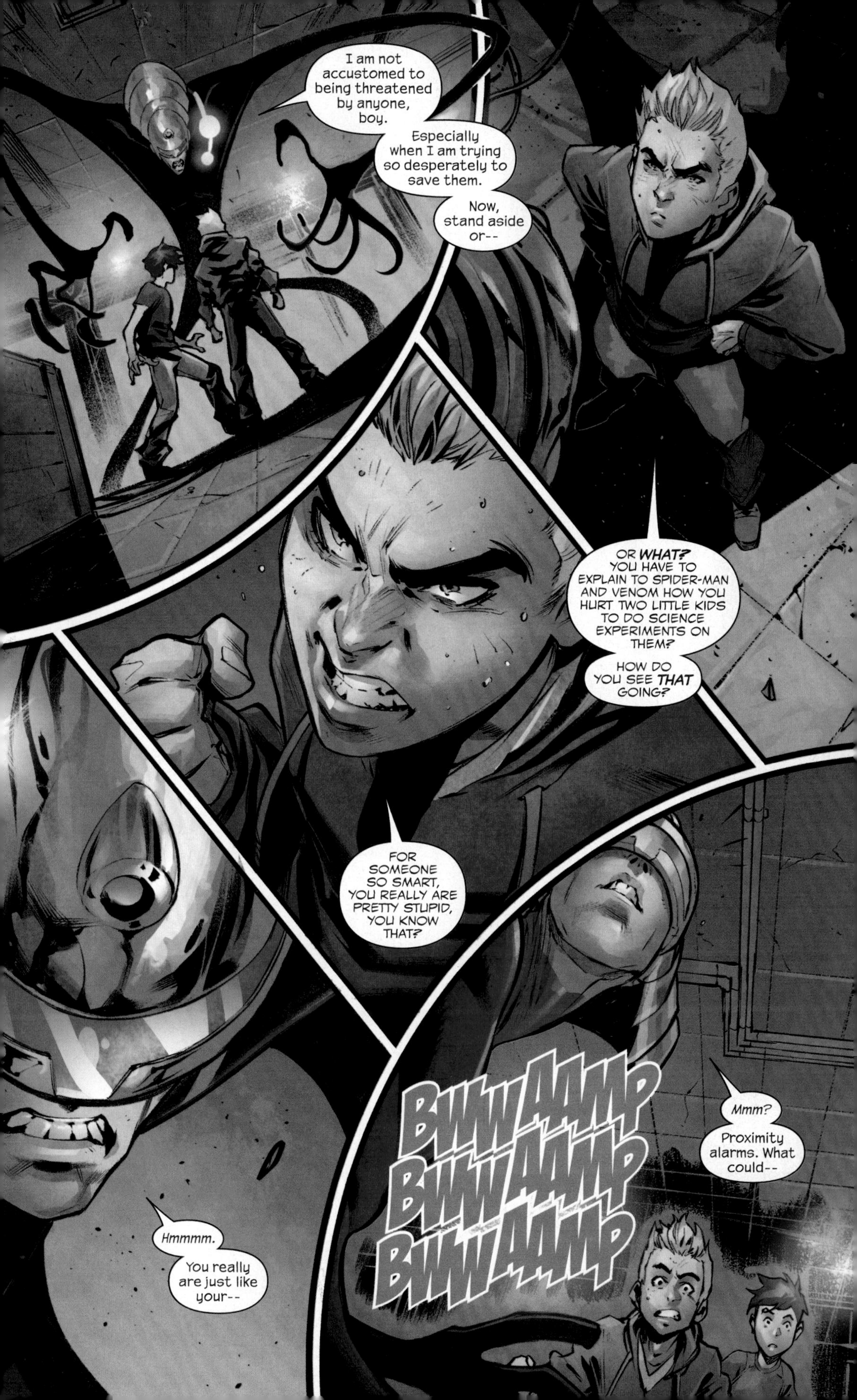
I am not accustomed to being threatened by anyone, boy.
Especially when I am trying so desperately to save them.
Now, stand aside or--
OR WHAT? YOU HAVE TO EXPLAIN TO SPIDER-MAN AND VENOM HOW YOU HURT TWO LITTLE KIDS TO DO SCIENCE EXPERIMENTS ON THEM?
HOW DO YOU SEE THAT GOING?
FOR SOMEONE SO SMART, YOU REALLY ARE PRETTY STUPID, YOU KNOW THAT?
Hmmmm.
You really are just like your--
BWW AAMP
BWW AAMP
BWW AAMP
Mmm?
Proximity alarms. What could--

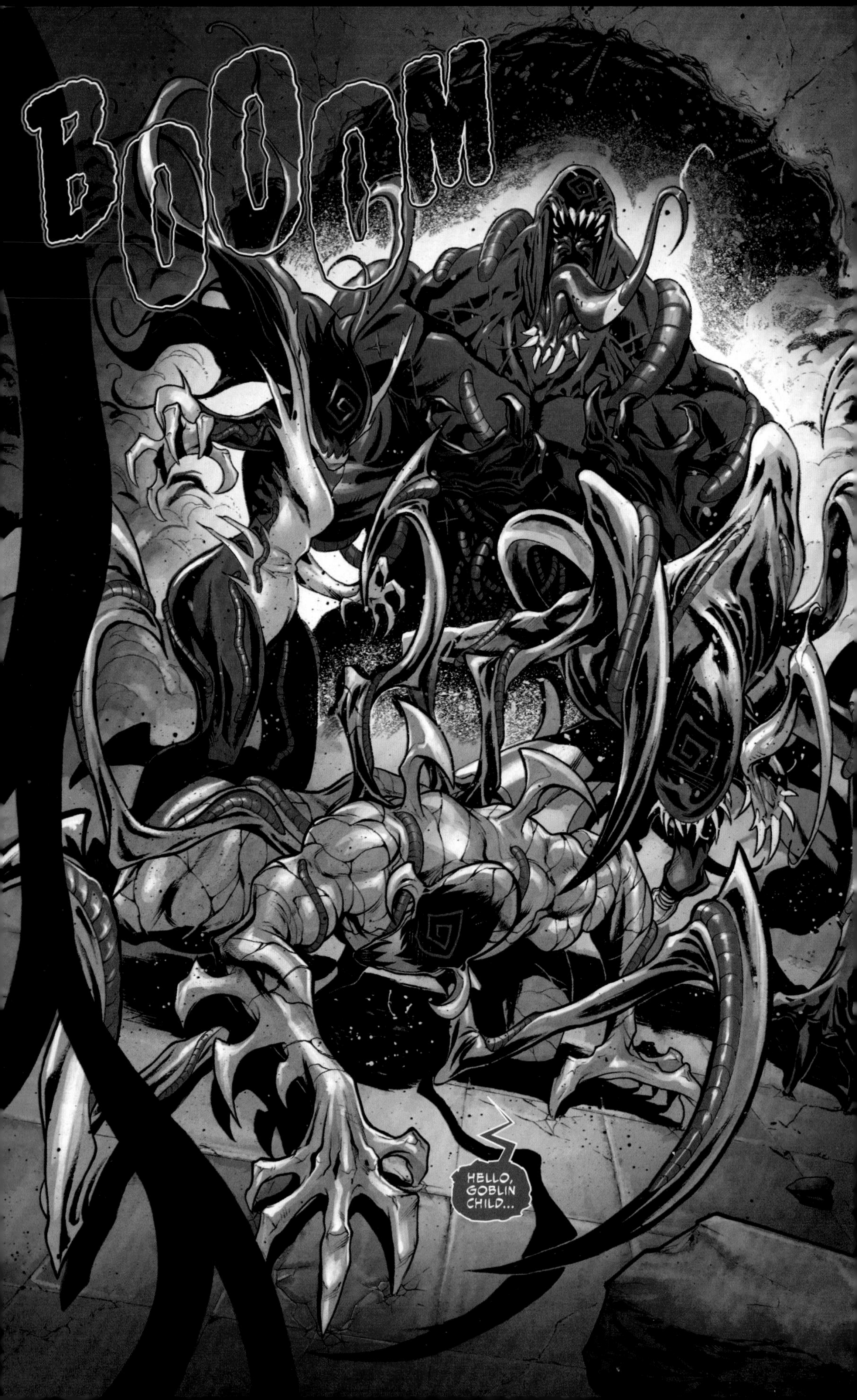
BOOOM
HELLO, GOBLIN CHILD...

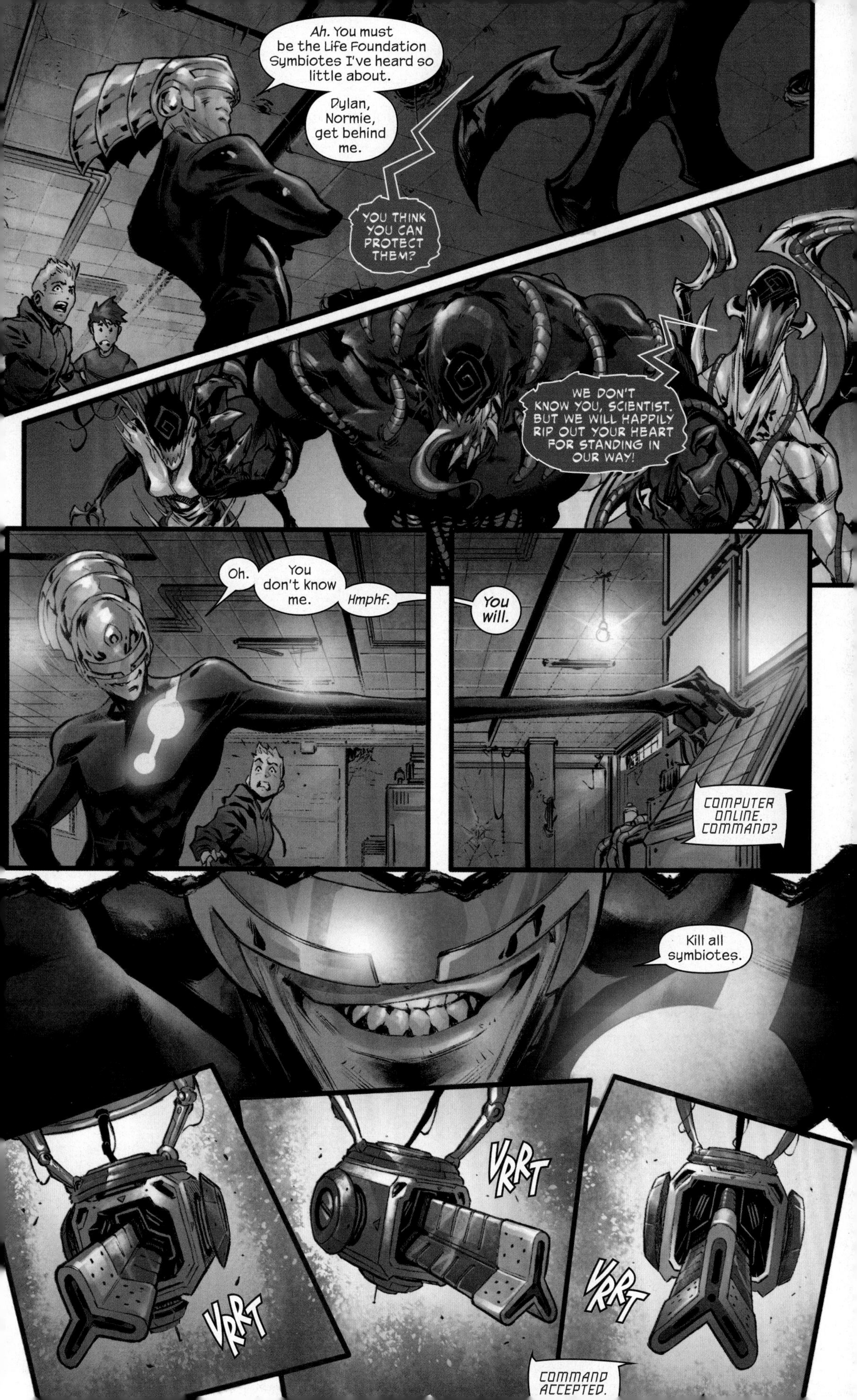

Ah. You must be the Life Foundation Symbiotes I've heard so little about.
Dylan, Normie, get behind me.
YOU THINK YOU CAN PROTECT THEM?
WE DON'T KNOW YOU, SCIENTIST. BUT WE WILL HAPPILY RIP OUT YOUR HEART FOR STANDING IN OUR WAY!
Oh.
You don't know me.
Hmphf.
You will.
COMPUTER ONLINE. COMMAND?
Kill all symbiotes.
VRRT
VRRT
VRRT
COMMAND ACCEPTED.

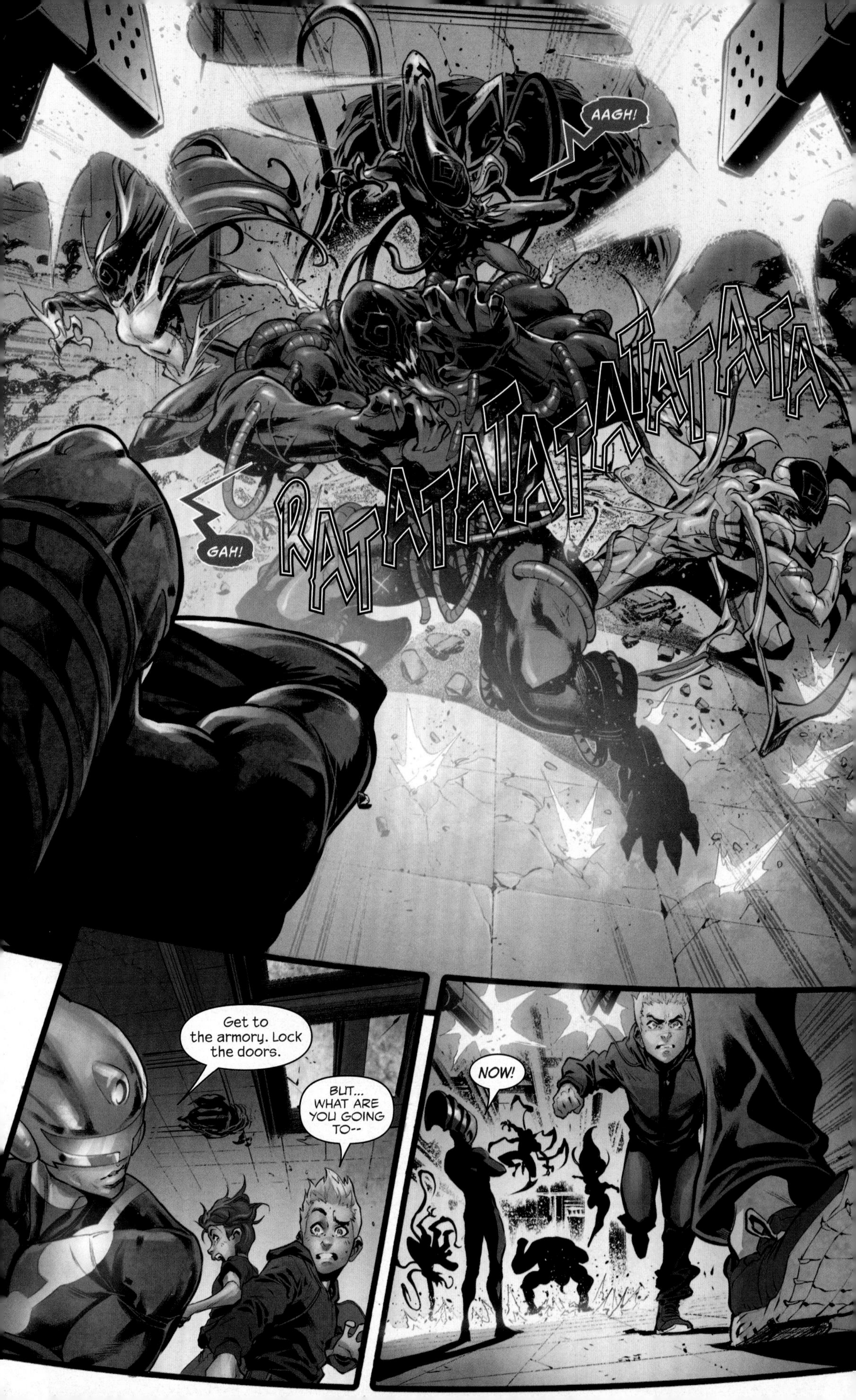
AAGH!
GAH!
RATATATATATATATA
Get to the armory. Lock the doors.
BUT... WHAT ARE YOU GOING TO--
NOW!

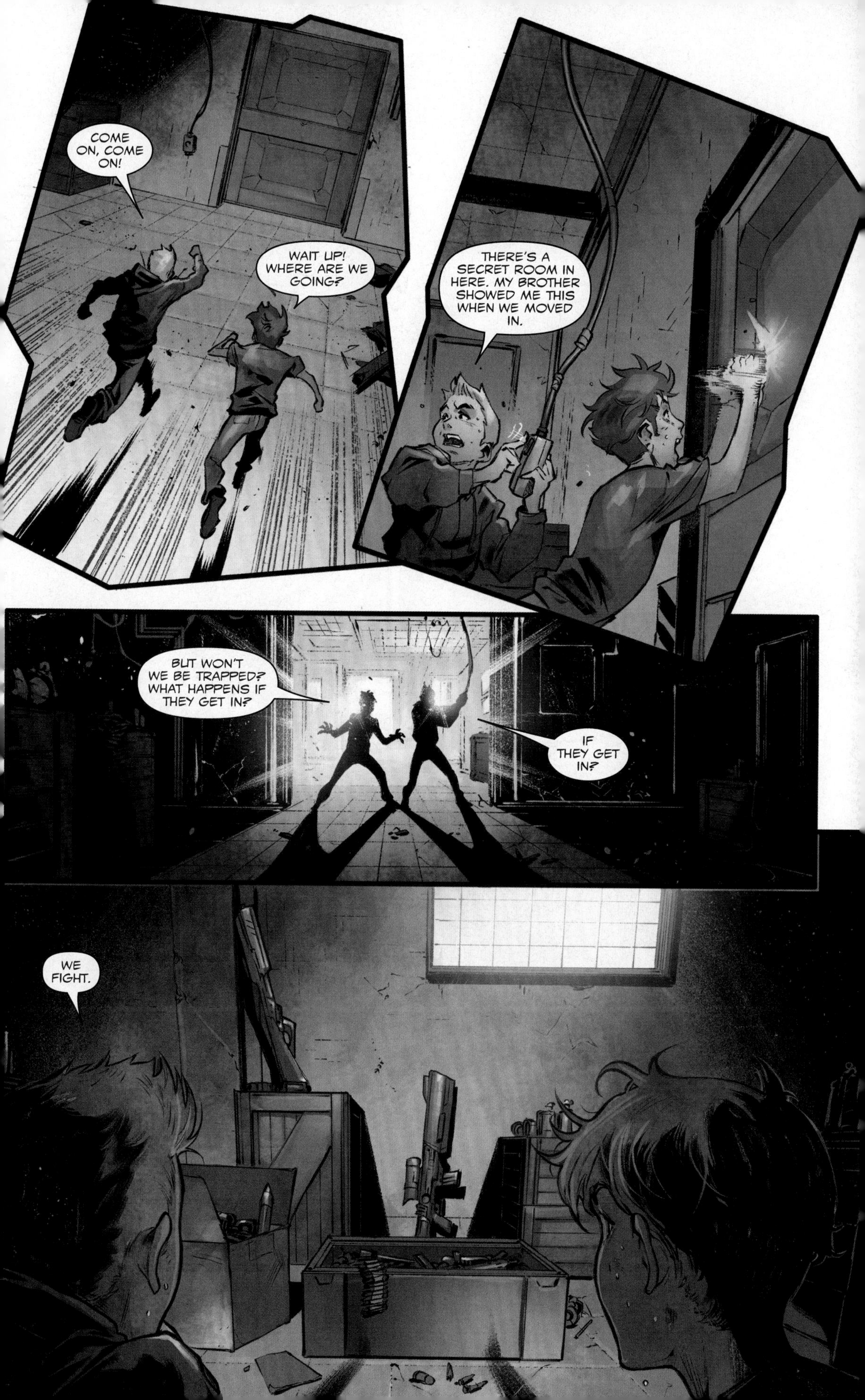
COME ON, COME ON!
WAIT UP! WHERE ARE WE GOING?
THERE'S A SECRET ROOM IN HERE. MY BROTHER SHOWED ME THIS WHEN WE MOVED IN.
BUT WON'T WE BE TRAPPED? WHAT HAPPENS IF THEY GET IN?
IF THEY GET IN?
WE FIGHT.

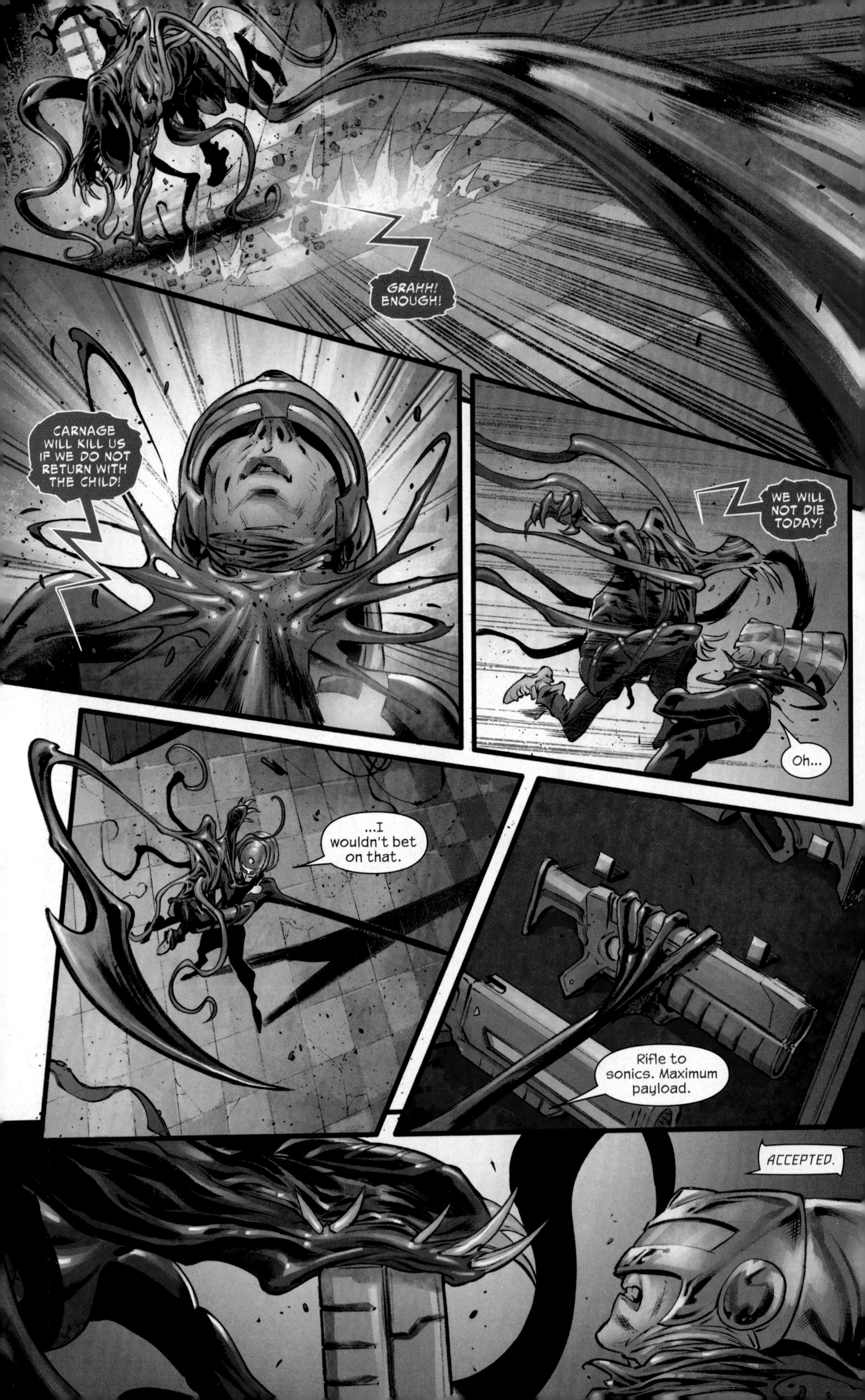
GRAHH! ENOUGH!
CARNAGE WILL KILL US IF WE DO NOT RETURN WITH THE CHILD!
WE WILL NOT DIE TODAY!
Oh...
...I wouldn't bet on that.
Rifle to sonics. Maximum payload.
ACCEPTED.

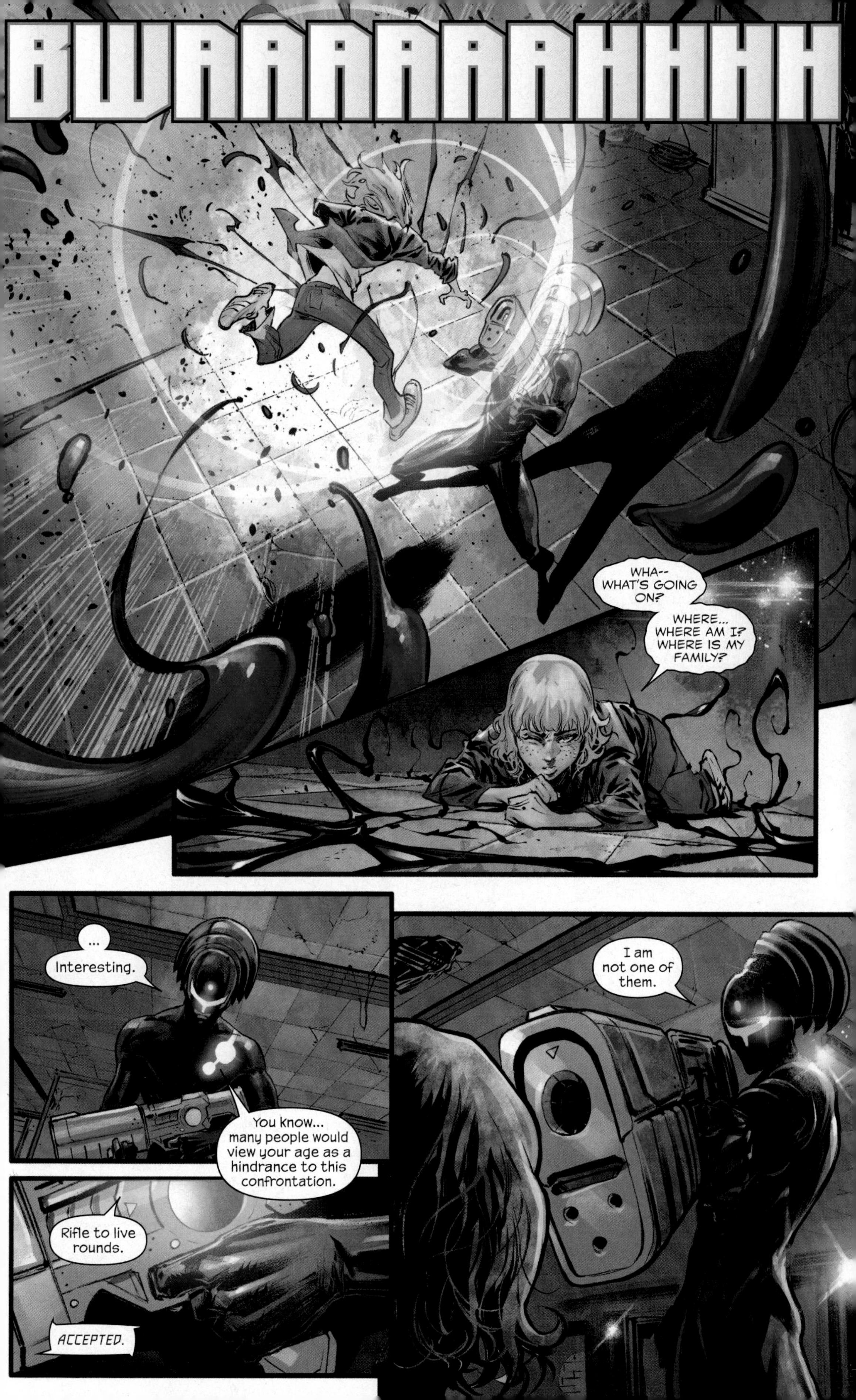
BWAAAAAAAHHHH
WHA-- WHAT'S GOING ON?
WHERE... WHERE AM I? WHERE IS MY FAMILY?
... Interesting.
You know... many people would view your age as a hindrance to this confrontation.
I am not one of them.
Rifle to live rounds.
ACCEPTED.

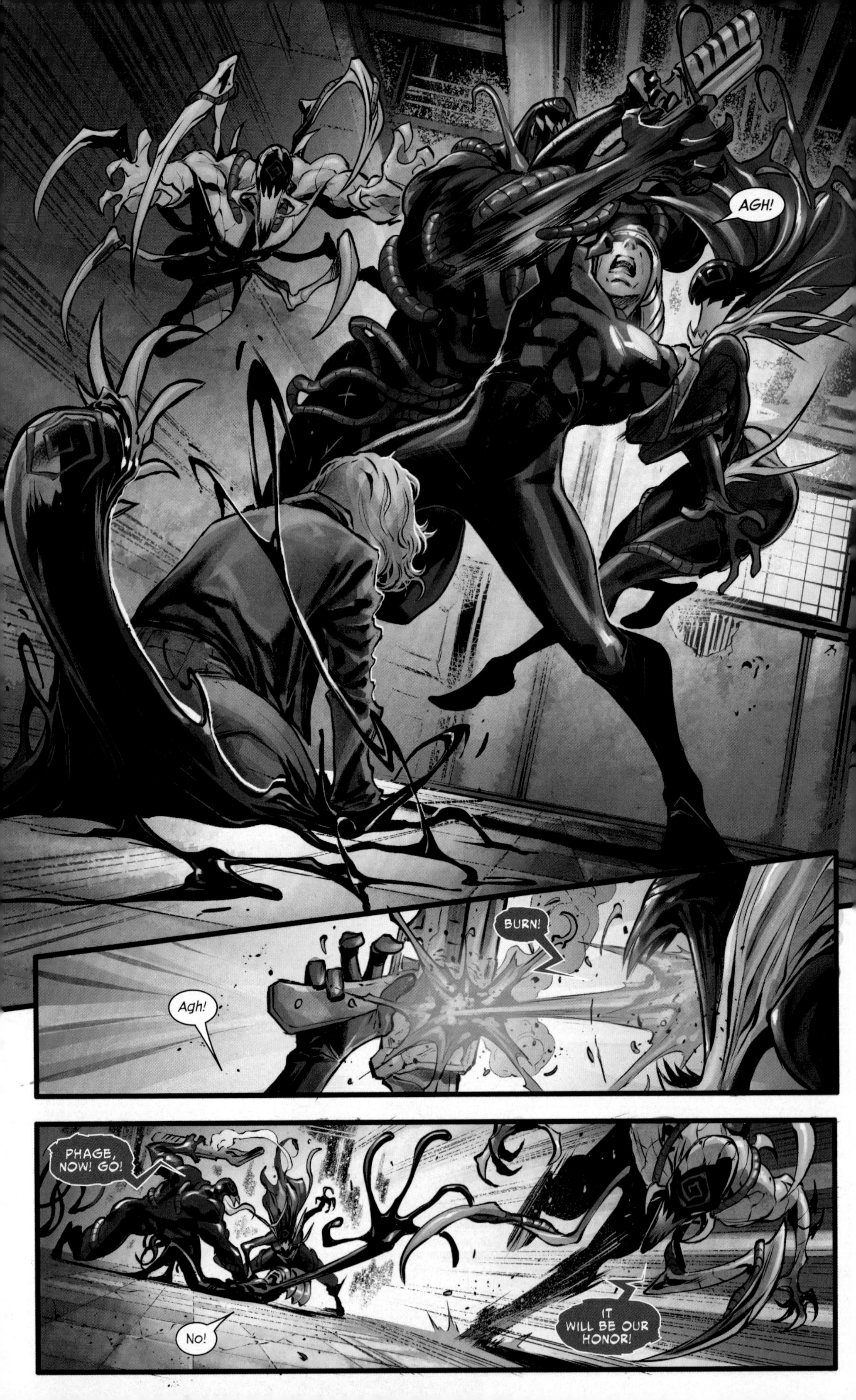
AGH!
BURN!
Agh!
PHAGE, NOW! GO!
No!
IT WILL BE OUR HONOR!

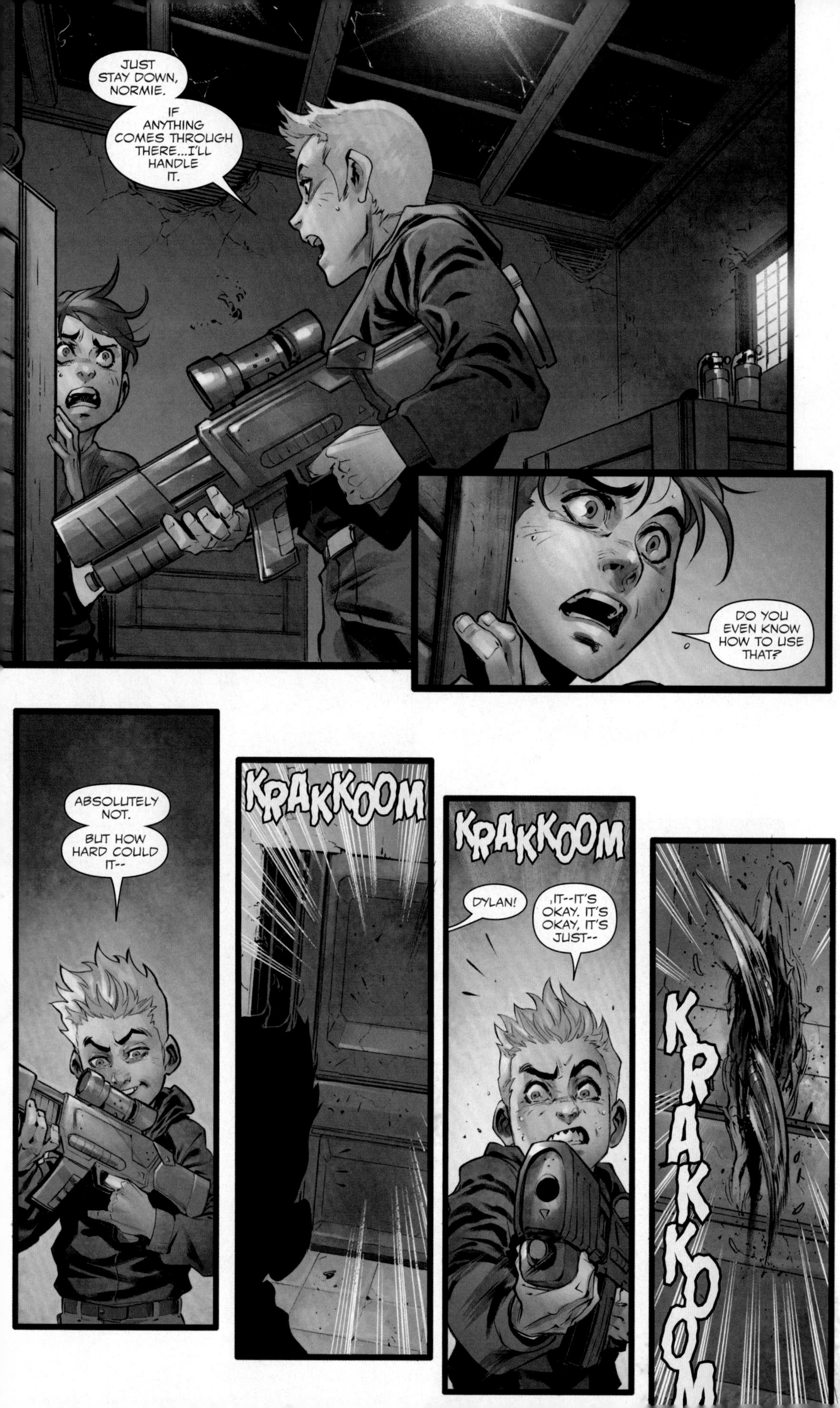
JUST STAY DOWN, NORMIE.
IF ANYTHING COMES THROUGH THERE...I'LL HANDLE IT.
DO YOU EVEN KNOW HOW TO USE THAT?
ABSOLUTELY NOT.
BUT HOW HARD COULD IT--
KRAKKOOM
KRAKKOOM
DYLAN!
IT--IT'S OKAY. IT'S OKAY, IT'S JUST--
KRAKKOOM

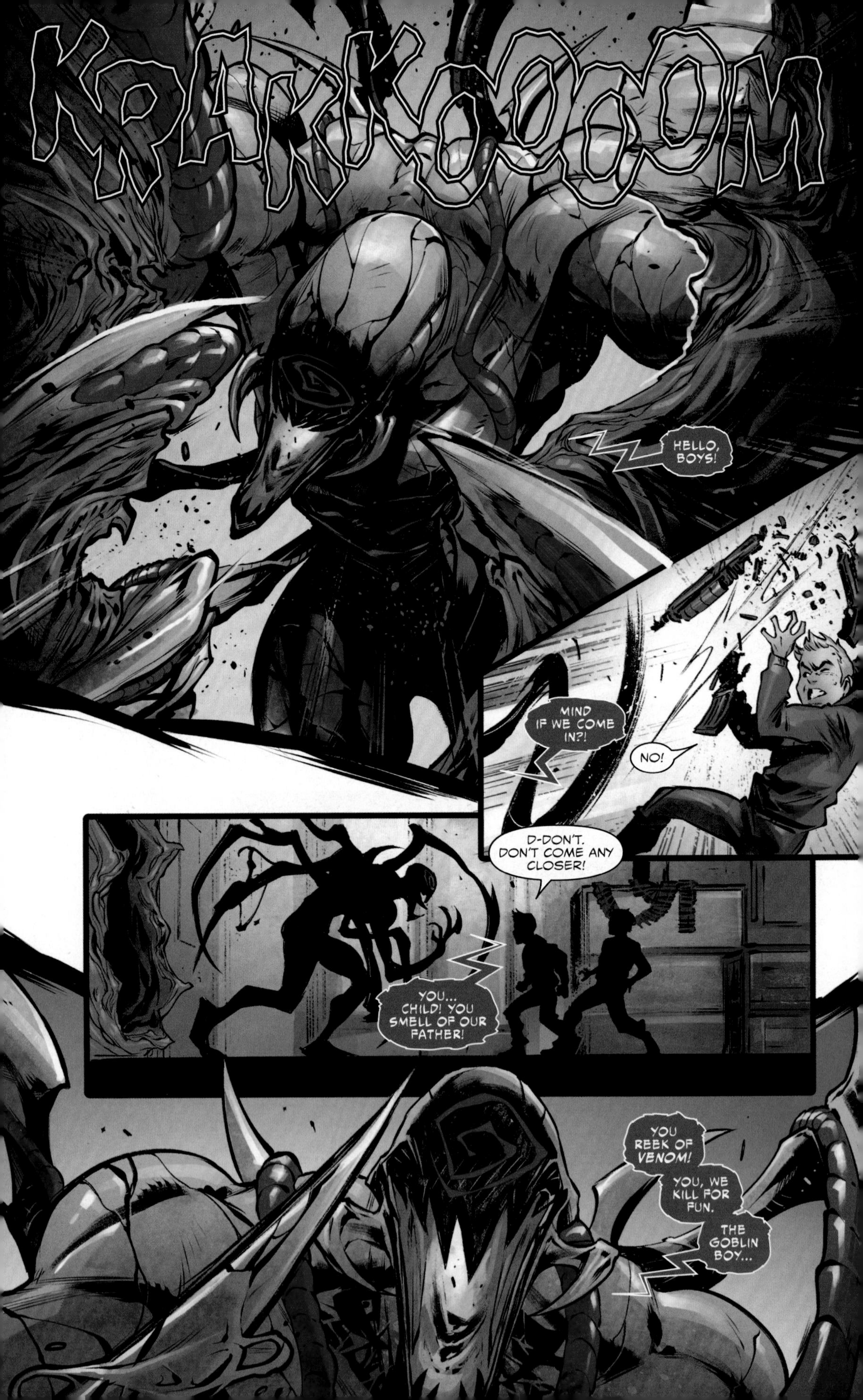
KRAKKOOOOOM
HELLO, BOYS!
MIND IF WE COME IN?!
NO!
D-DON'T. DON'T COME ANY CLOSER!
YOU... CHILD! YOU SMELL OF OUR FATHER!
YOU REEK OF *VENOM!*
YOU, WE KILL FOR FUN.
THE GOBLIN BOY...

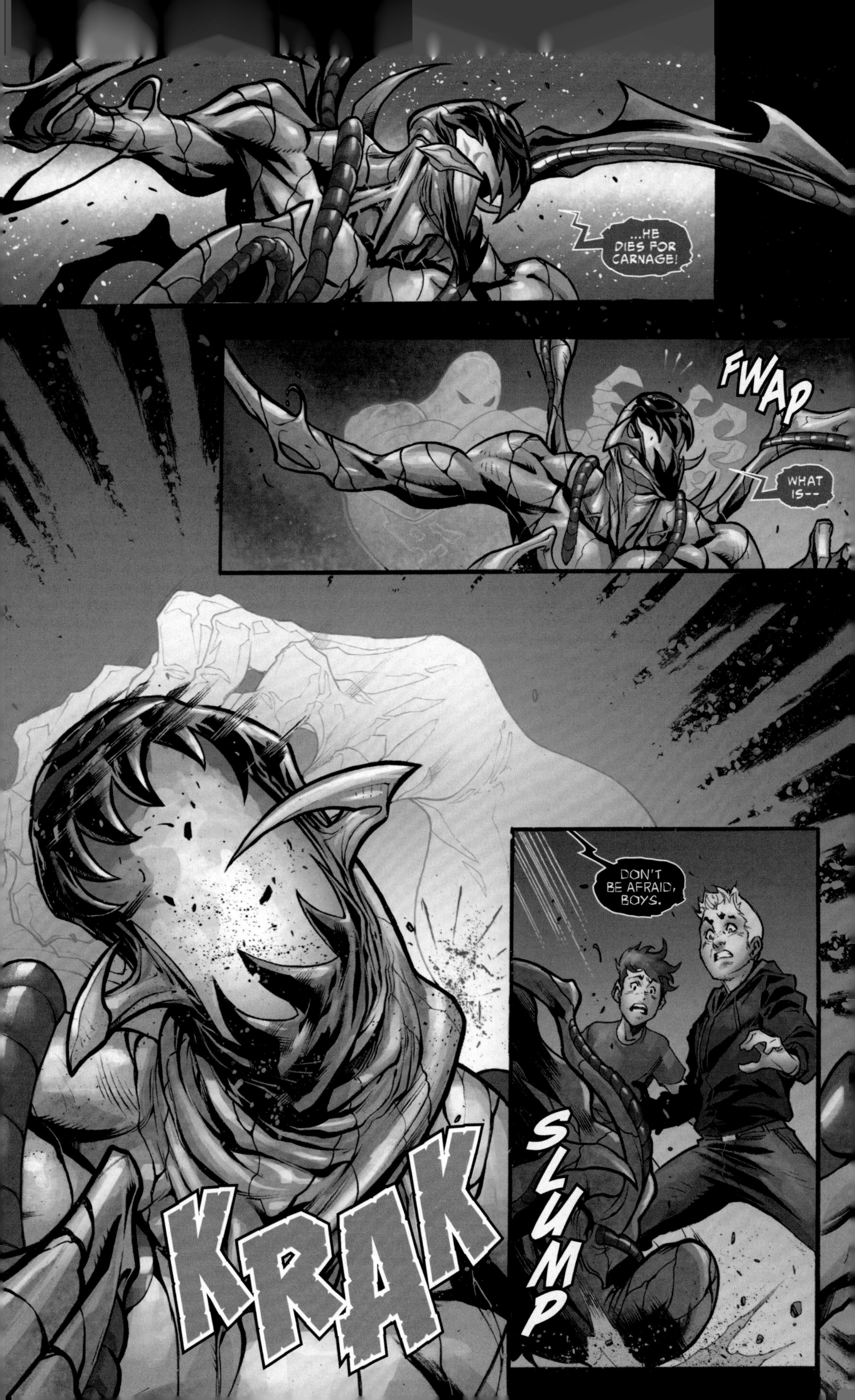
...HE
DIES FOR
CARNAGE!
FWAP
WHAT IS--
DON'T BE AFRAID, BOYS.
KRAK
SLUMP

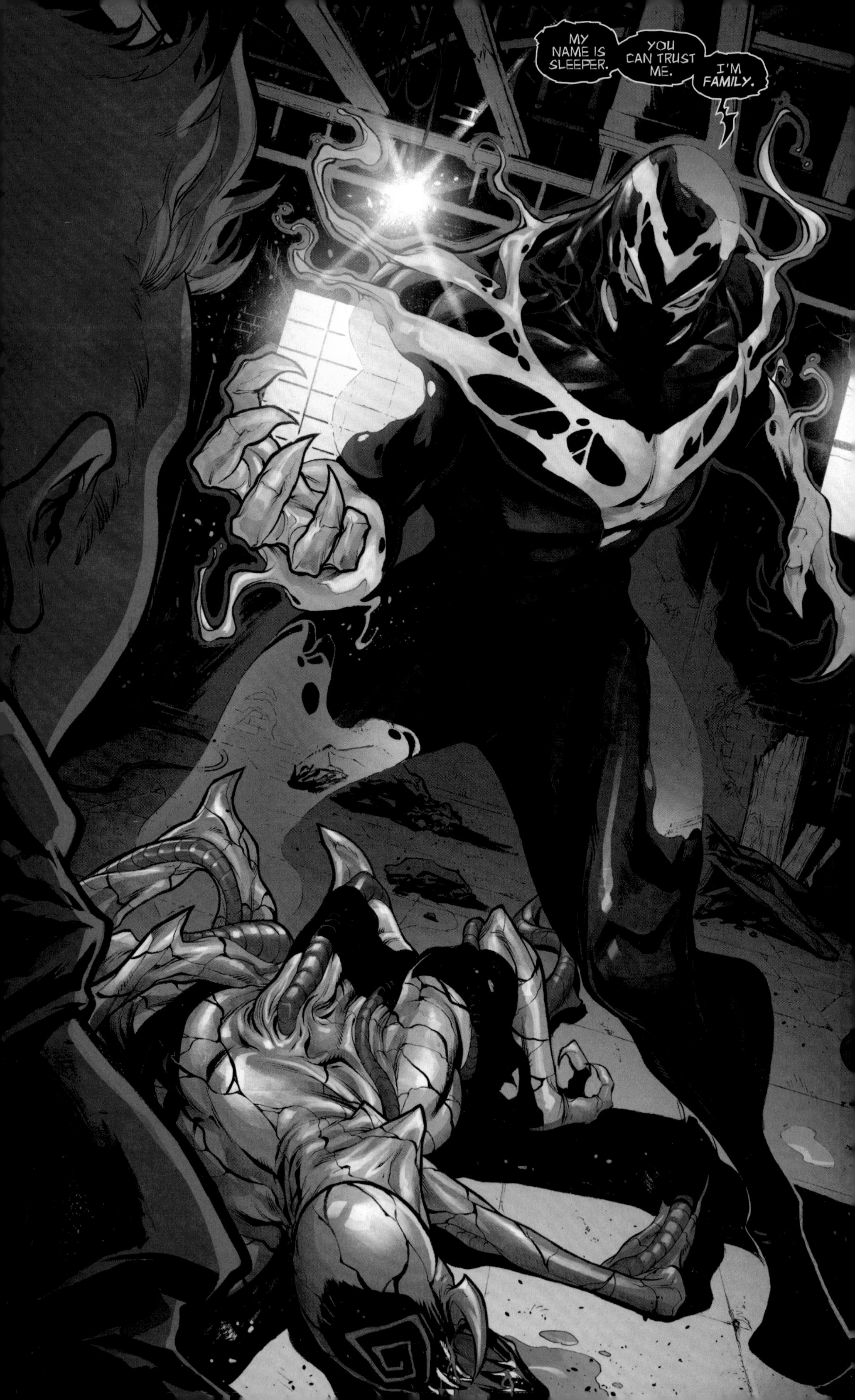
MY NAME IS SLEEPER.
YOU CAN TRUST ME.
I'M FAMILY.

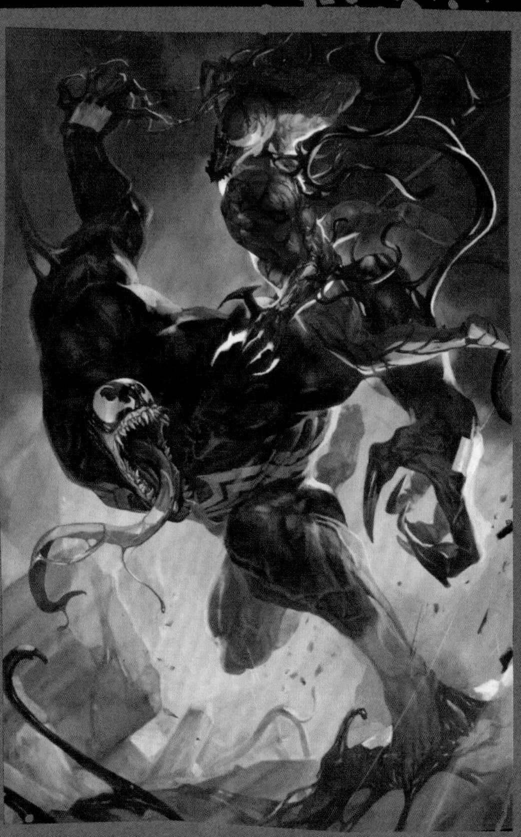

#17 BRING ON THE BAD GUYS VARIANT
BY **SUNGHAN YUNE**

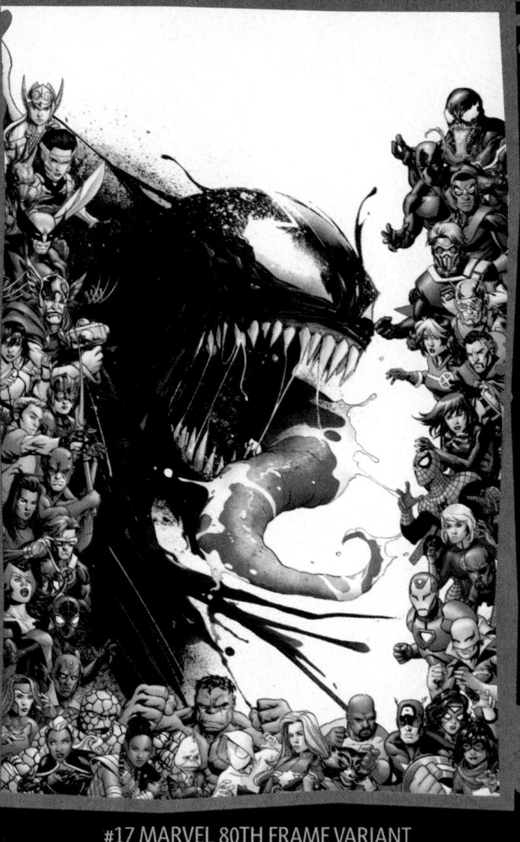

#17 MARVEL 80TH FRAME VARIANT
BY **LEE GARBETT**
WITH **MIKE McKONE** & **EDGAR DELGADO**

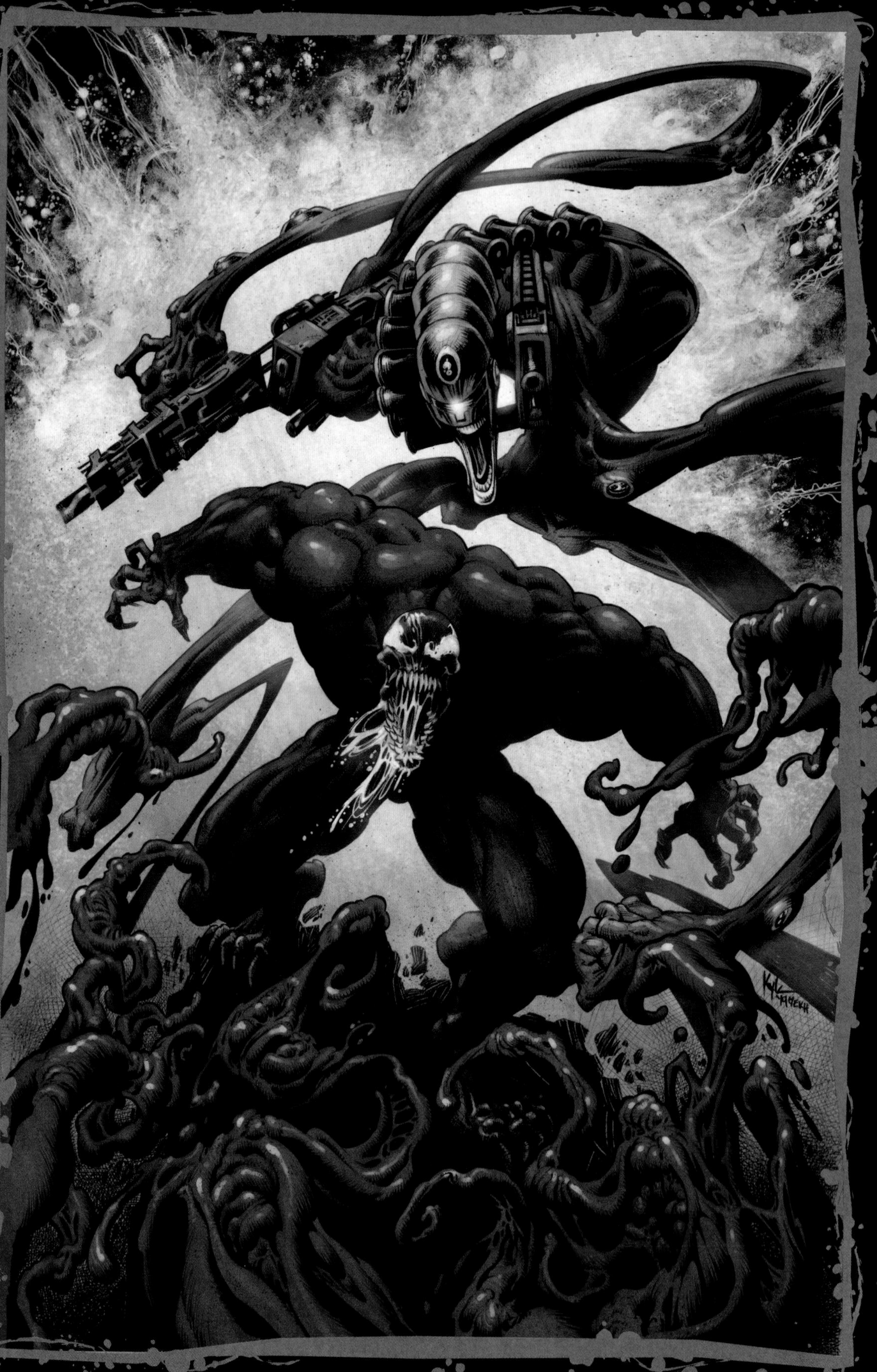

18

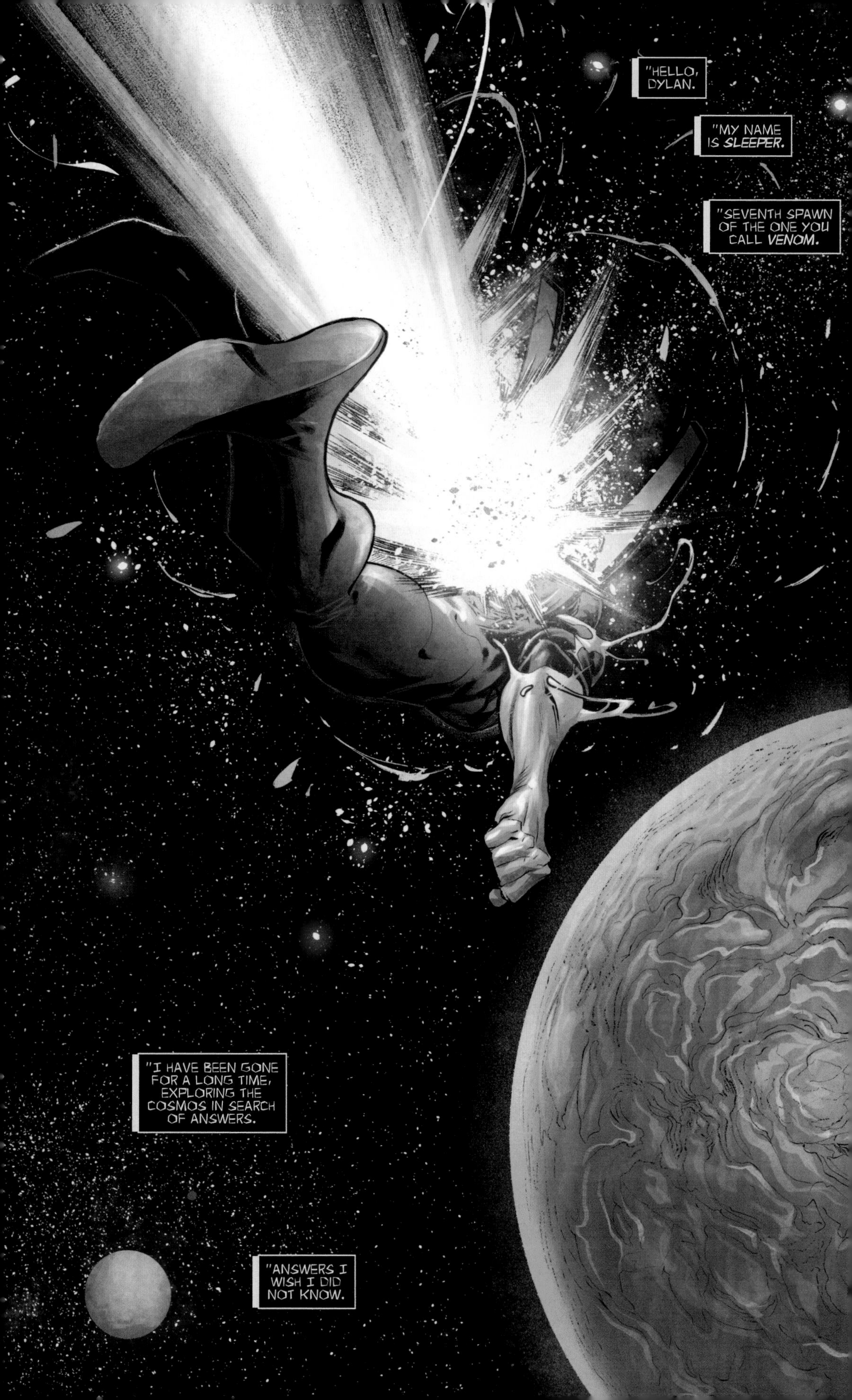
"HELLO, DYLAN.
"MY NAME IS SLEEPER.
"SEVENTH SPAWN OF THE ONE YOU CALL VENOM.
"I HAVE BEEN GONE FOR A LONG TIME, EXPLORING THE COSMOS IN SEARCH OF ANSWERS.
"ANSWERS I WISH I DID NOT KNOW.

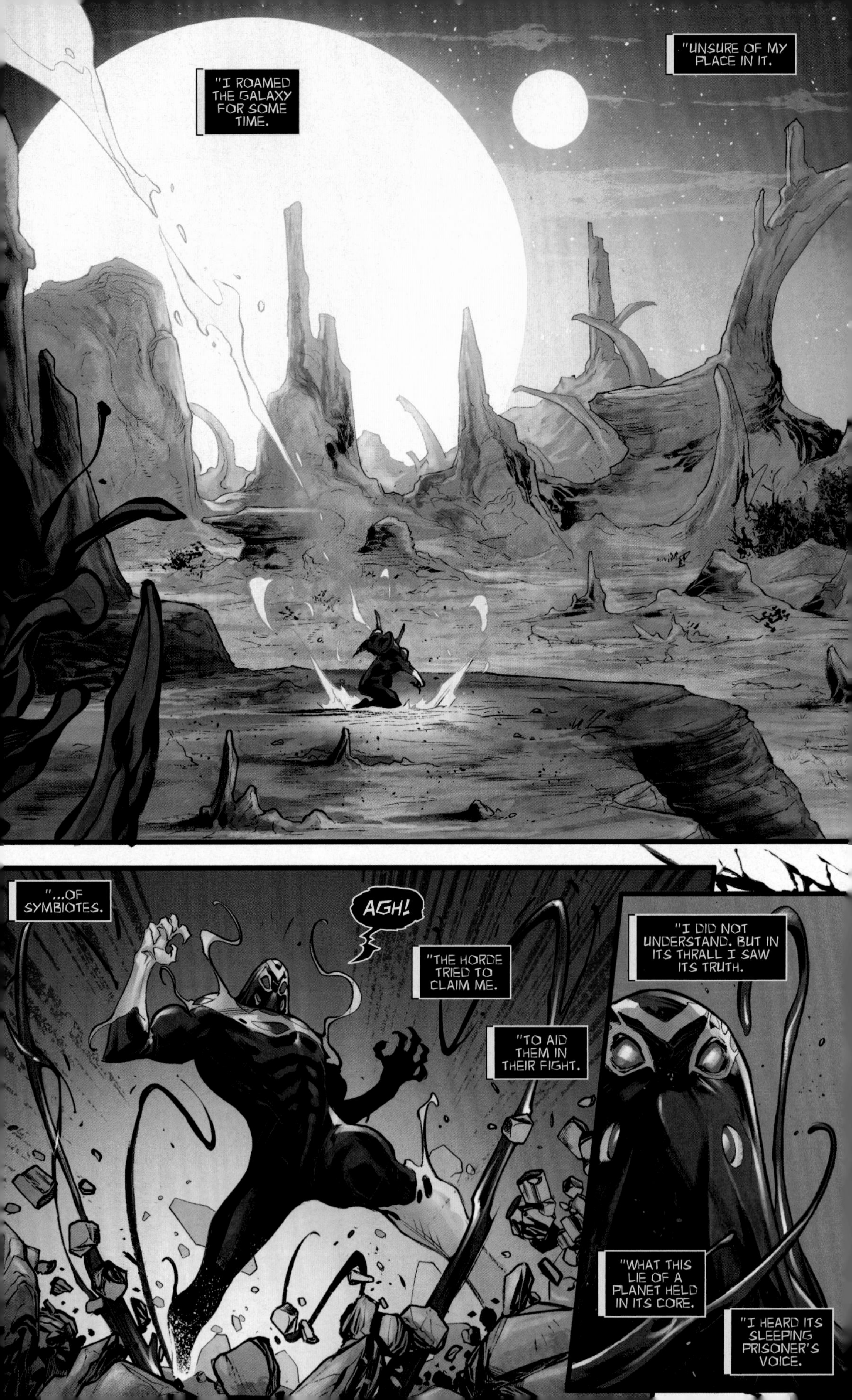
"I ROAMED THE GALAXY FOR SOME TIME.
"UNSURE OF MY PLACE IN IT.
"...OF SYMBIOTES.
AGH!
"THE HORDE TRIED TO CLAIM ME.
"TO AID THEM IN THEIR FIGHT.
"I DID NOT UNDERSTAND. BUT IN ITS THRALL I SAW ITS TRUTH.
"WHAT THIS LIE OF A PLANET HELD IN ITS CORE.
"I HEARD ITS SLEEPING PRISONER'S VOICE.

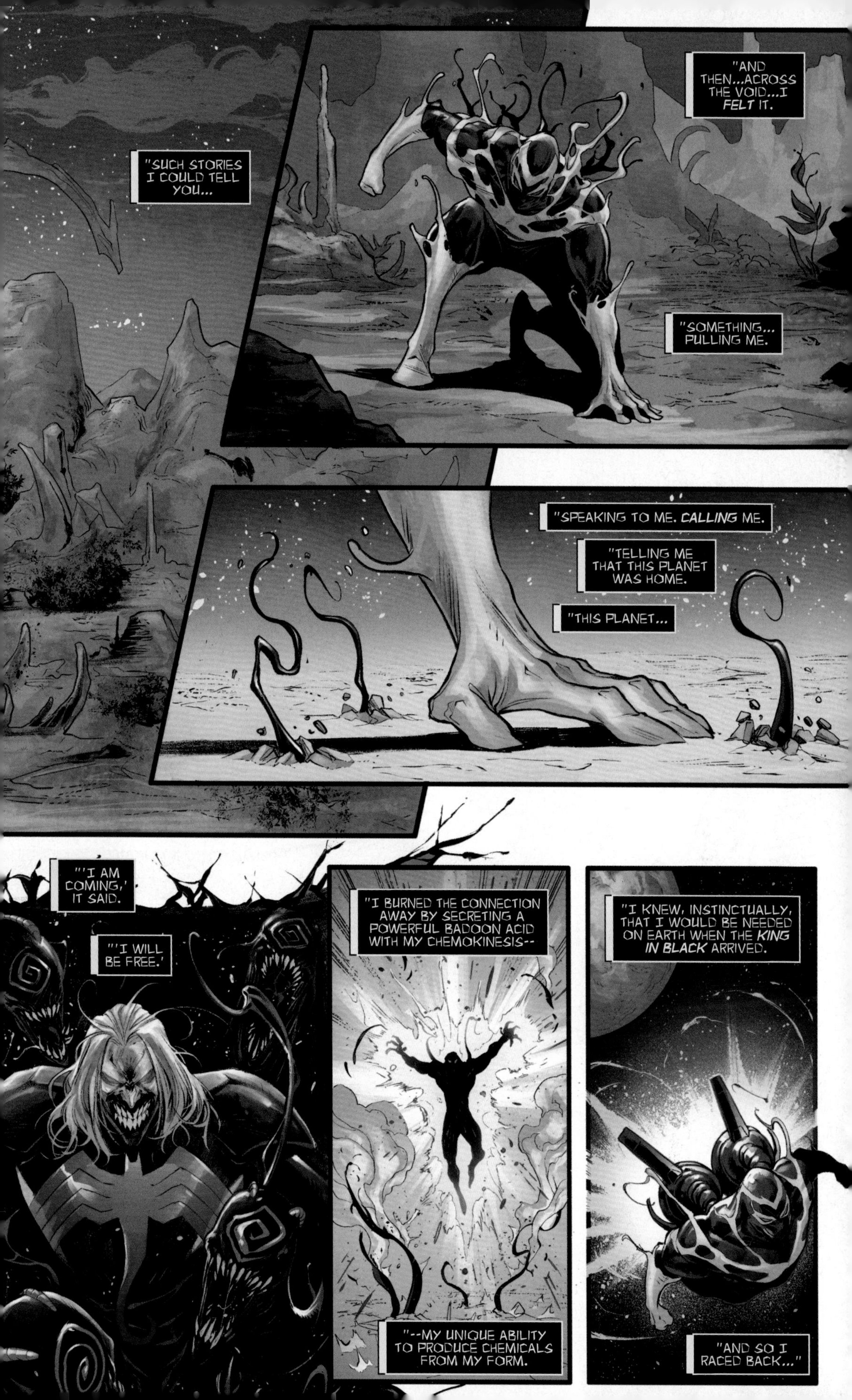
"SUCH STORIES I COULD TELL YOU...
"AND THEN...ACROSS THE VOID...I *FELT* IT.
"SOMETHING... PULLING ME.
"SPEAKING TO ME. *CALLING* ME.
"TELLING ME THAT THIS PLANET WAS HOME.
"THIS PLANET...
"'I AM COMING,' IT SAID.
"'I WILL BE FREE.'
"I BURNED THE CONNECTION AWAY BY SECRETING A POWERFUL BADOON ACID WITH MY CHEMOKINESIS--
"--MY UNIQUE ABILITY TO PRODUCE CHEMICALS FROM MY FORM.
"I KNEW, INSTINCTUALLY, THAT I WOULD BE NEEDED ON EARTH WHEN THE *KING IN BLACK* ARRIVED.
"AND SO I RACED BACK..."

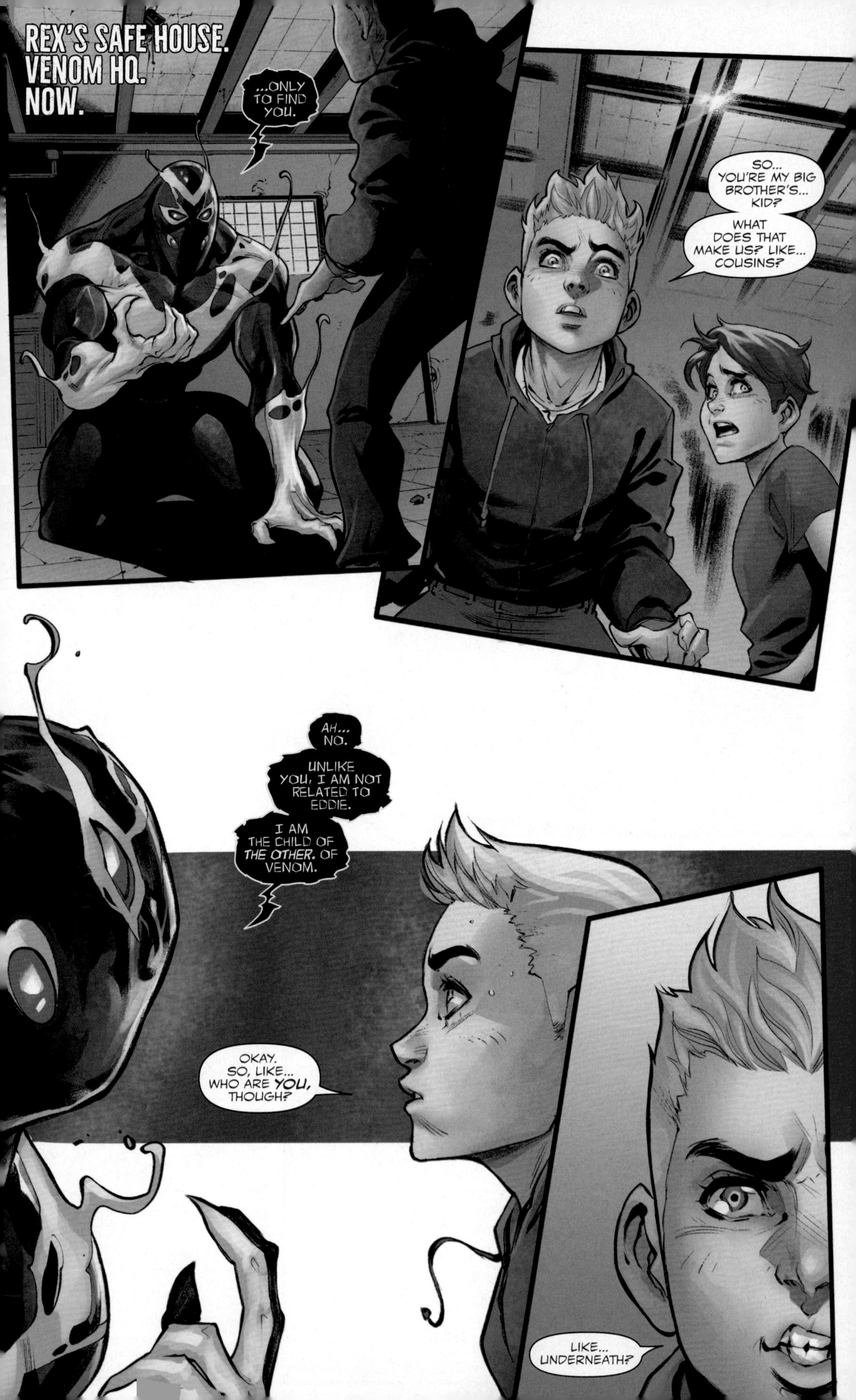
REX'S SAFE HOUSE. VENOM HQ. NOW.
...ONLY TO FIND YOU.
SO... YOU'RE MY BIG BROTHER'S... KID?
WHAT DOES THAT MAKE US? LIKE... COUSINS?
AH... NO.
UNLIKE YOU, I AM NOT RELATED TO EDDIE.
I AM THE CHILD OF THE OTHER. OF VENOM.
OKAY. SO, LIKE... WHO ARE YOU, THOUGH?
LIKE... UNDERNEATH?

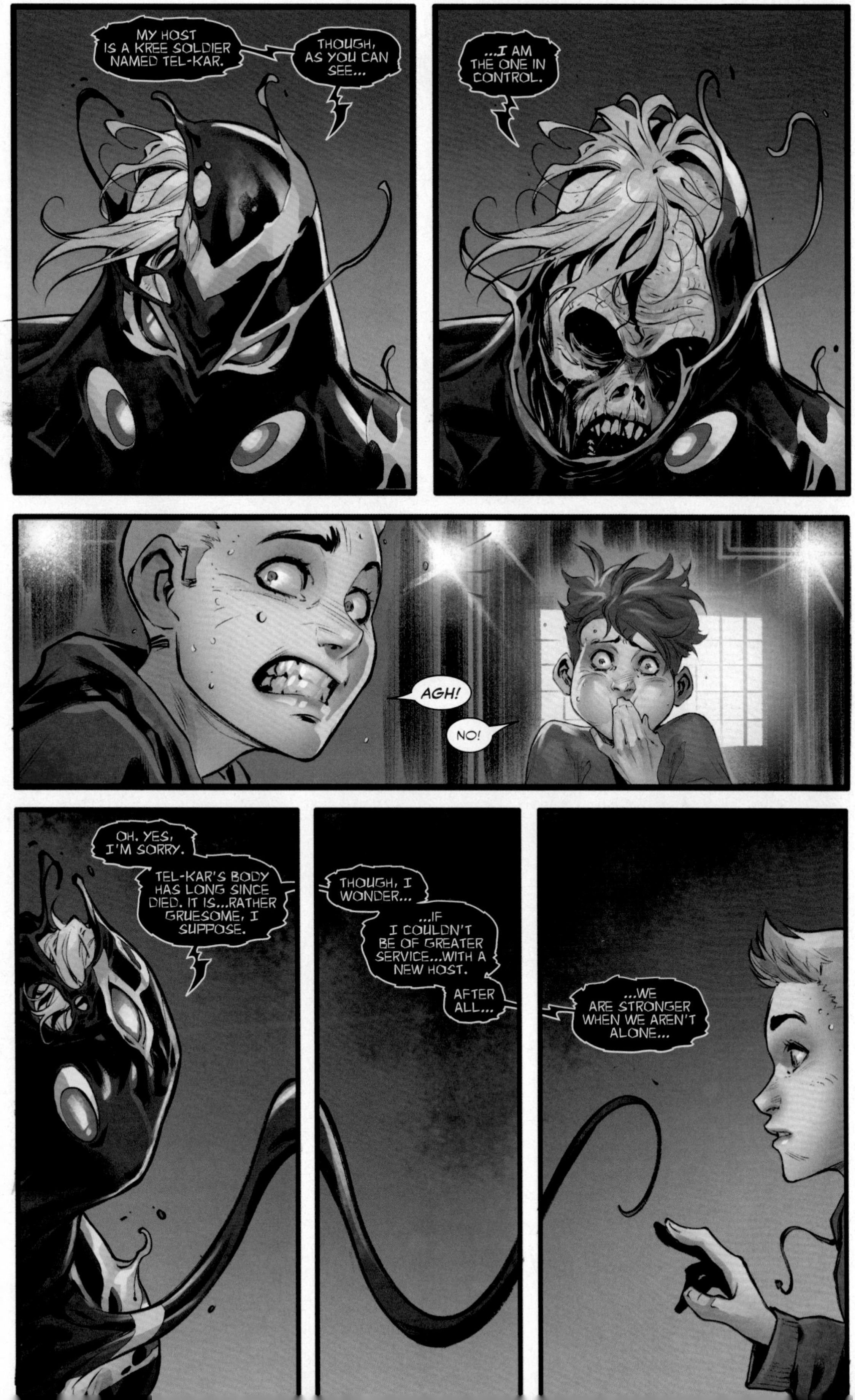
MY HOST IS A KREE SOLDIER NAMED TEL-KAR.
THOUGH, AS YOU CAN SEE...
...I AM THE ONE IN CONTROL.
AGH!
NO!
OH. YES, I'M SORRY.
TEL-KAR'S BODY HAS LONG SINCE DIED. IT IS...RATHER GRUESOME, I SUPPOSE.
THOUGH, I WONDER...
...IF I COULDN'T BE OF GREATER SERVICE...WITH A NEW HOST.
AFTER ALL...
...WE ARE STRONGER WHEN WE AREN'T ALONE...

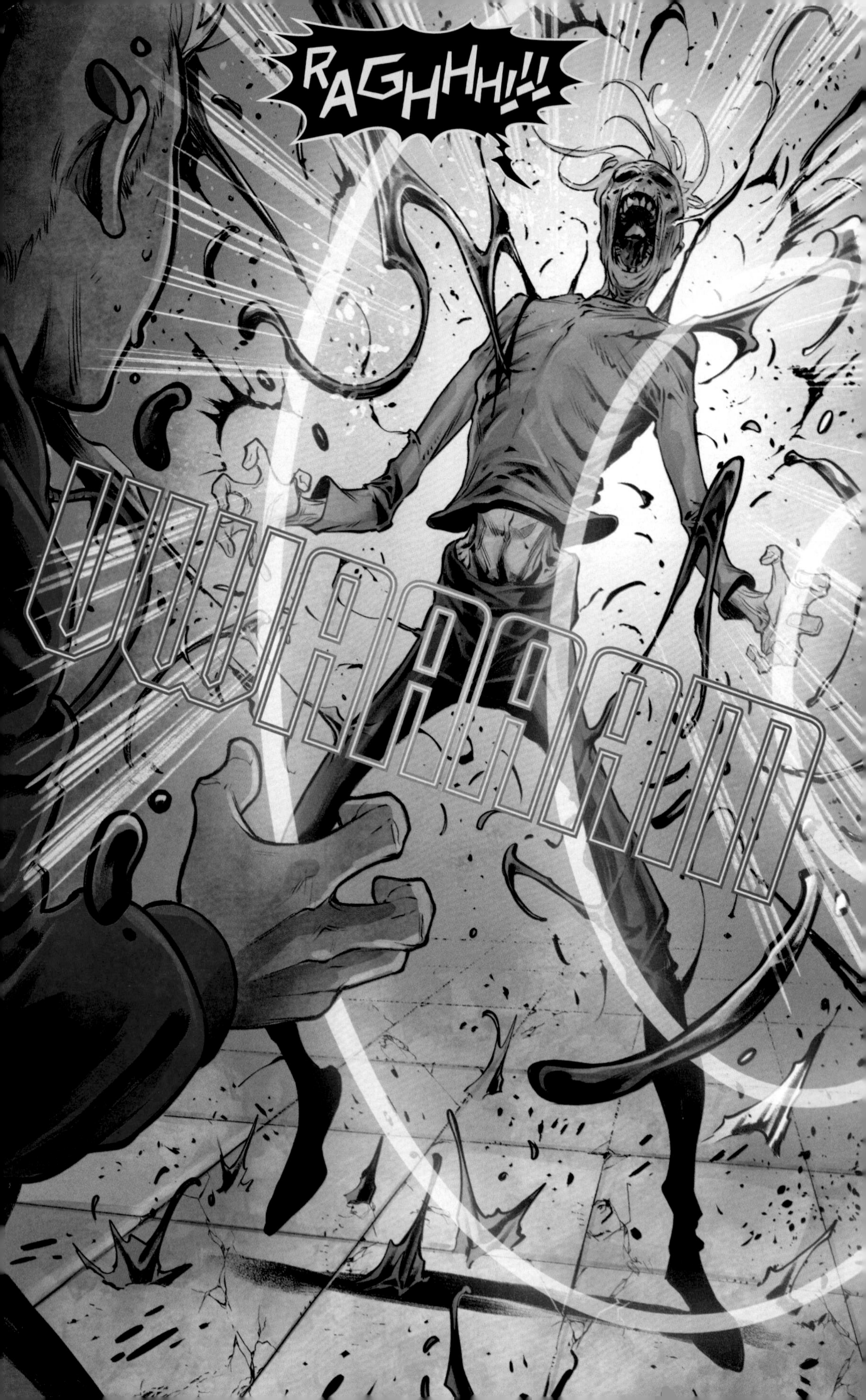
RAGHHH!!!
VWAAAAM

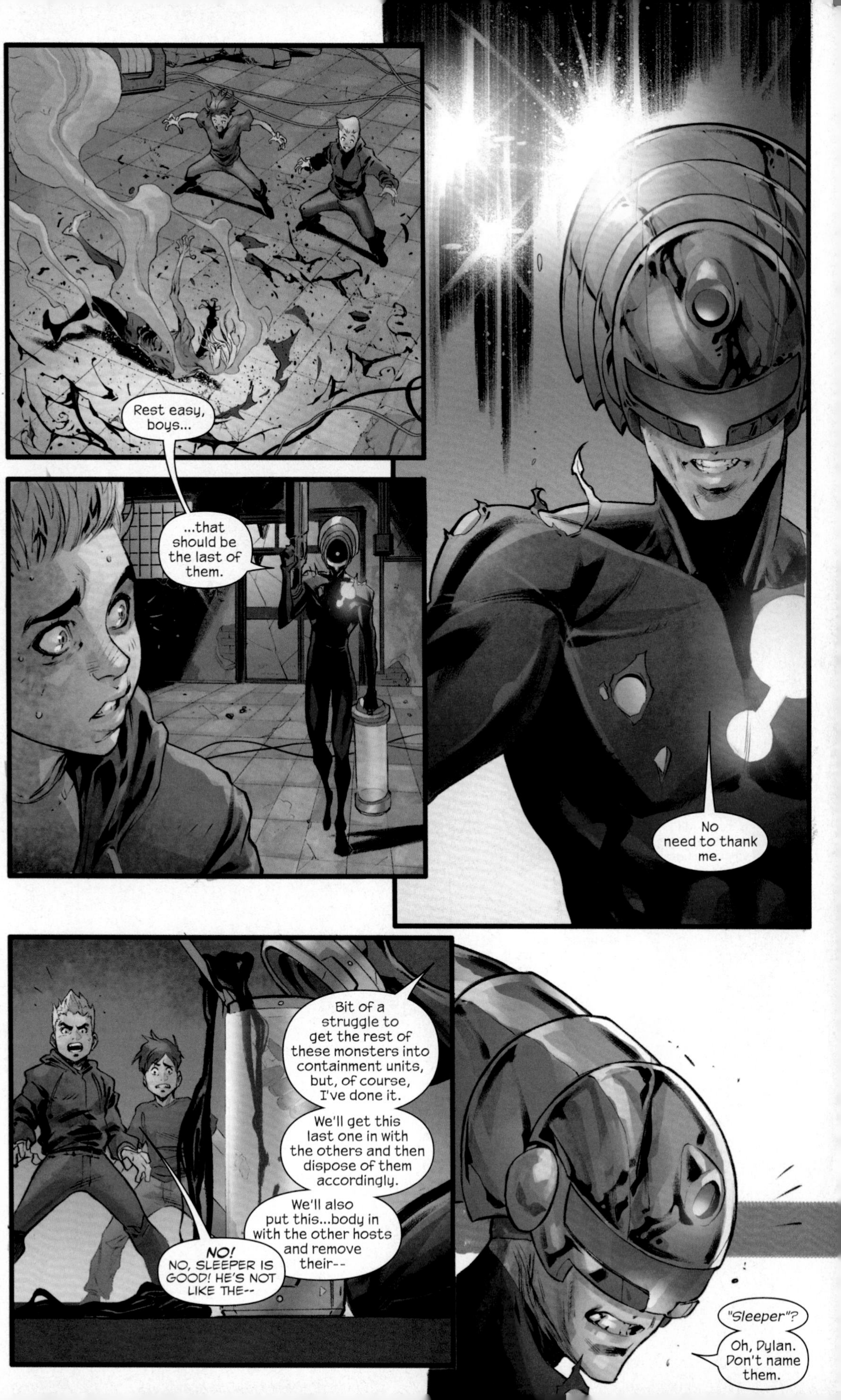
Rest easy, boys...
...that should be the last of them.
No need to thank me.
Bit of a struggle to get the rest of these monsters into containment units, but, of course, I've done it.
We'll get this last one in with the others and then dispose of them accordingly.
We'll also put this...body in with the other hosts and remove their--
NO! NO, SLEEPER IS GOOD! HE'S NOT LIKE THE--
"Sleeper"?
Oh, Dylan. Don't name them.

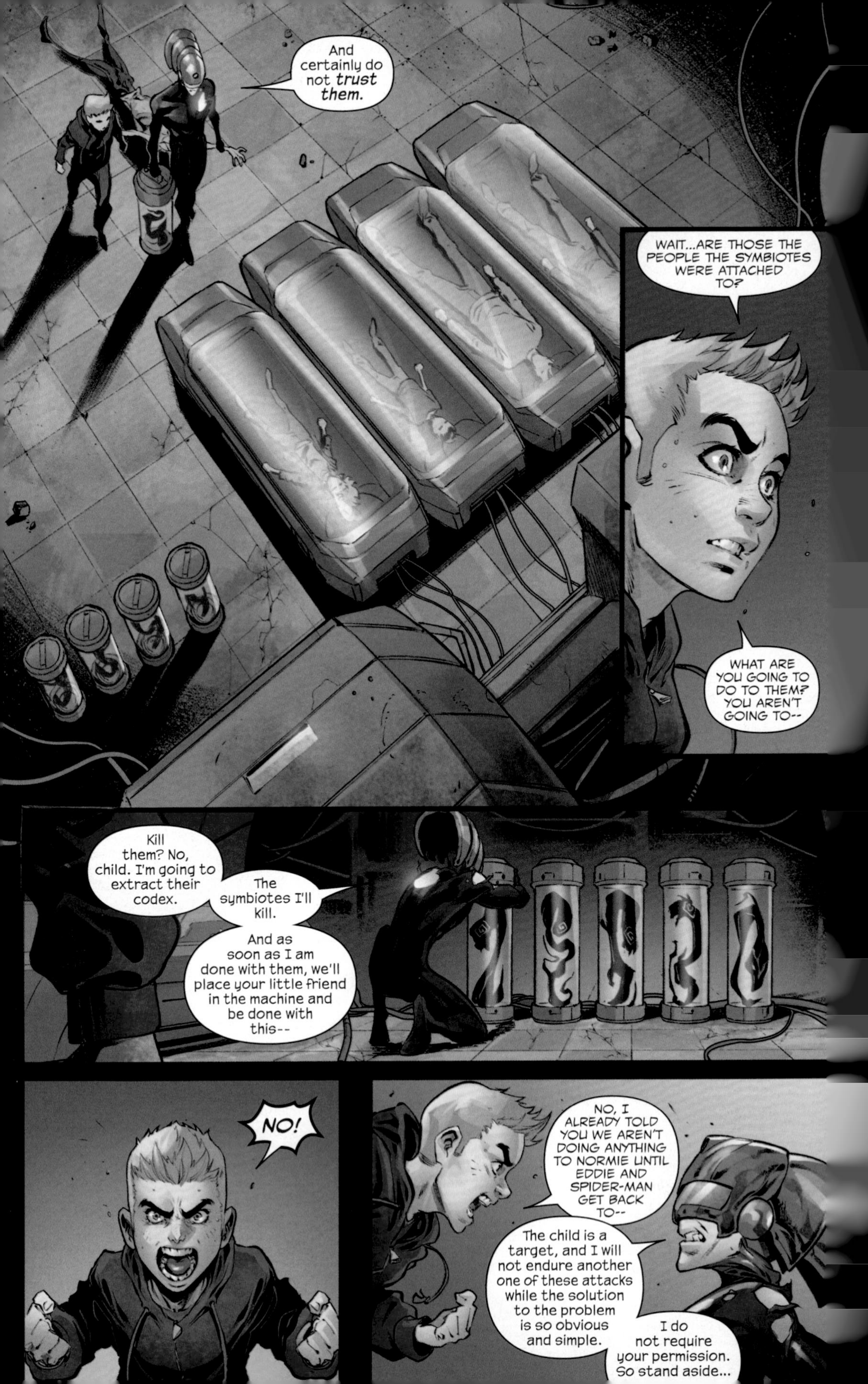
And certainly do not *trust them.*
WAIT...ARE THOSE THE PEOPLE THE SYMBIOTES WERE ATTACHED TO?
WHAT ARE YOU GOING TO DO TO THEM? YOU AREN'T GOING TO--
Kill them? No, child. I'm going to extract their codex.
The symbiotes I'll kill.
And as soon as I am done with them, we'll place your little friend in the machine and be done with this--
NO!
NO, I ALREADY TOLD YOU WE AREN'T DOING ANYTHING TO NORMIE UNTIL EDDIE AND SPIDER-MAN GET BACK TO--
The child is a target, and I will not endure another one of these attacks while the solution to the problem is so obvious and simple.
I do not require your permission. So stand aside...

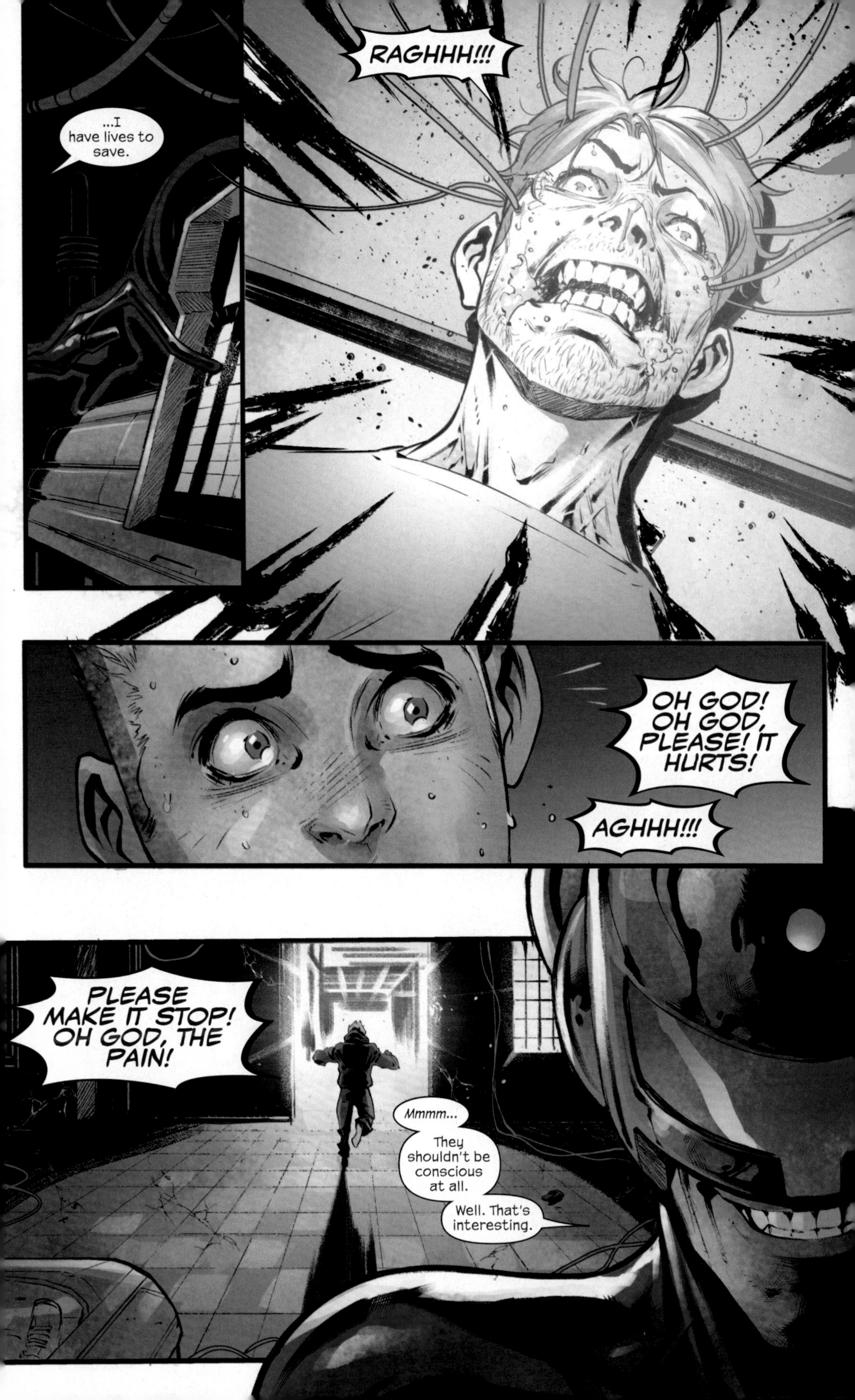

...I have lives to save.
RAGHHH!!!
OH GOD! OH GOD, PLEASE! IT HURTS!
AGHHH!!!
PLEASE MAKE IT STOP! OH GOD, THE PAIN!
Mmmm...
They shouldn't be conscious at all.
Well. That's interesting.

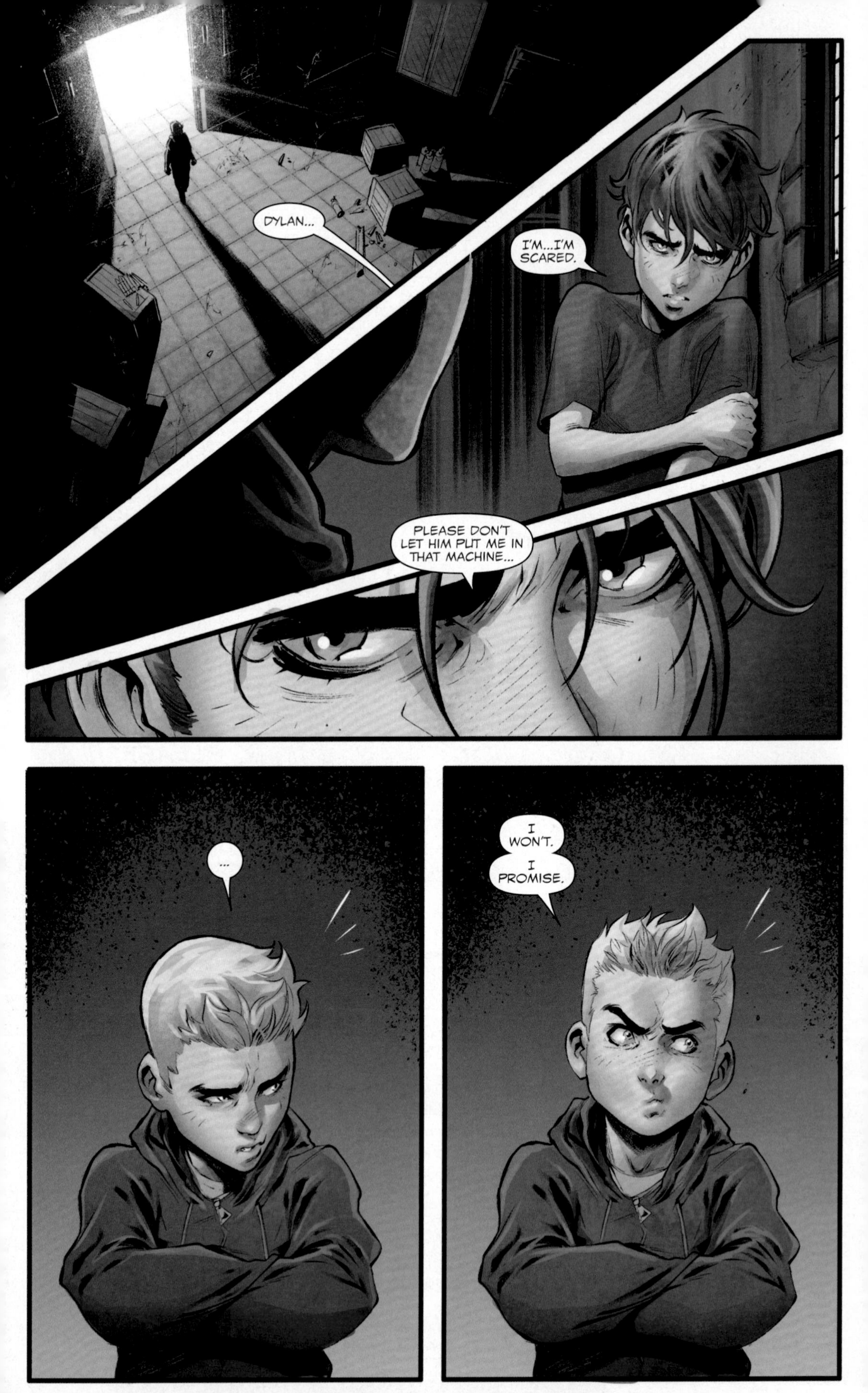
DYLAN...
I'M...I'M SCARED.
PLEASE DON'T LET HIM PUT ME IN THAT MACHINE...
...
I WON'T.
I PROMISE.

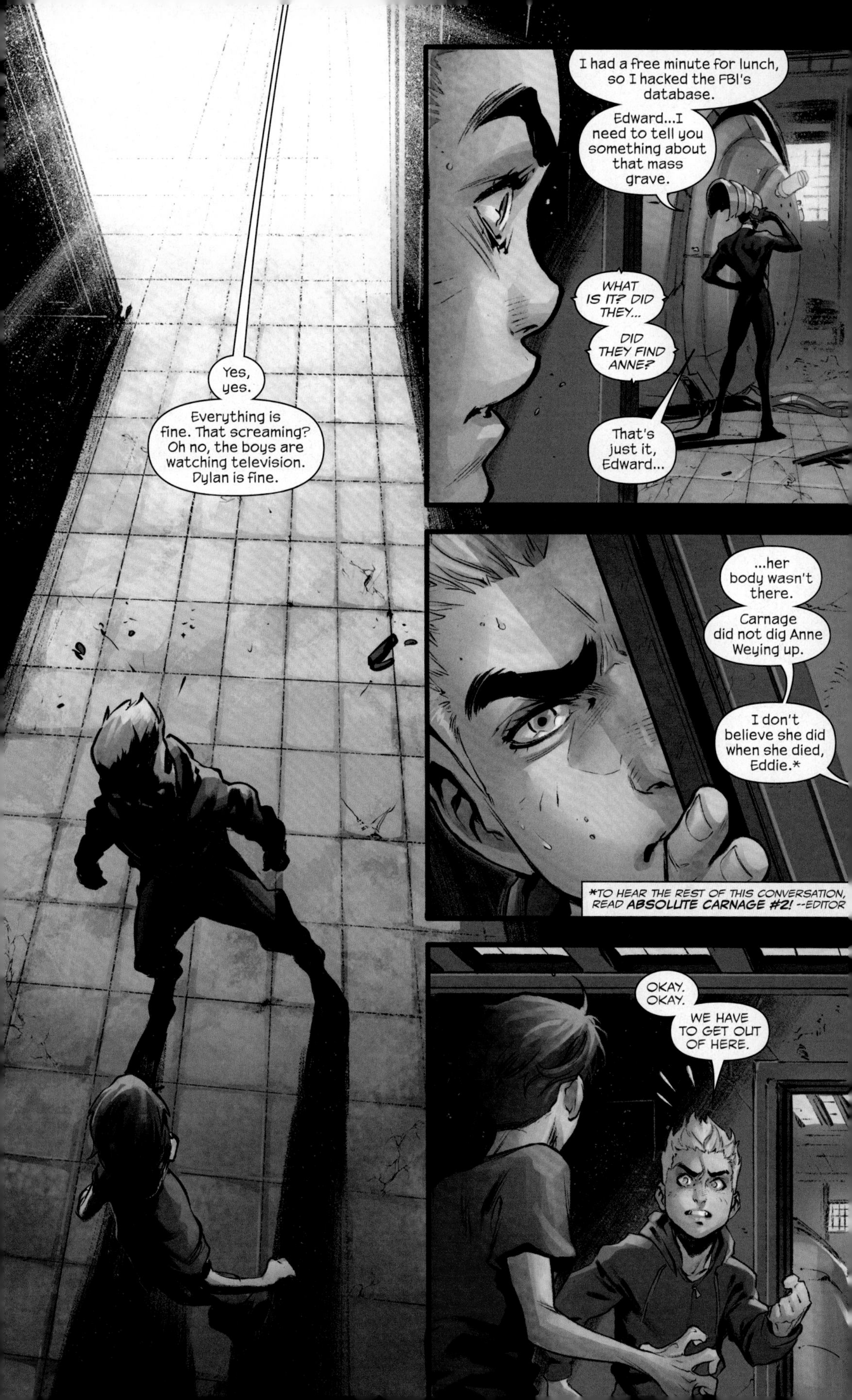

Yes, yes.
Everything is fine. That screaming? Oh no, the boys are watching television. Dylan is fine.
I had a free minute for lunch, so I hacked the FBI's database.
Edward...I need to tell you something about that mass grave.
WHAT IS IT? DID THEY...
DID THEY FIND ANNE?
That's just it, Edward...
...her body wasn't there.
Carnage did not dig Anne Weying up.
I don't believe she did when she died, Eddie.*
*TO HEAR THE REST OF THIS CONVERSATION, READ ABSOLUTE CARNAGE #2! --EDITOR
OKAY. OKAY.
WE HAVE TO GET OUT OF HERE.

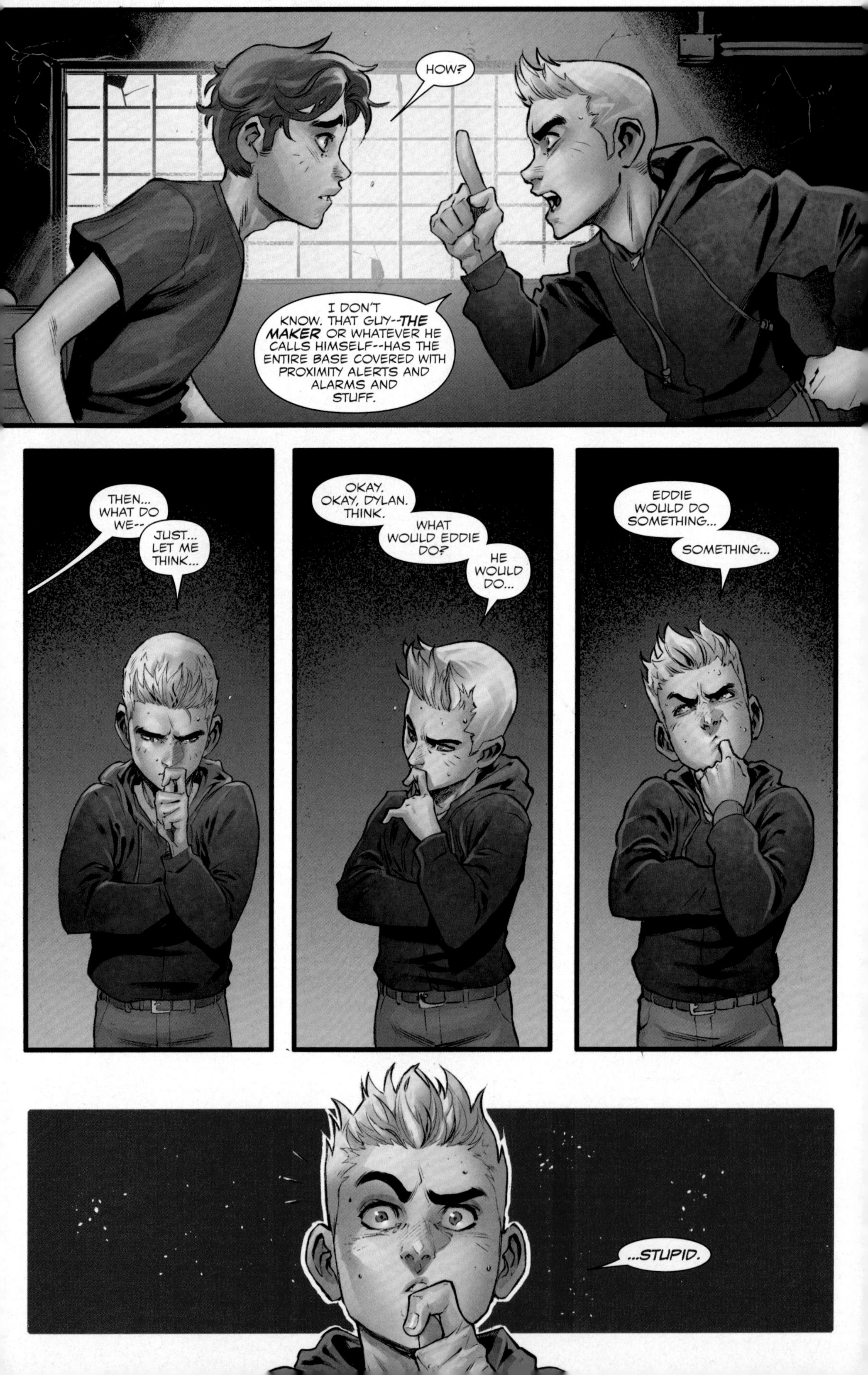
HOW?
I DON'T KNOW. THAT GUY--THE MAKER OR WHATEVER HE CALLS HIMSELF--HAS THE ENTIRE BASE COVERED WITH PROXIMITY ALERTS AND ALARMS AND STUFF.
THEN... WHAT DO WE--
JUST... LET ME THINK...
OKAY. OKAY, DYLAN. THINK.
WHAT WOULD EDDIE DO?
HE WOULD DO...
EDDIE WOULD DO SOMETHING...
SOMETHING...
...STUPID.

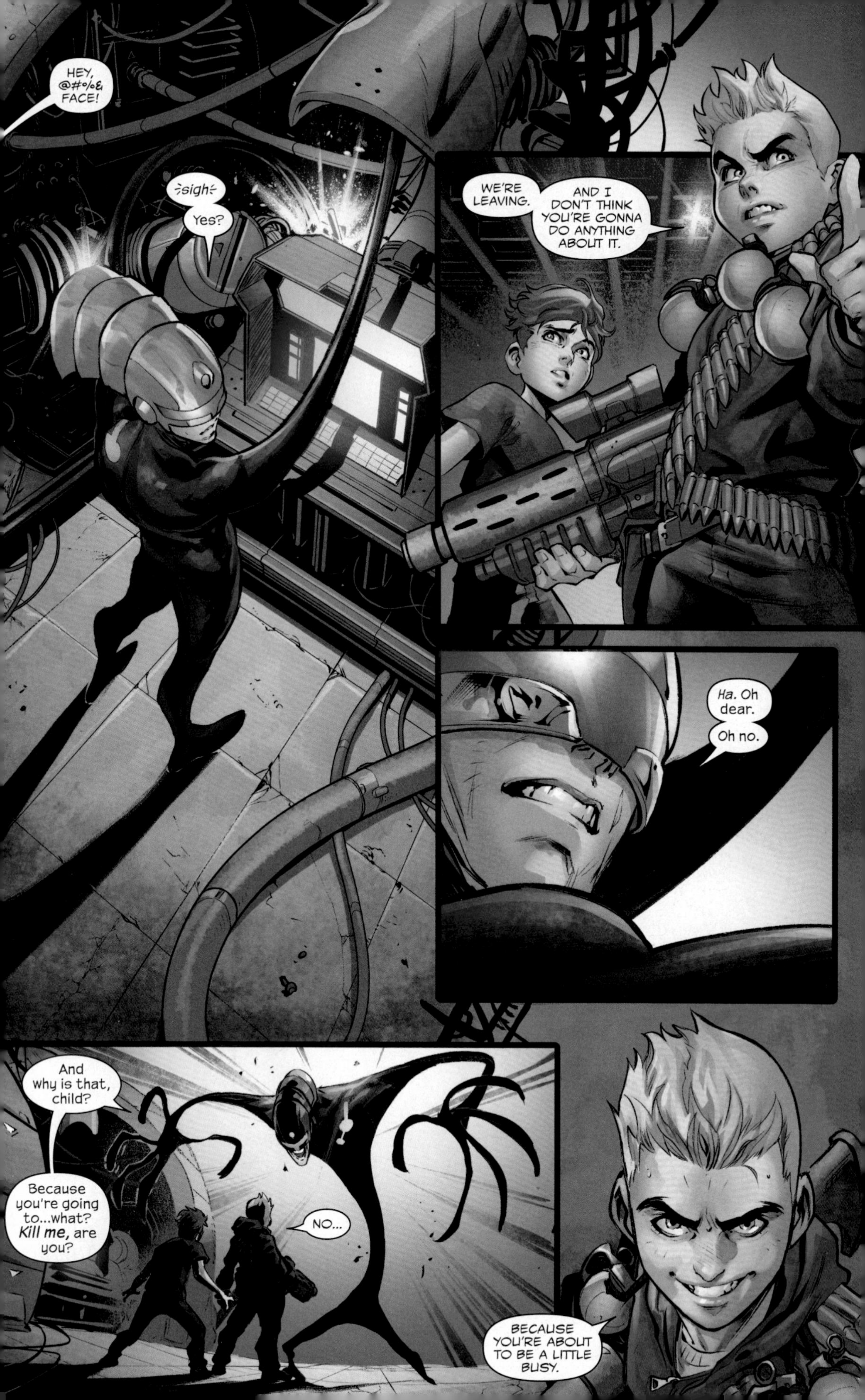
HEY, @#%& FACE!
-sigh-
Yes?
WE'RE LEAVING.
AND I DON'T THINK YOU'RE GONNA DO ANYTHING ABOUT IT.
Ha. Oh dear.
Oh no.
And why is that, child?
Because you're going to...what? Kill me, are you?
NO...
BECAUSE YOU'RE ABOUT TO BE A LITTLE BUSY.

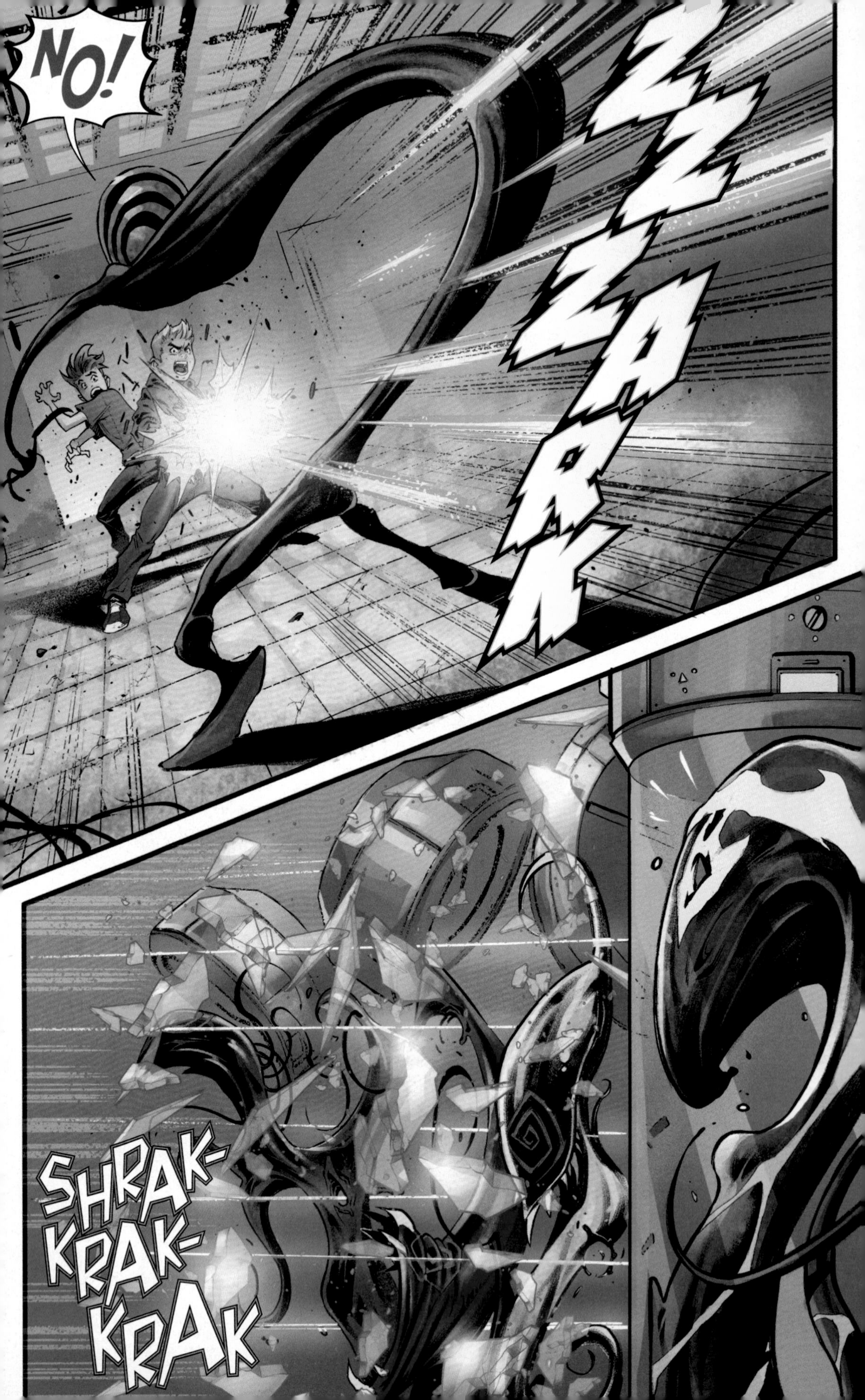
NO!
ZZZAARK
SHRAK-
KRAK-
KRAK

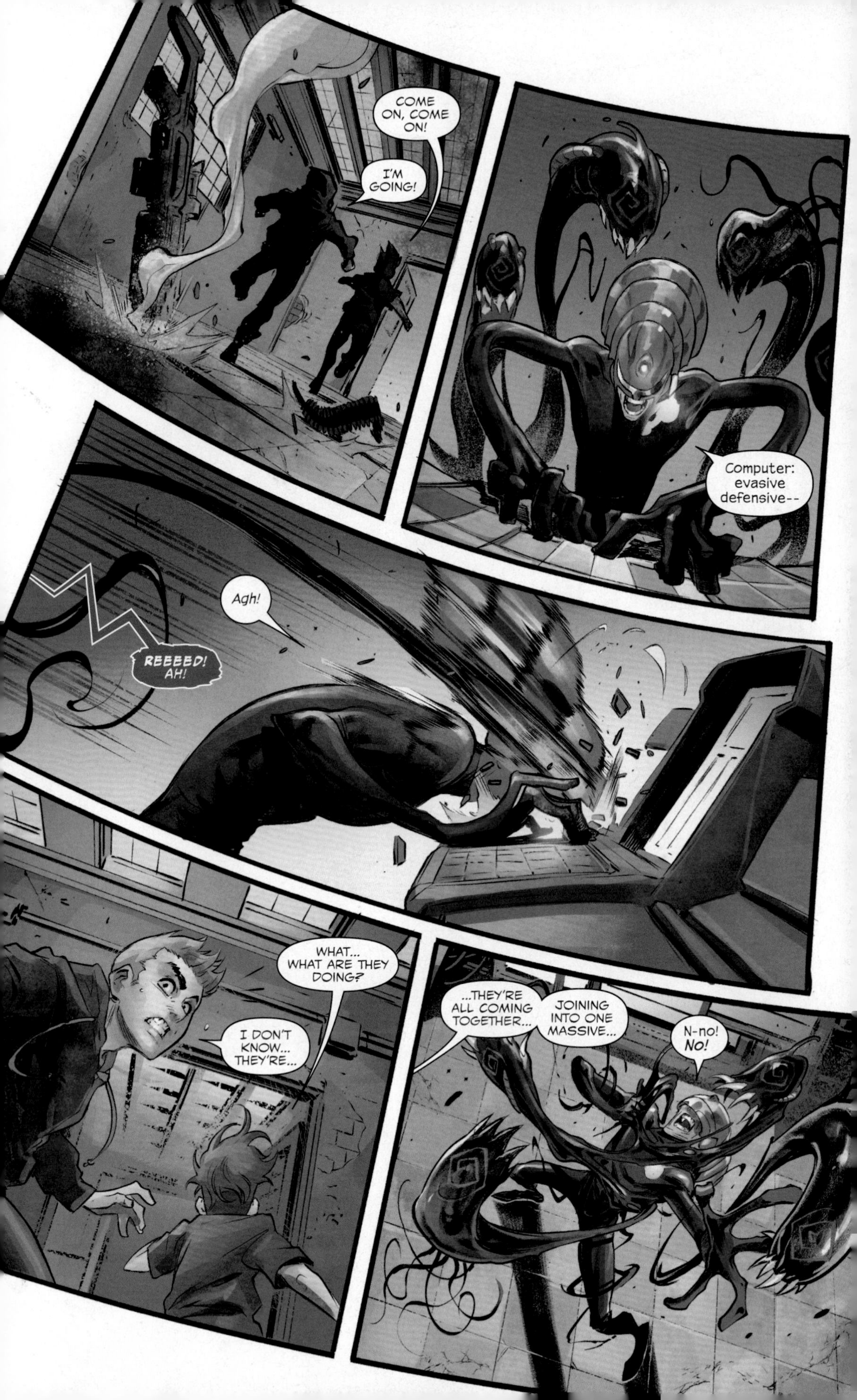
COME ON, COME ON!
I'M GOING!
Computer: evasive defensive--
Agh!
REEEED! AH!
WHAT... WHAT ARE THEY DOING?
I DON'T KNOW... THEY'RE...
...THEY'RE ALL COMING TOGETHER...
JOINING INTO ONE MASSIVE...
N-no! No!

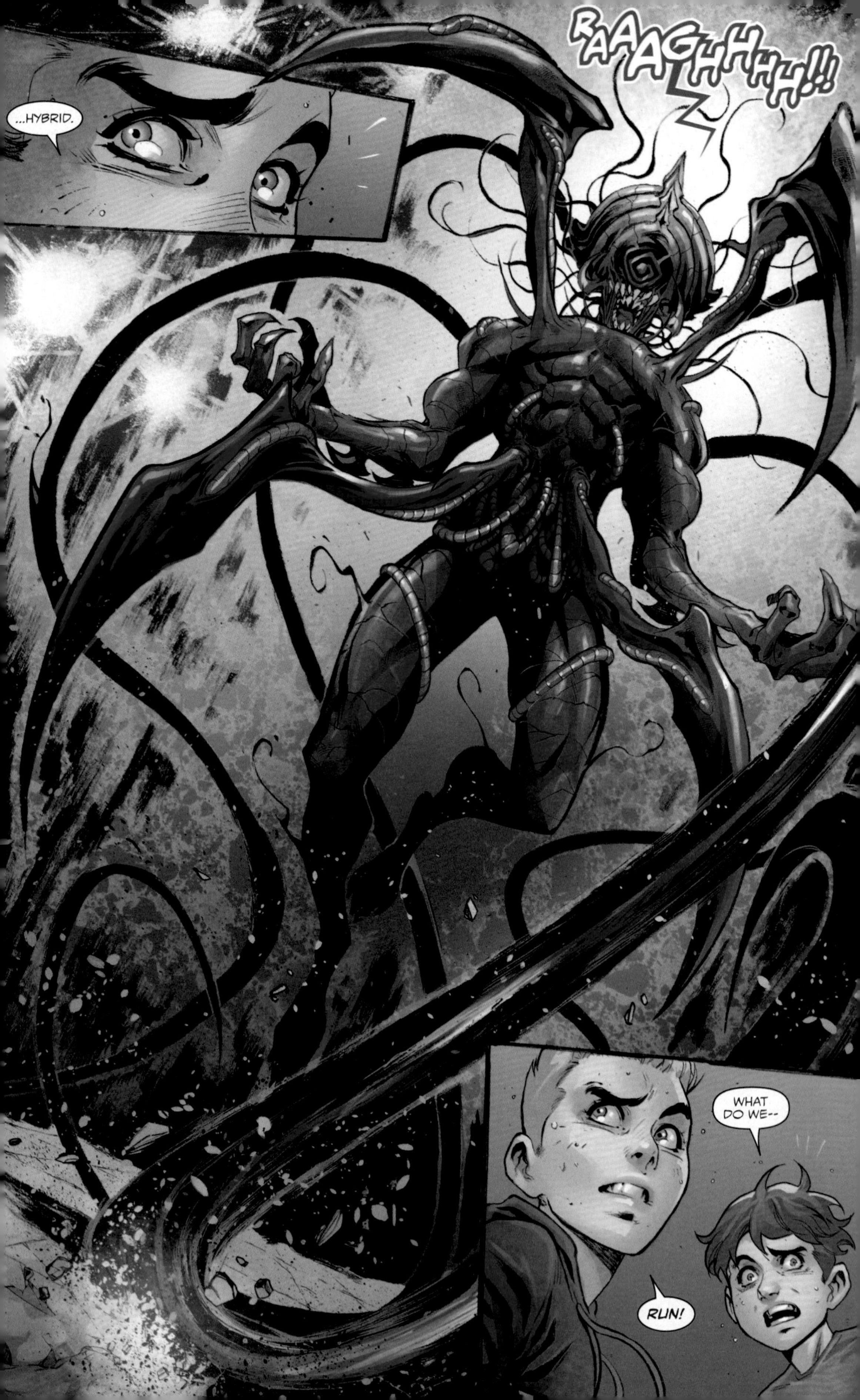
...HYBRID.
RAAAGHHHHH!!
WHAT DO WE--
RUN!

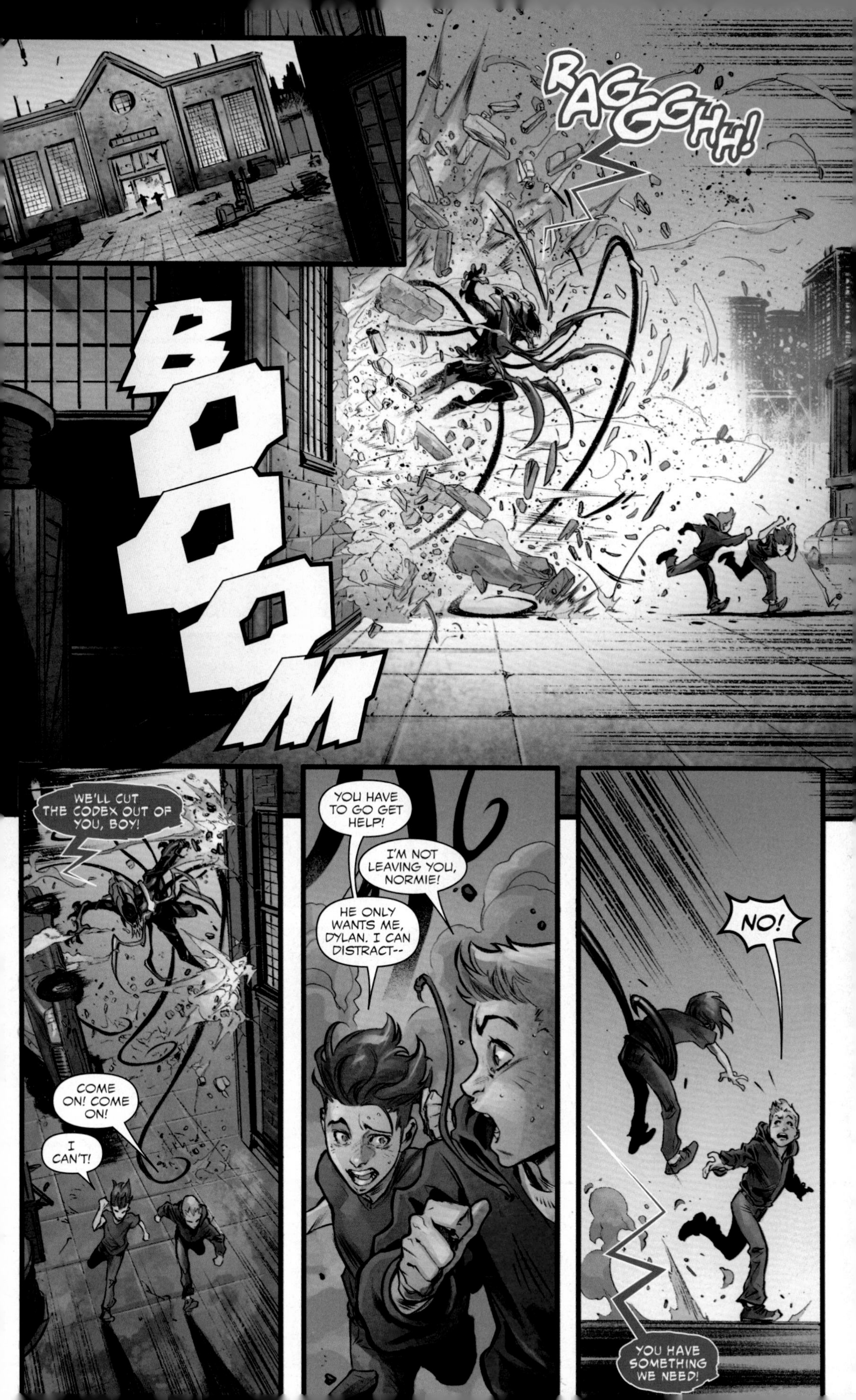
RAGGGHHH!
BOOOOM
WE'LL CUT THE CODEX OUT OF YOU, BOY!
COME ON! COME ON!
I CAN'T!
YOU HAVE TO GO GET HELP!
I'M NOT LEAVING YOU, NORMIE!
HE ONLY WANTS ME, DYLAN. I CAN DISTRACT--
NO!
YOU HAVE SOMETHING WE NEED!

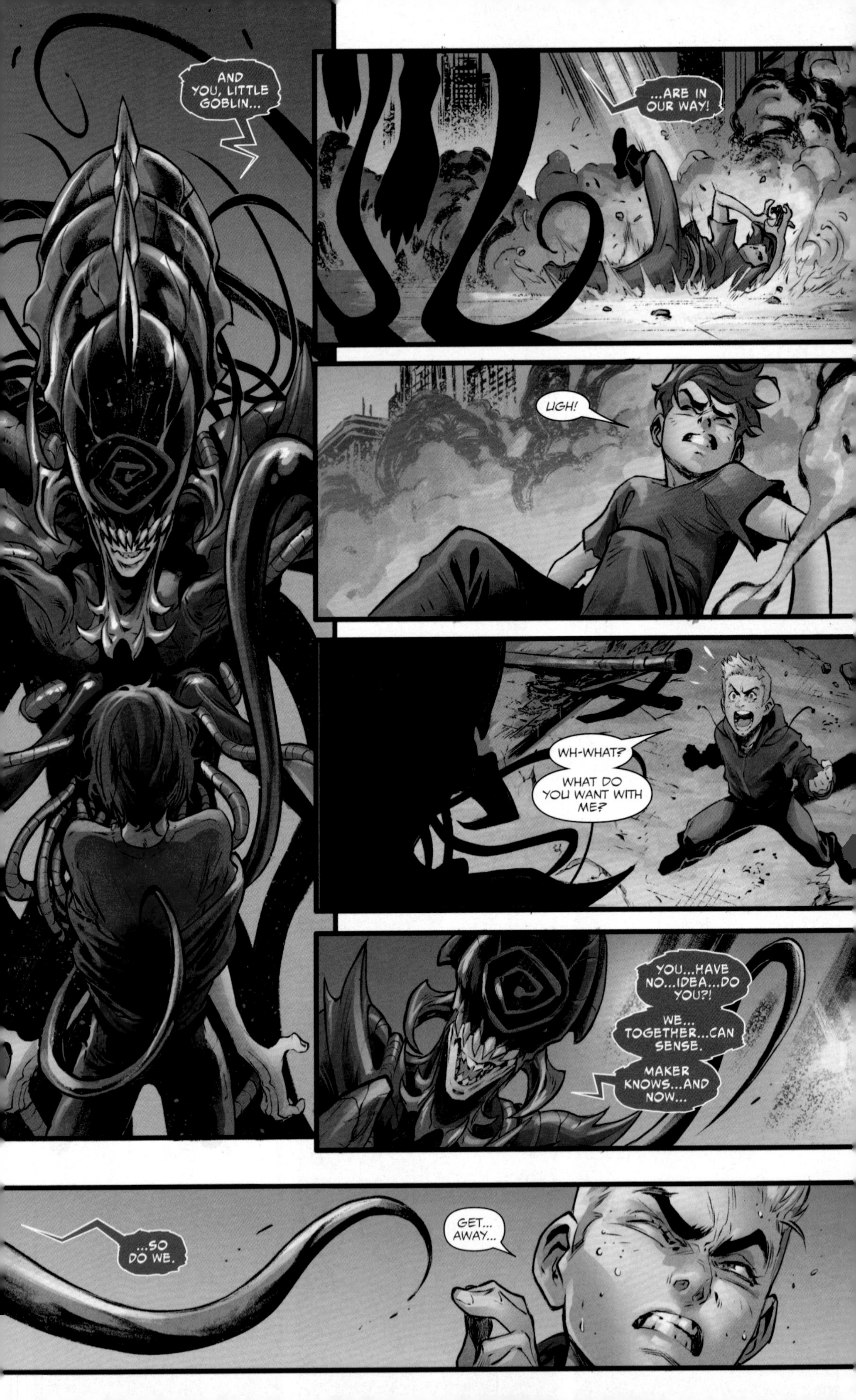
AND YOU, LITTLE GOBLIN...
...ARE IN OUR WAY!
UGH!
WH-WHAT?
WHAT DO YOU WANT WITH ME?
YOU...HAVE NO...IDEA...DO YOU?!
WE... TOGETHER...CAN SENSE.
MAKER KNOWS...AND NOW...
...SO DO WE.
GET... AWAY...

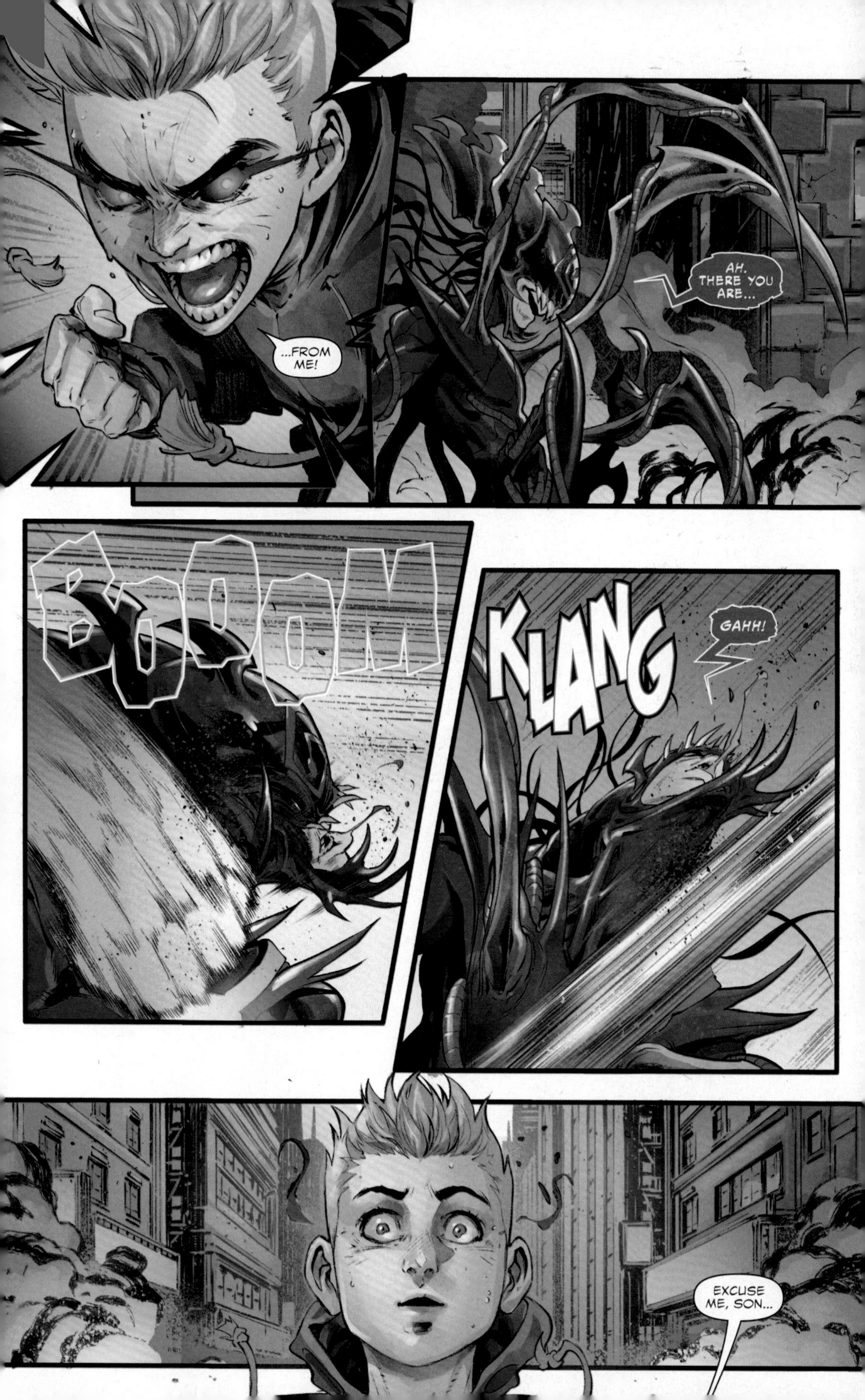
...FROM ME!
AH. THERE YOU ARE...
BOOOM
KLANG
GAHH!
EXCUSE ME, SON...

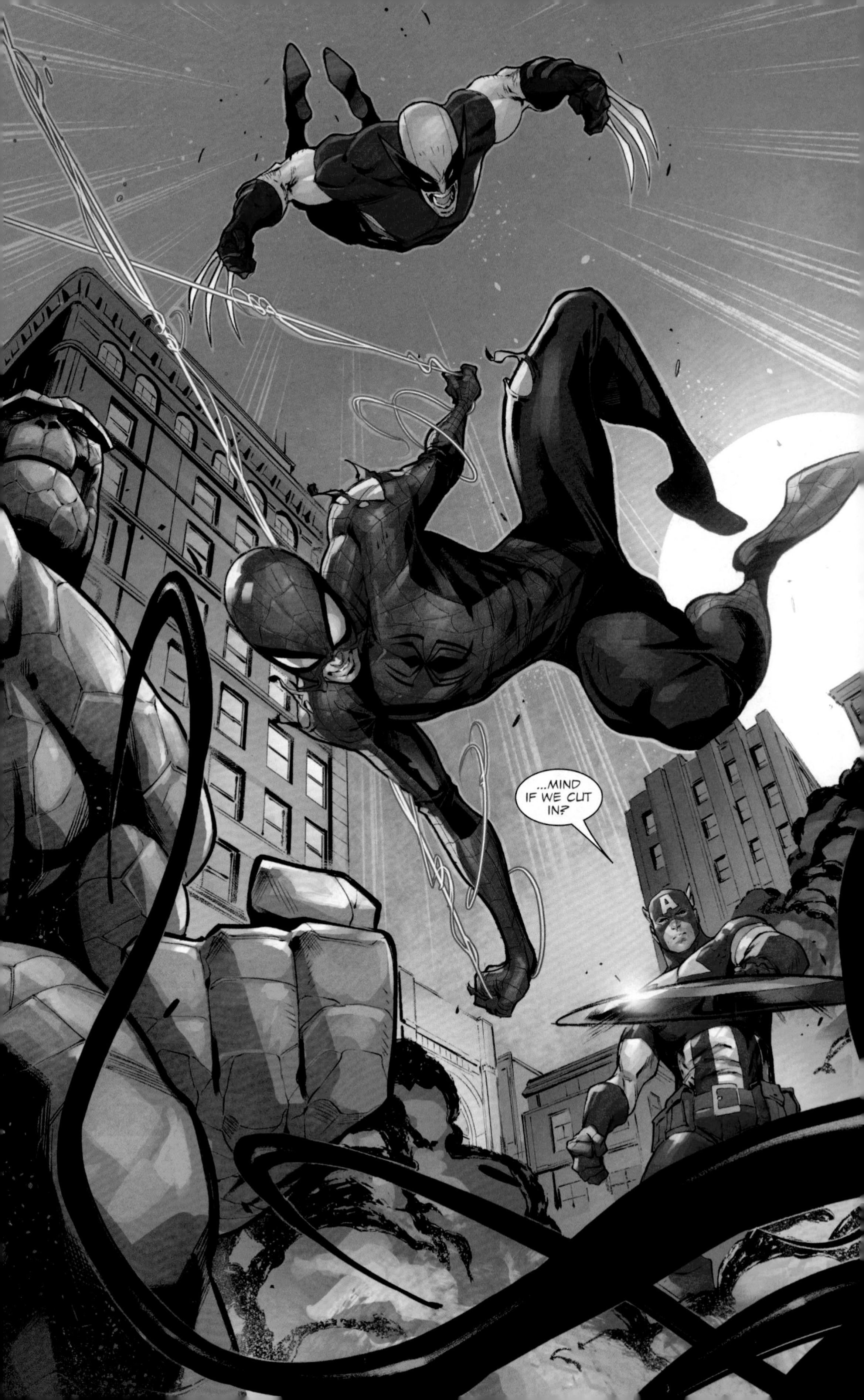
...MIND IF WE CUT IN?

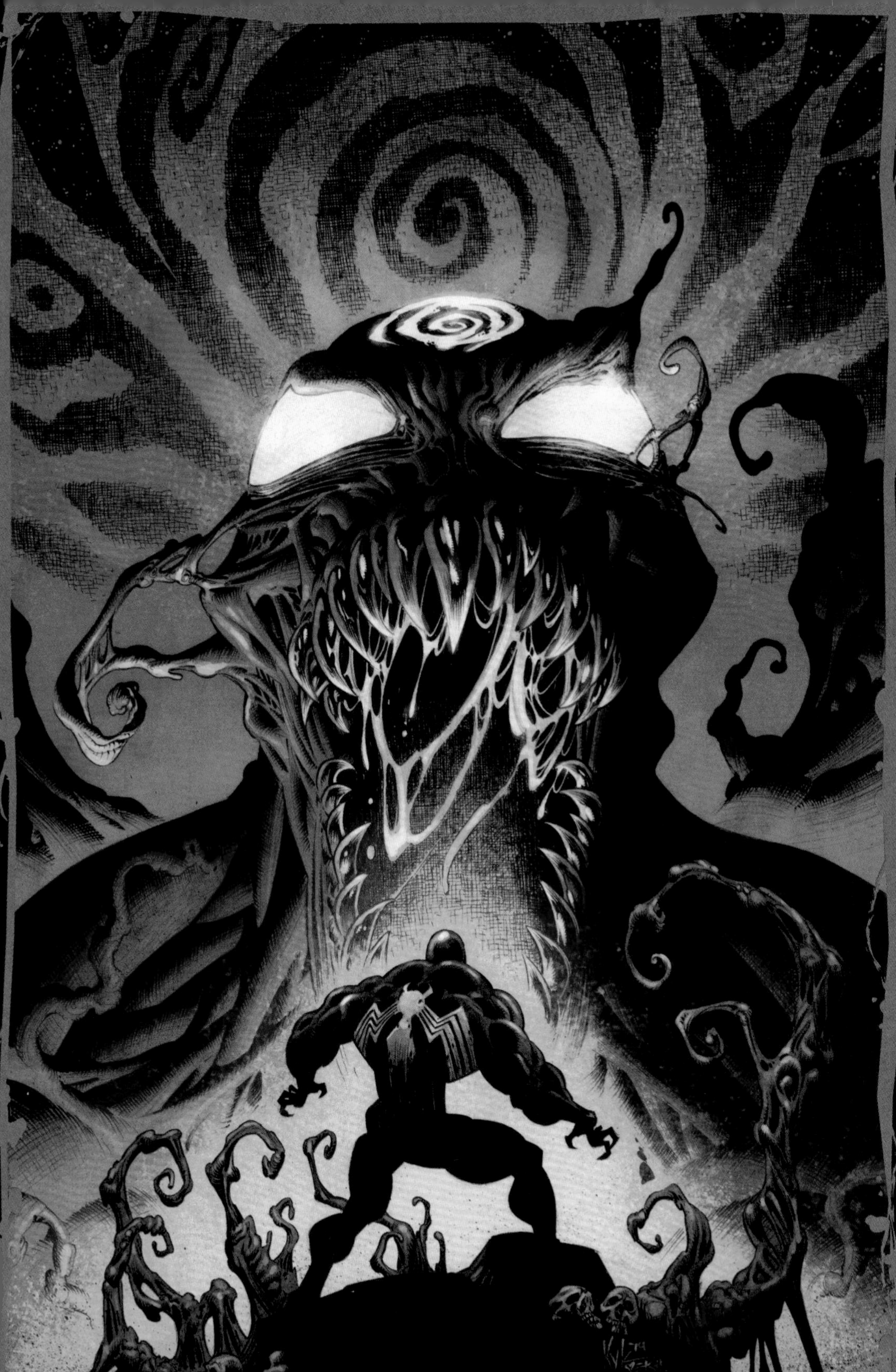

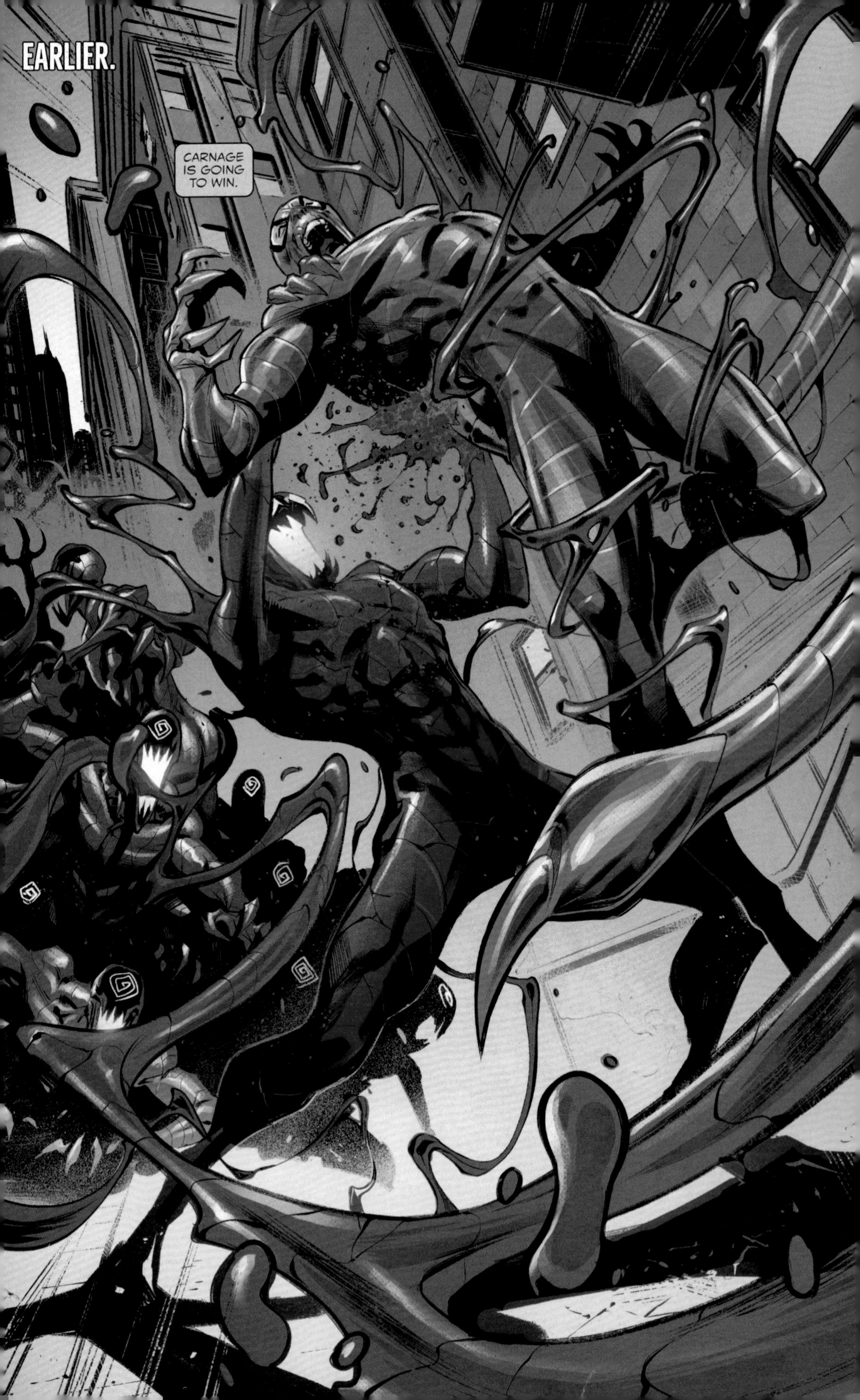
EARLIER.
CARNAGE IS GOING TO WIN.

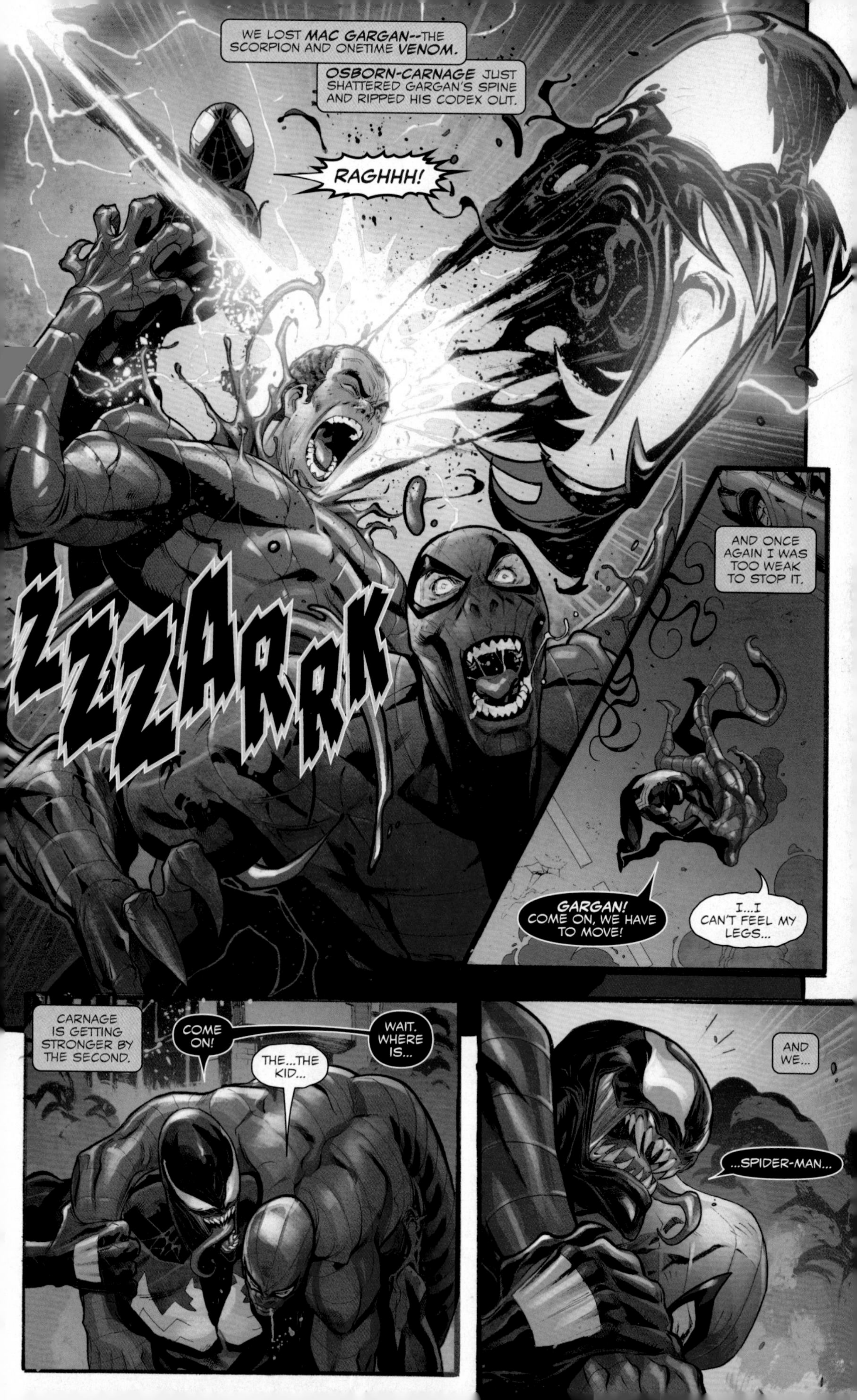
WE LOST MAC GARGAN--THE SCORPION AND ONETIME VENOM.
OSBORN-CARNAGE JUST SHATTERED GARGAN'S SPINE AND RIPPED HIS CODEX OUT.
RAGHHH!
ZZZARRK
AND ONCE AGAIN I WAS TOO WEAK TO STOP IT.
GARGAN! COME ON, WE HAVE TO MOVE!
I...I CAN'T FEEL MY LEGS...
CARNAGE IS GETTING STRONGER BY THE SECOND.
COME ON!
WAIT. WHERE IS...
THE...THE KID...
AND WE...
...SPIDER-MAN...

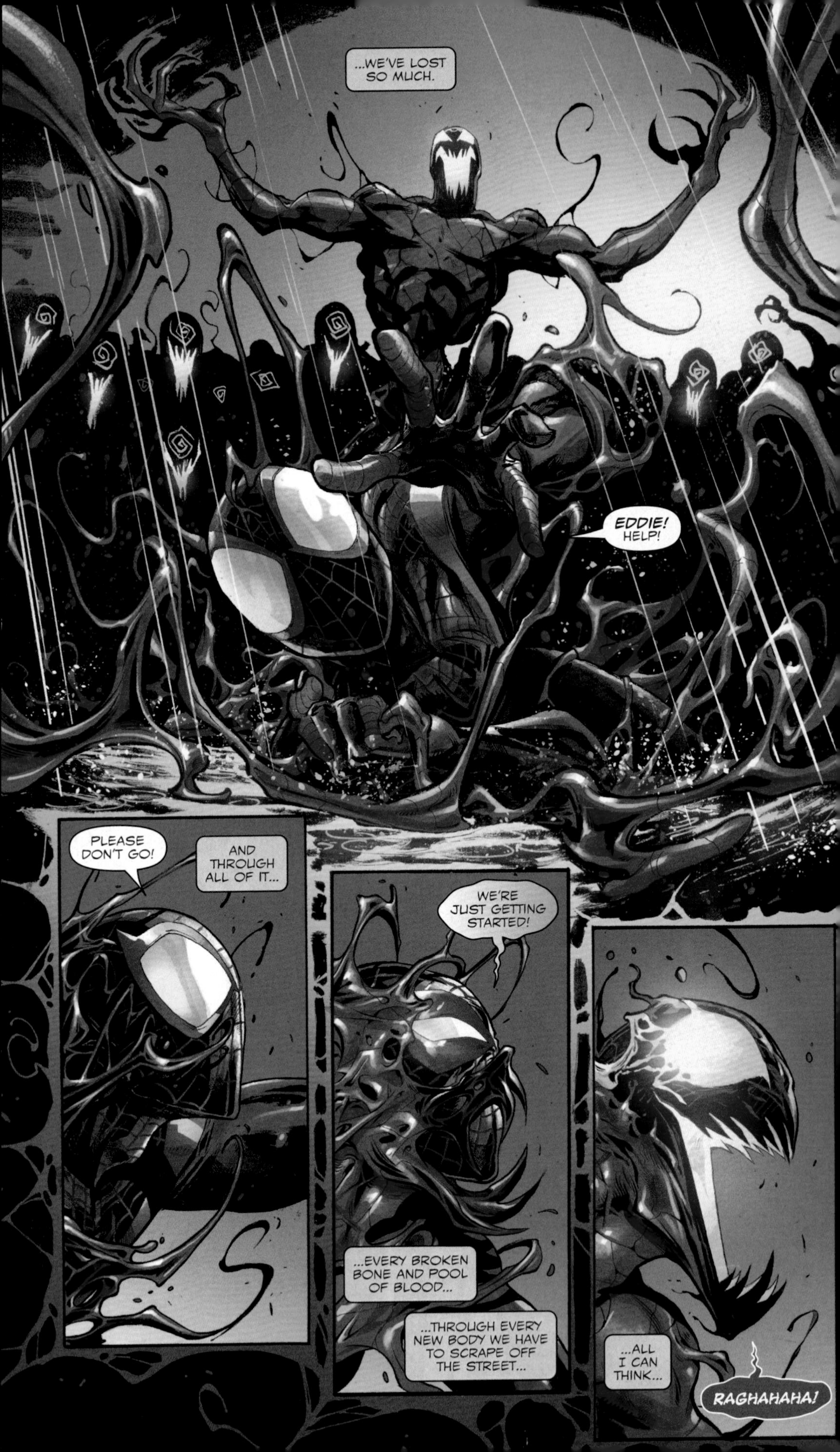
...WE'VE LOST SO MUCH.
EDDIE! HELP!
PLEASE DON'T GO!
AND THROUGH ALL OF IT...
WE'RE JUST GETTING STARTED!
...EVERY BROKEN BONE AND POOL OF BLOOD...
...THROUGH EVERY NEW BODY WE HAVE TO SCRAPE OFF THE STREET...
...ALL I CAN THINK...
RAGHAHAHA!

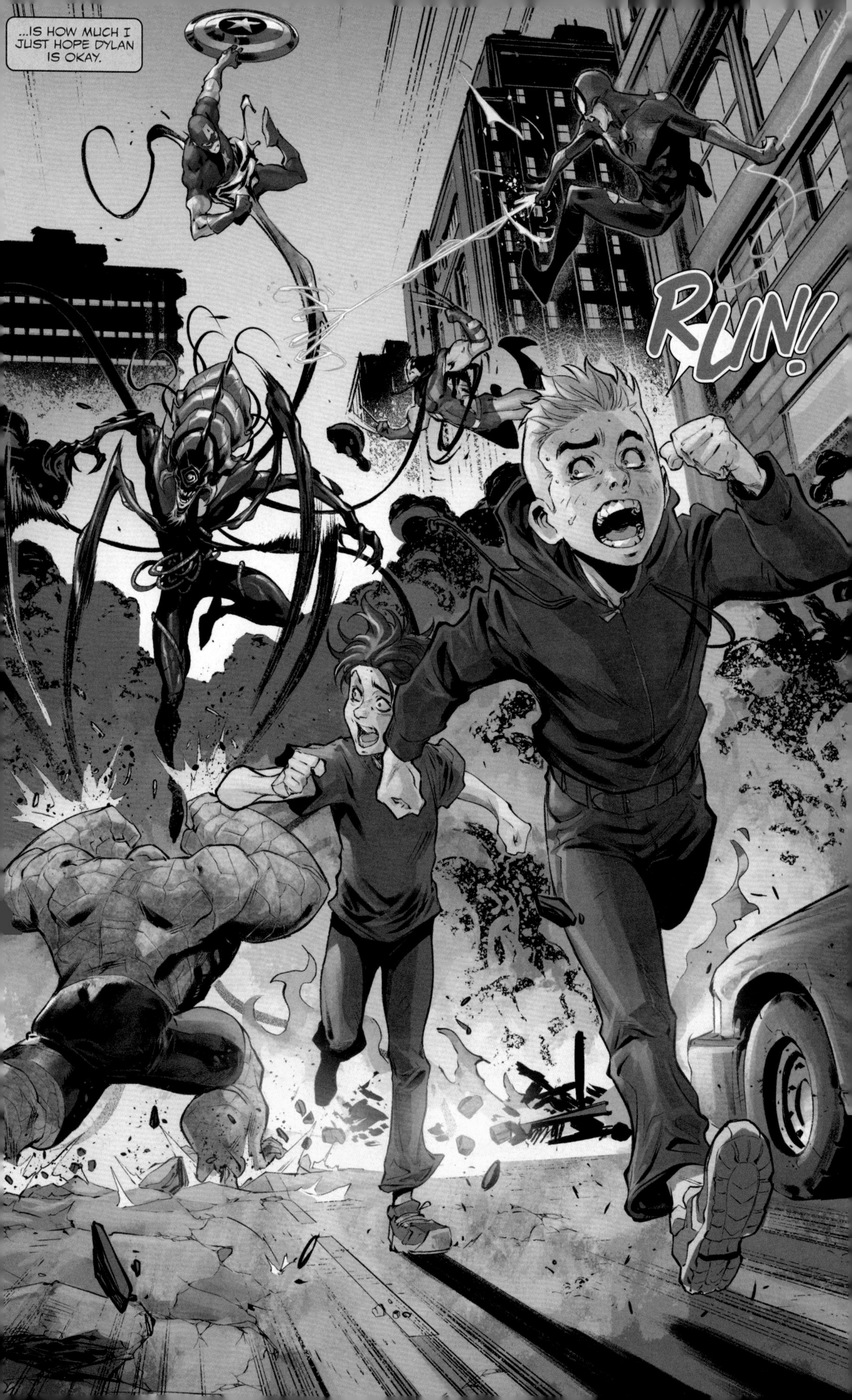
...IS HOW MUCH I JUST HOPE DYLAN IS OKAY.
RUN!

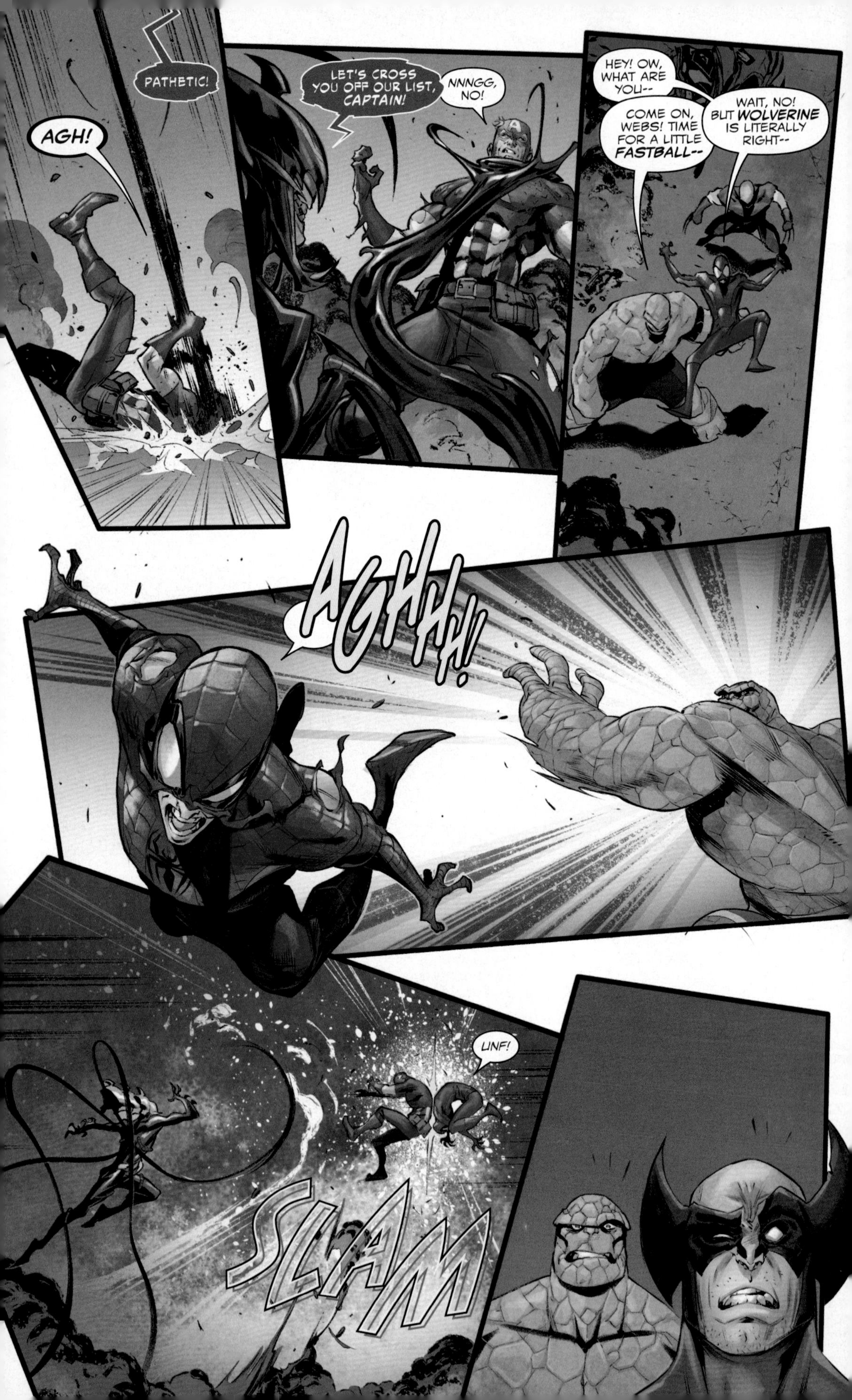

PATHETIC!
AGH!
LET'S CROSS YOU OFF OUR LIST, CAPTAIN!
NNNGG, NO!
HEY! OW, WHAT ARE YOU--
COME ON, WEBS! TIME FOR A LITTLE FASTBALL--
WAIT, NO! BUT WOLVERINE IS LITERALLY RIGHT--
AGHHH!
UNF!
SLAM

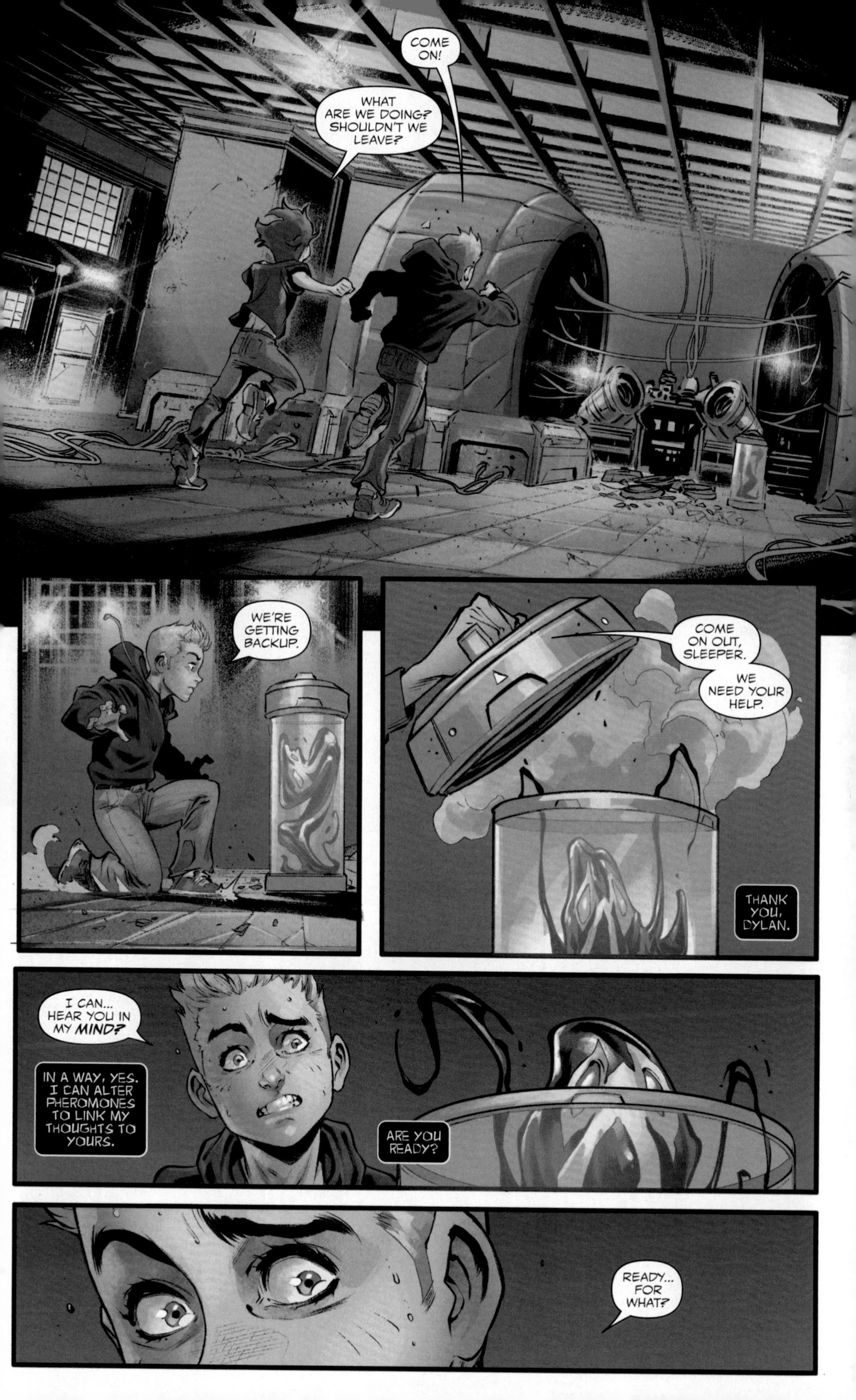
COME ON!
WHAT ARE WE DOING? SHOULDN'T WE LEAVE?
WE'RE GETTING BACKUP.
COME ON OUT, SLEEPER.
WE NEED YOUR HELP.
THANK YOU, DYLAN.
I CAN... HEAR YOU IN MY MIND?
IN A WAY, YES. I CAN ALTER PHEROMONES TO LINK MY THOUGHTS TO YOURS.
ARE YOU READY?
READY... FOR WHAT?

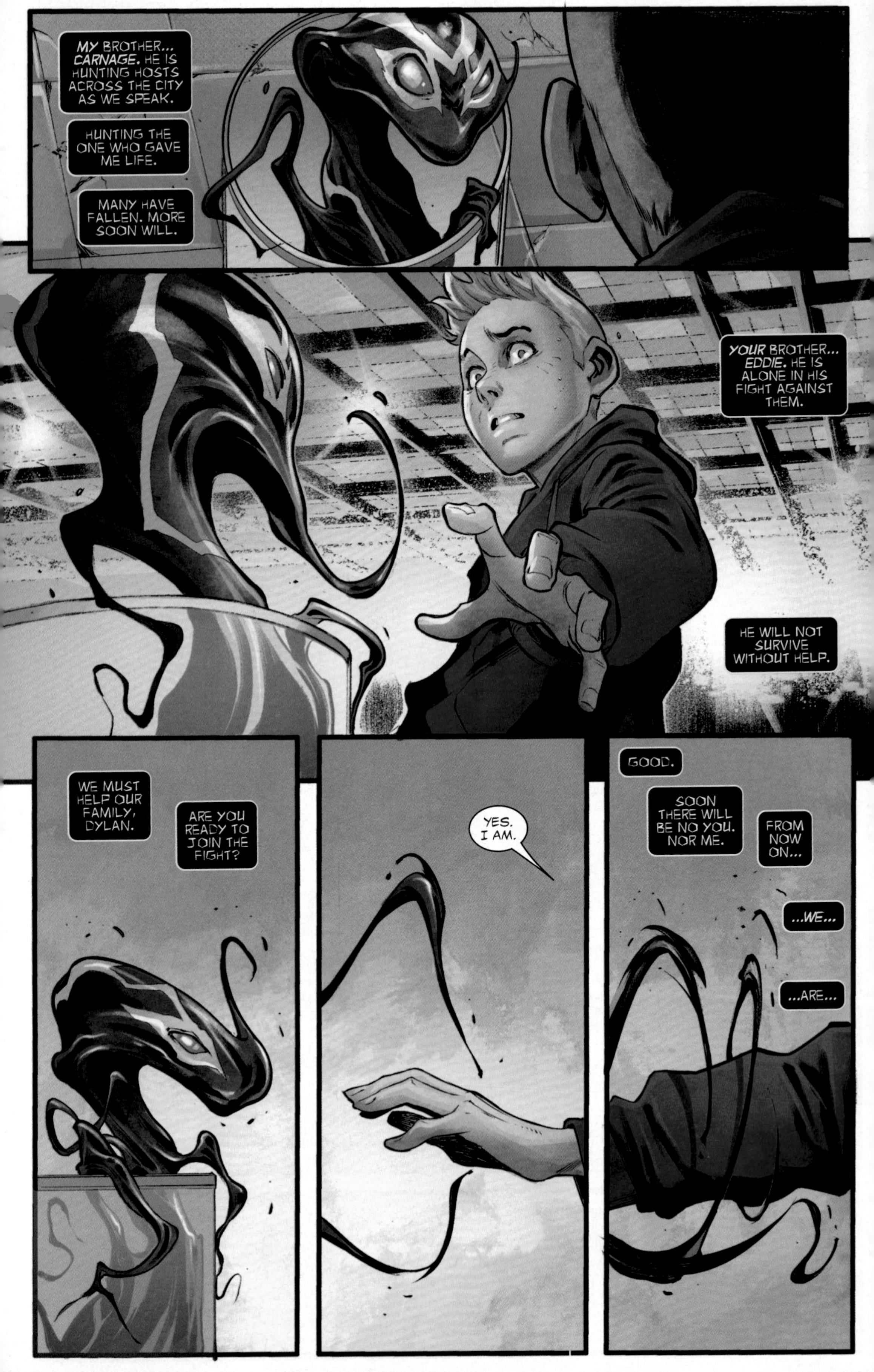
MY BROTHER... CARNAGE. HE IS HUNTING HOSTS ACROSS THE CITY AS WE SPEAK.
HUNTING THE ONE WHO GAVE ME LIFE.
MANY HAVE FALLEN. MORE SOON WILL.
YOUR BROTHER... EDDIE. HE IS ALONE IN HIS FIGHT AGAINST THEM.
HE WILL NOT SURVIVE WITHOUT HELP.
WE MUST HELP OUR FAMILY, DYLAN.
ARE YOU READY TO JOIN THE FIGHT?
YES. I AM.
GOOD.
SOON THERE WILL BE NO YOU. NOR ME.
FROM NOW ON...
...WE...
...ARE...

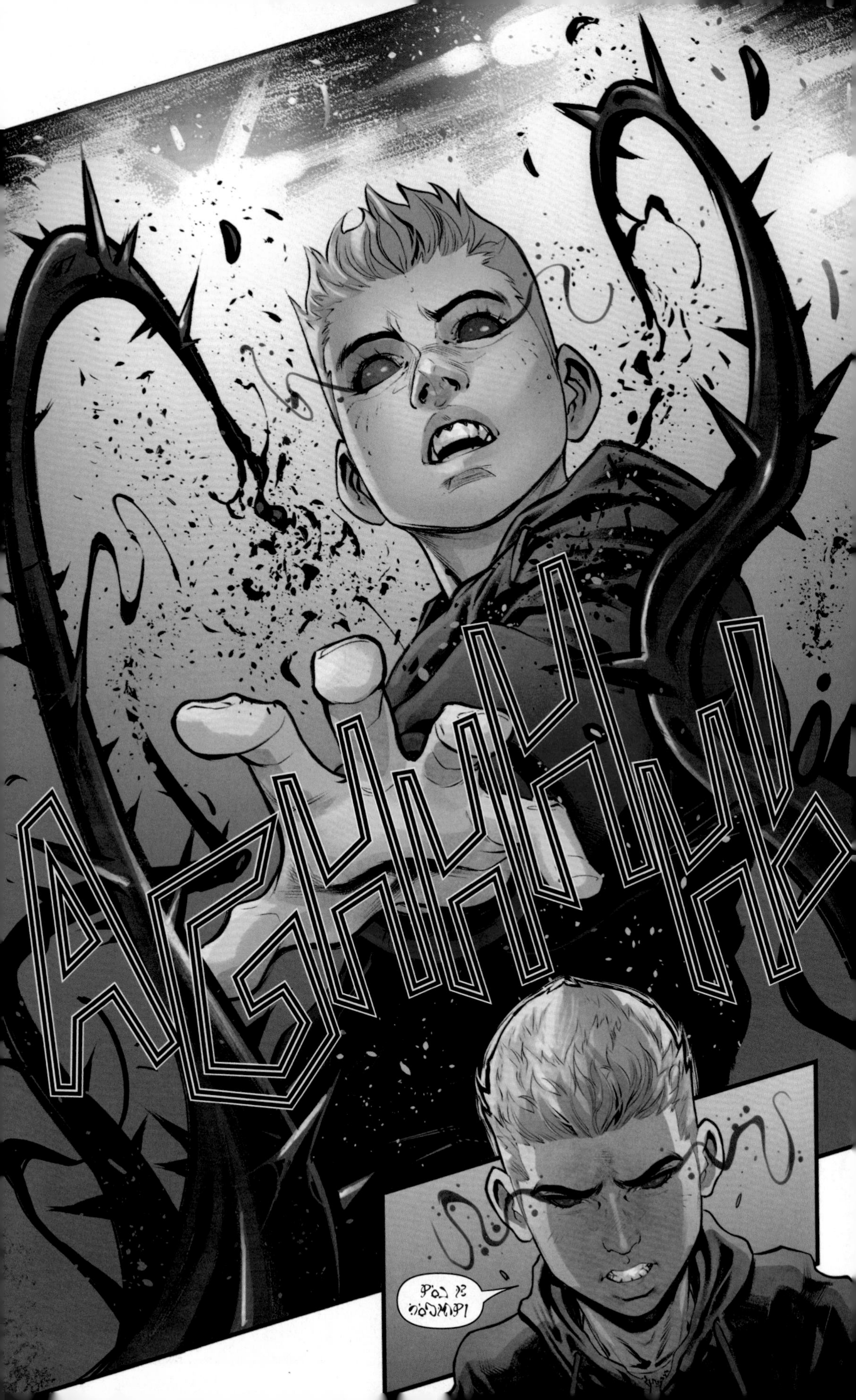
AGHHHHK

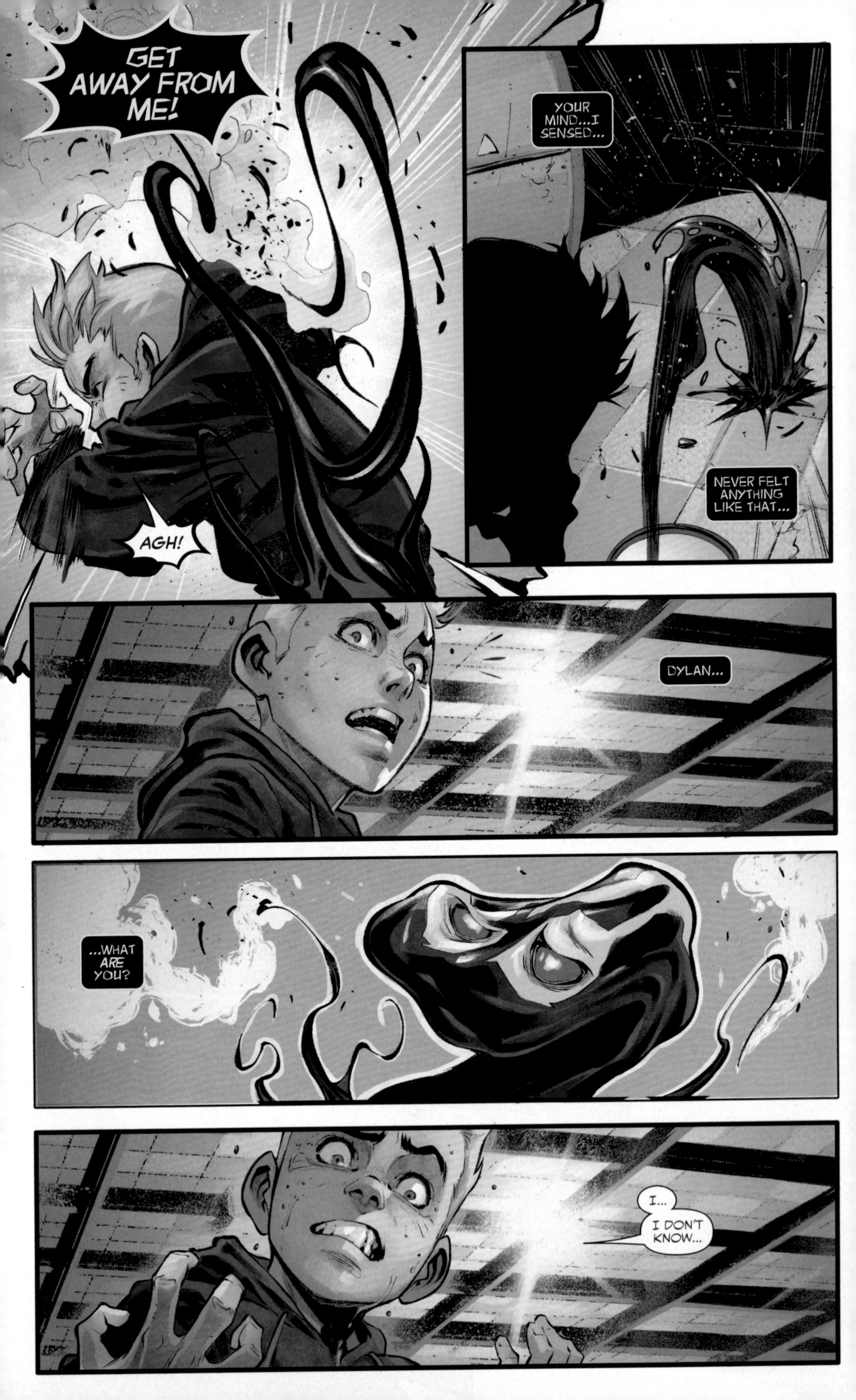
GET AWAY FROM ME!
AGH!
YOUR MIND...I SENSED...
NEVER FELT ANYTHING LIKE THAT...
DYLAN...
...WHAT ARE YOU?
I...
I DON'T KNOW...

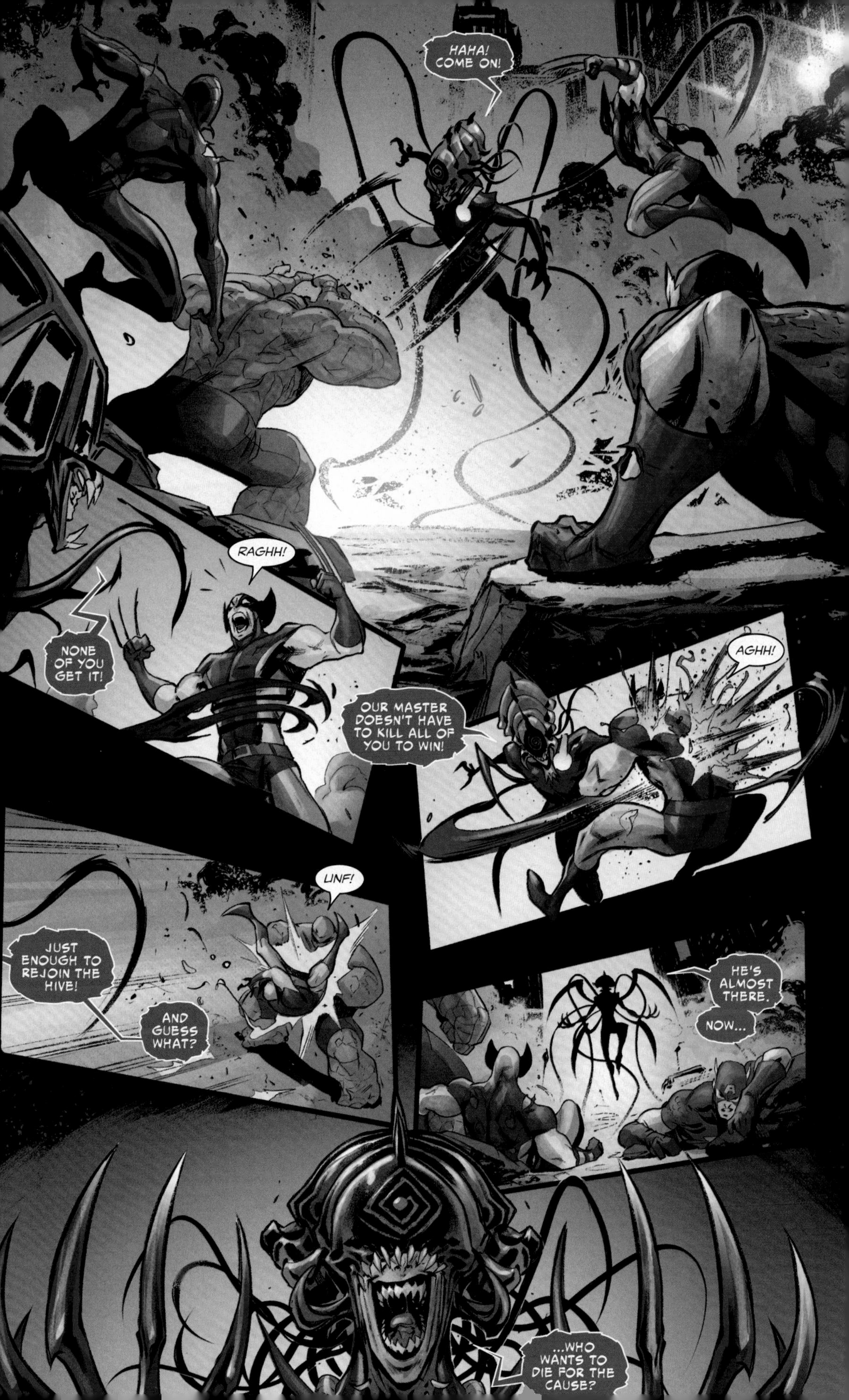
HAHA! COME ON!
RAGHH!
NONE OF YOU GET IT!
OUR MASTER DOESN'T HAVE TO KILL ALL OF YOU TO WIN!
AGHH!
UNF!
JUST ENOUGH TO REJOIN THE HIVE!
AND GUESS WHAT?
HE'S ALMOST THERE.
NOW...
...WHO WANTS TO DIE FOR THE CAUSE?

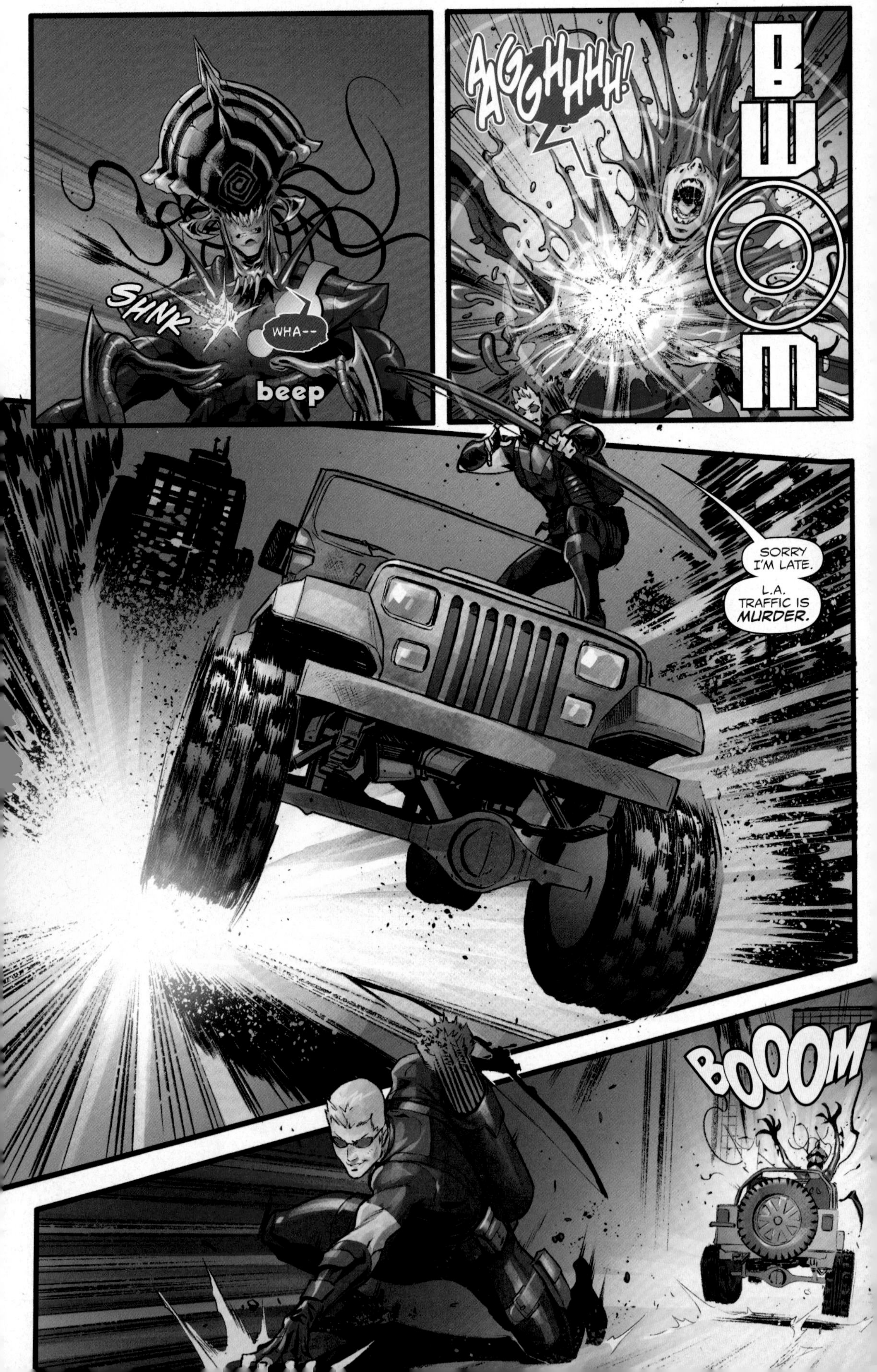
SHNK
WHA--
beep
AAGHHHH!
BWOOM
SORRY I'M LATE.
L.A. TRAFFIC IS MURDER.
BOOOM

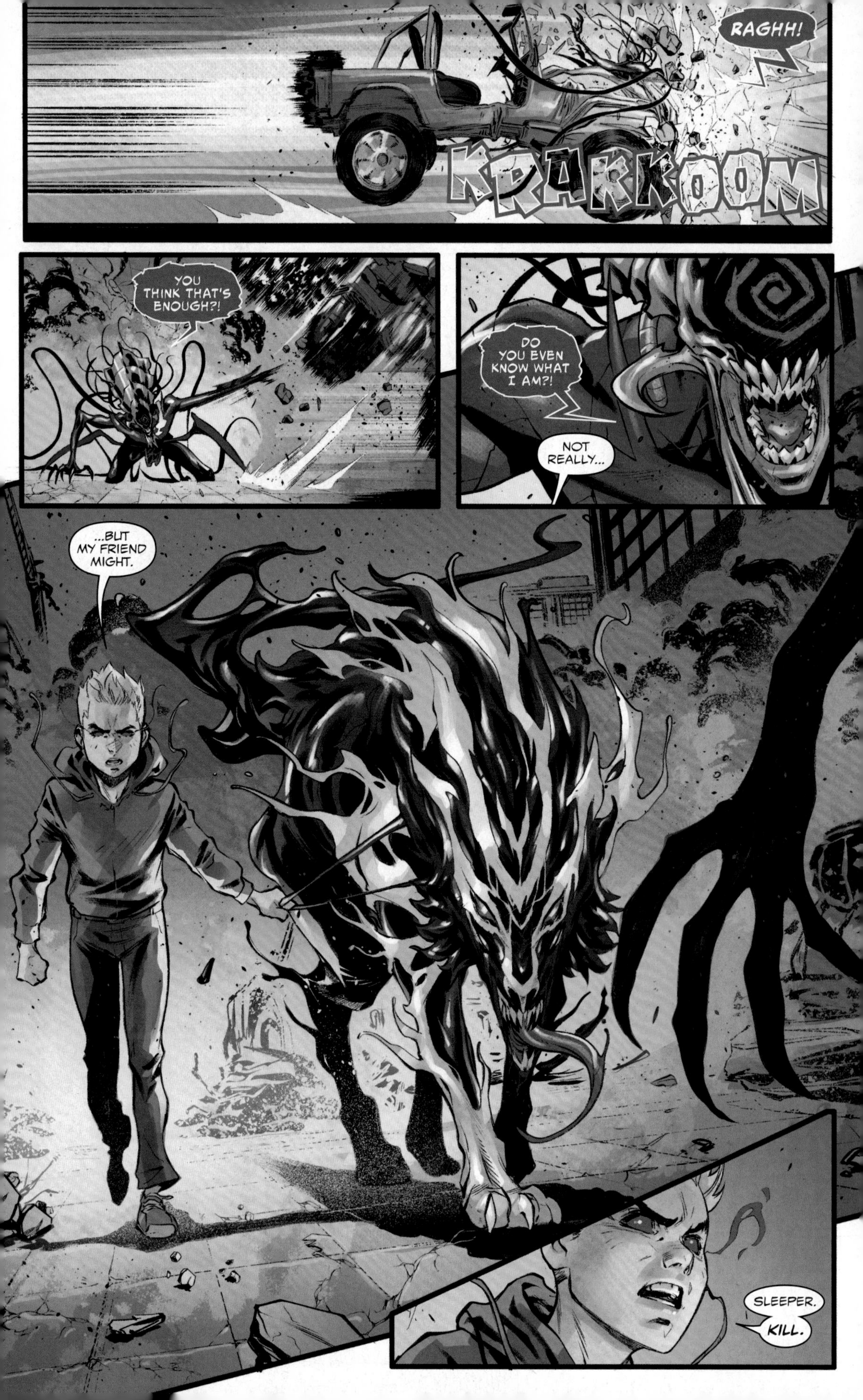
RAGHH!
KRAKKOOM
YOU THINK THAT'S ENOUGH?!
DO YOU EVEN KNOW WHAT I AM?!
NOT REALLY...
...BUT MY FRIEND MIGHT.
SLEEPER.
KILL.

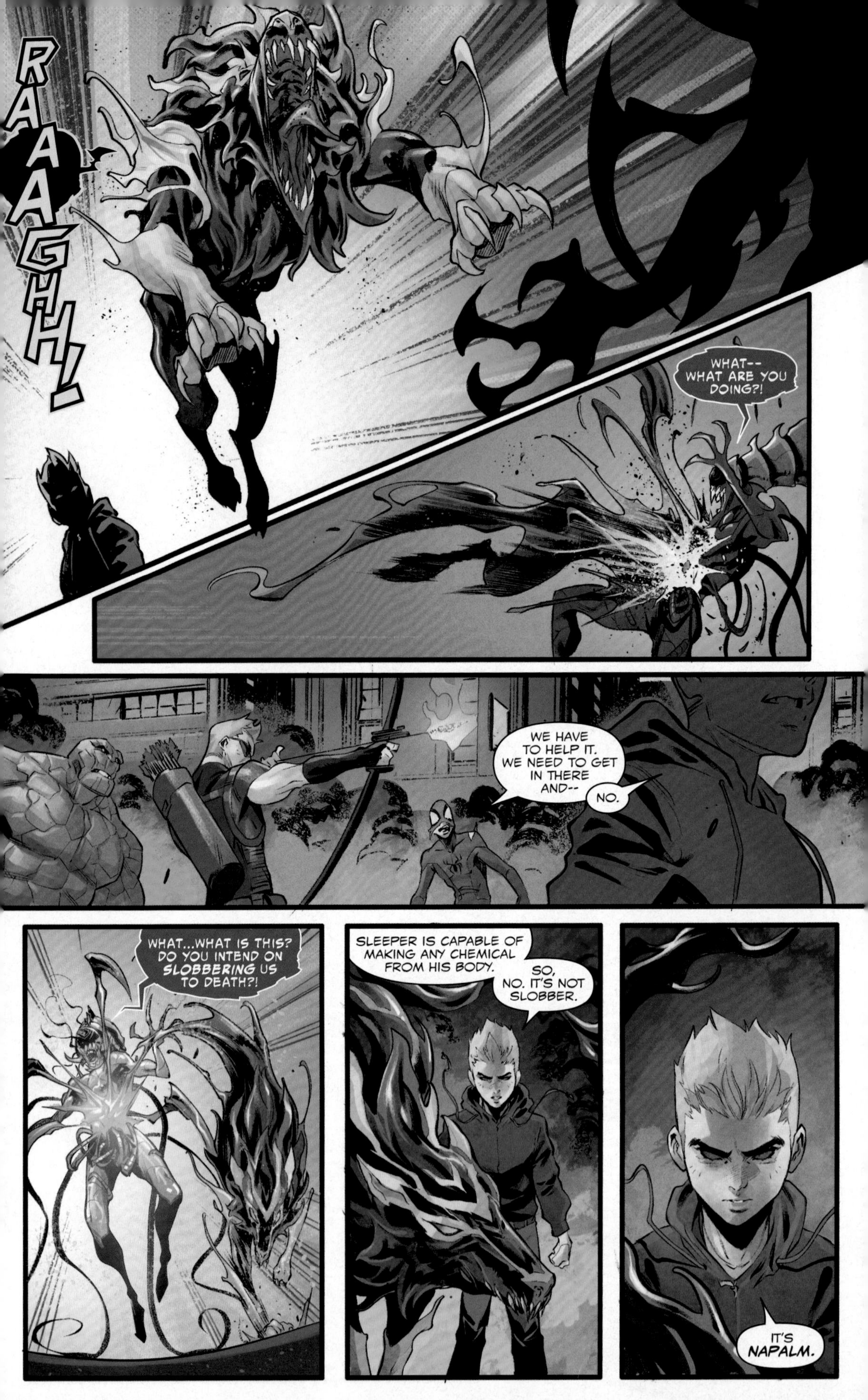

RAAAGHH!
WHAT-- WHAT ARE YOU DOING?!
WE HAVE TO HELP IT. WE NEED TO GET IN THERE AND--
NO.
WHAT...WHAT IS THIS? DO YOU INTEND ON SLOBBERING US TO DEATH?!
SLEEPER IS CAPABLE OF MAKING ANY CHEMICAL FROM HIS BODY.
SO, NO. IT'S NOT SLOBBER.
IT'S NAPALM.

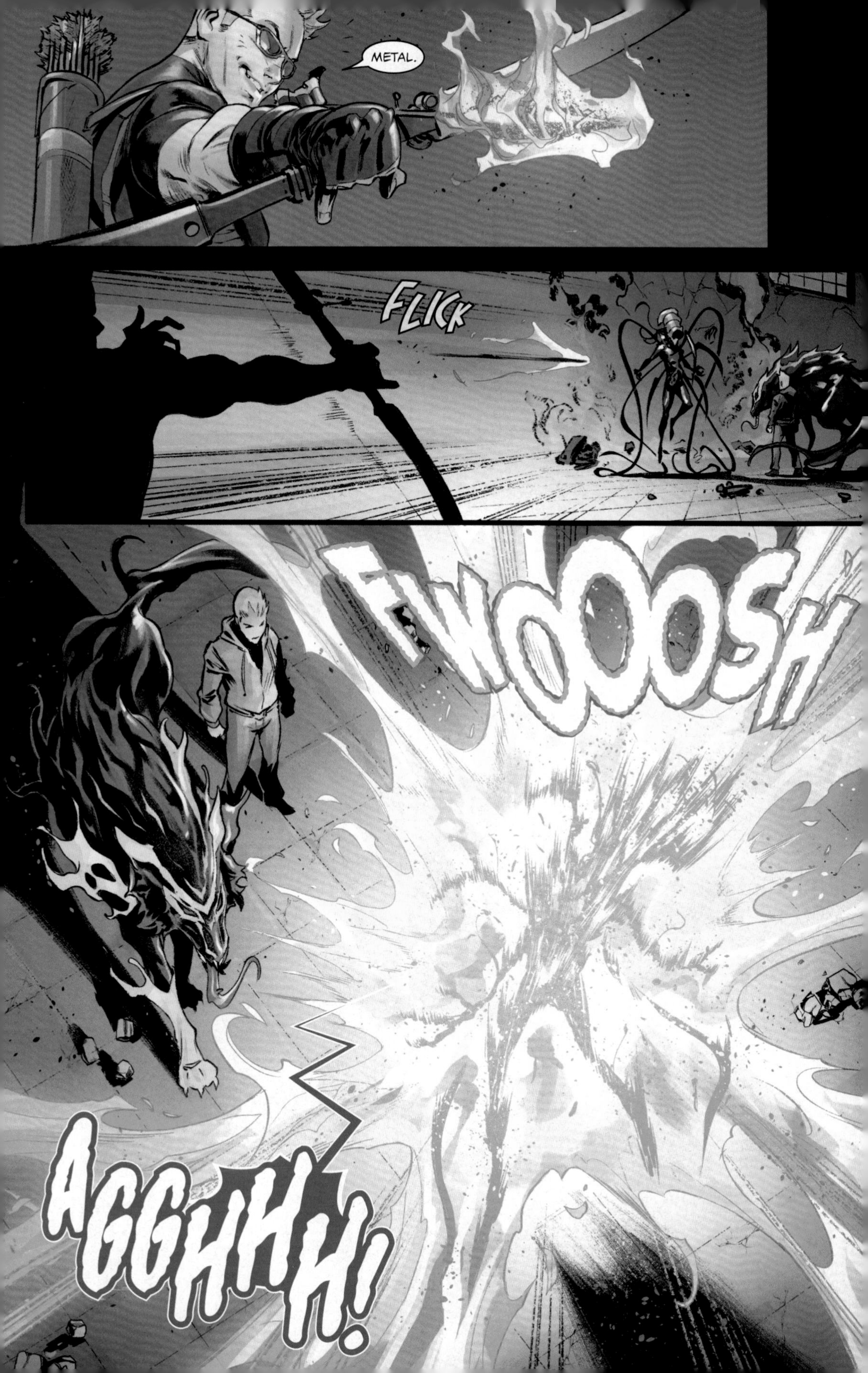
METAL.
FLICK
FWOOOSH
AGGHHH!

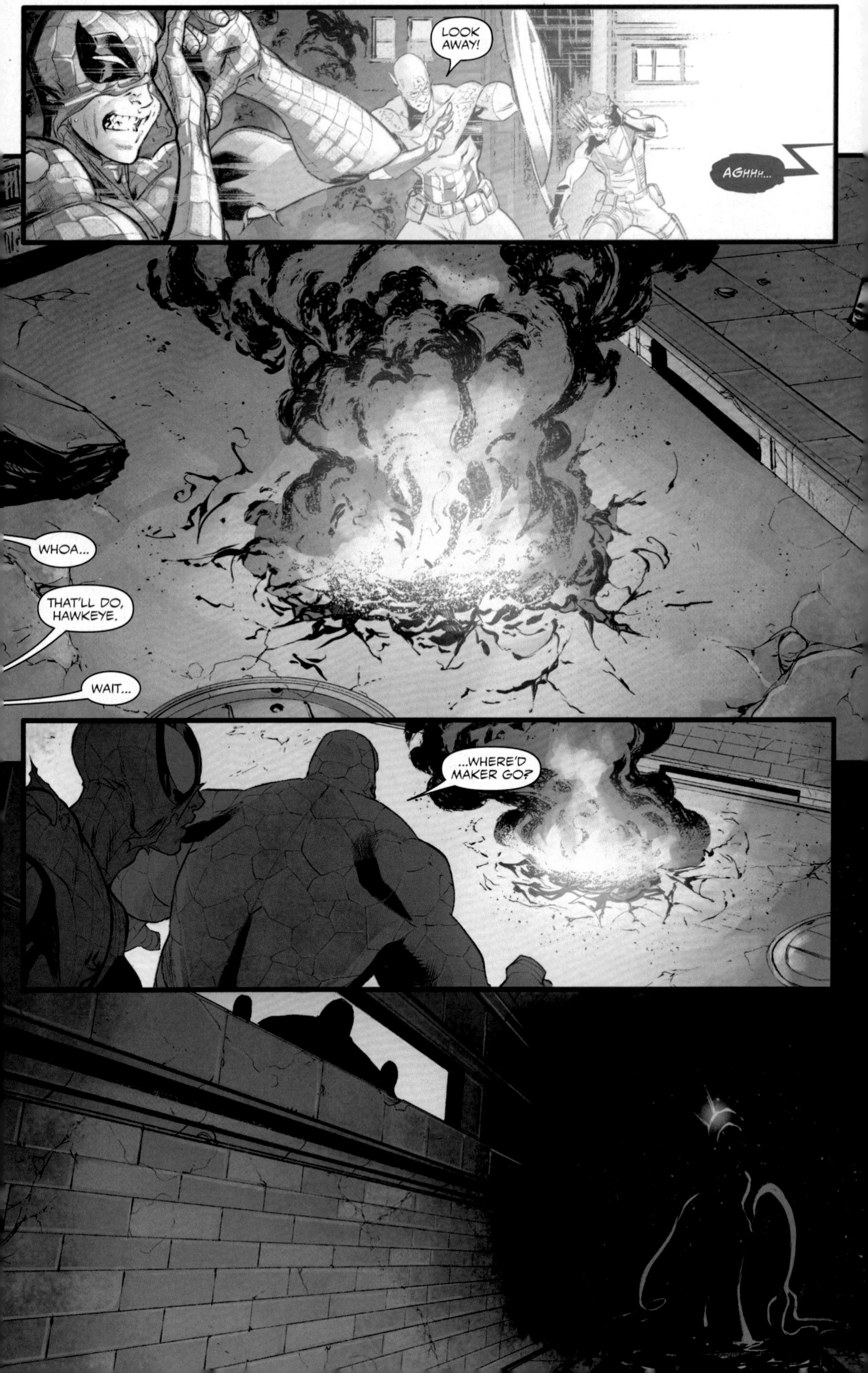
LOOK AWAY!
AGHHH...
WHOA...
THAT'LL DO, HAWKEYE.
WAIT...
...WHERE'D MAKER GO?

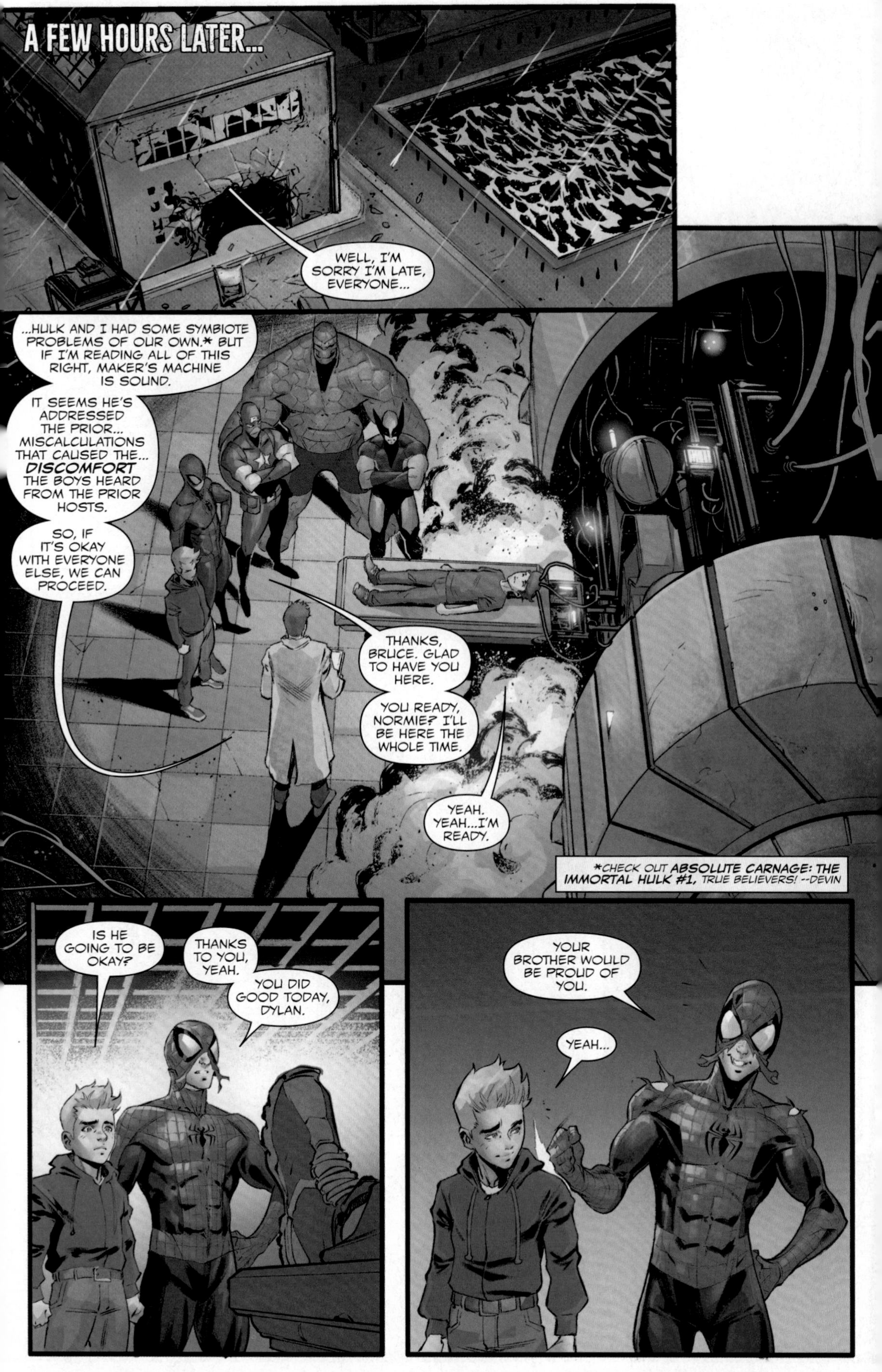
A FEW HOURS LATER...
WELL, I'M SORRY I'M LATE, EVERYONE...
...HULK AND I HAD SOME SYMBIOTE PROBLEMS OF OUR OWN.* BUT IF I'M READING ALL OF THIS RIGHT, MAKER'S MACHINE IS SOUND.
IT SEEMS HE'S ADDRESSED THE PRIOR... MISCALCULATIONS THAT CAUSED THE... DISCOMFORT THE BOYS HEARD FROM THE PRIOR HOSTS.
SO, IF IT'S OKAY WITH EVERYONE ELSE, WE CAN PROCEED.
THANKS, BRUCE. GLAD TO HAVE YOU HERE.
YOU READY, NORMIE? I'LL BE HERE THE WHOLE TIME.
YEAH. YEAH...I'M READY.
*CHECK OUT ABSOLUTE CARNAGE: THE IMMORTAL HULK #1, TRUE BELIEVERS! --DEVIN
IS HE GOING TO BE OKAY?
THANKS TO YOU, YEAH.
YOU DID GOOD TODAY, DYLAN.
YOUR BROTHER WOULD BE PROUD OF YOU.
YEAH...

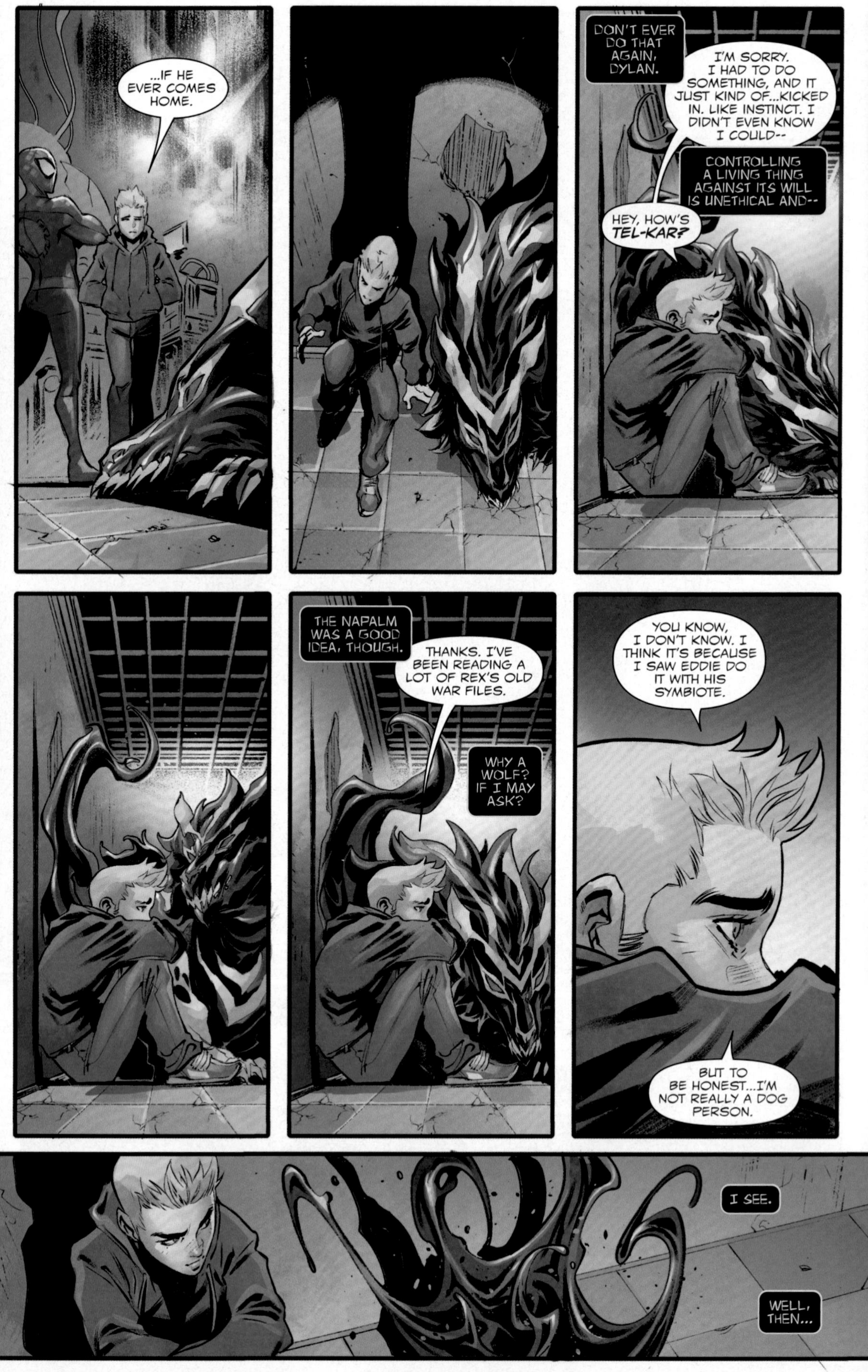
...IF HE EVER COMES HOME.
DON'T EVER DO THAT AGAIN, DYLAN.
I'M SORRY. I HAD TO DO SOMETHING, AND IT JUST KIND OF...KICKED IN. LIKE INSTINCT. I DIDN'T EVEN KNOW I COULD--
CONTROLLING A LIVING THING AGAINST ITS WILL IS UNETHICAL AND--
HEY, HOW'S TEL-KAR?
THE NAPALM WAS A GOOD IDEA, THOUGH.
THANKS. I'VE BEEN READING A LOT OF REX'S OLD WAR FILES.
WHY A WOLF? IF I MAY ASK?
YOU KNOW, I DON'T KNOW. I THINK IT'S BECAUSE I SAW EDDIE DO IT WITH HIS SYMBIOTE.
BUT TO BE HONEST...I'M NOT REALLY A DOG PERSON.
I SEE.
WELL, THEN...

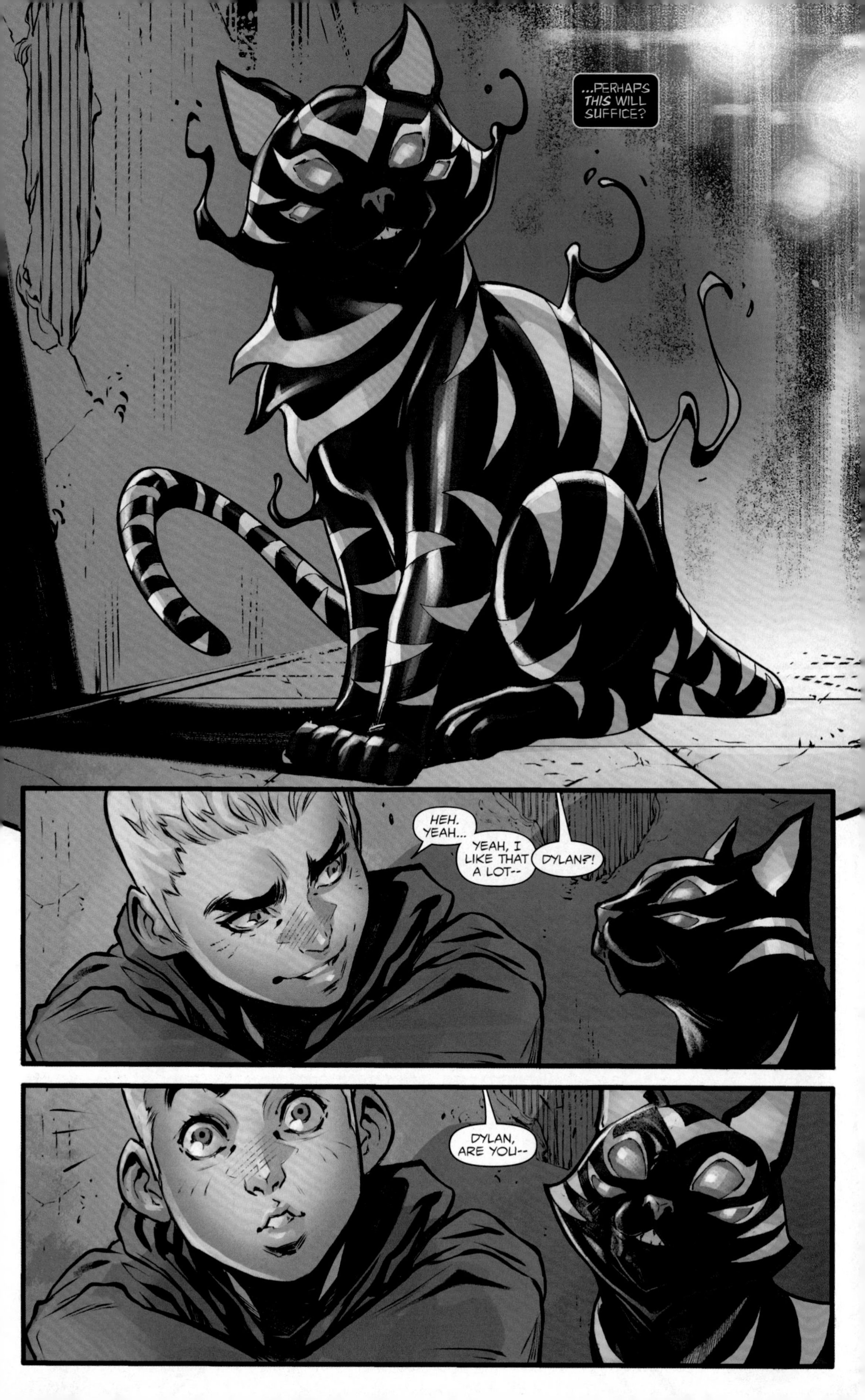
...PERHAPS THIS WILL SUFFICE?
HEH. YEAH...
YEAH, I LIKE THAT A LOT--
DYLAN?!
DYLAN, ARE YOU--

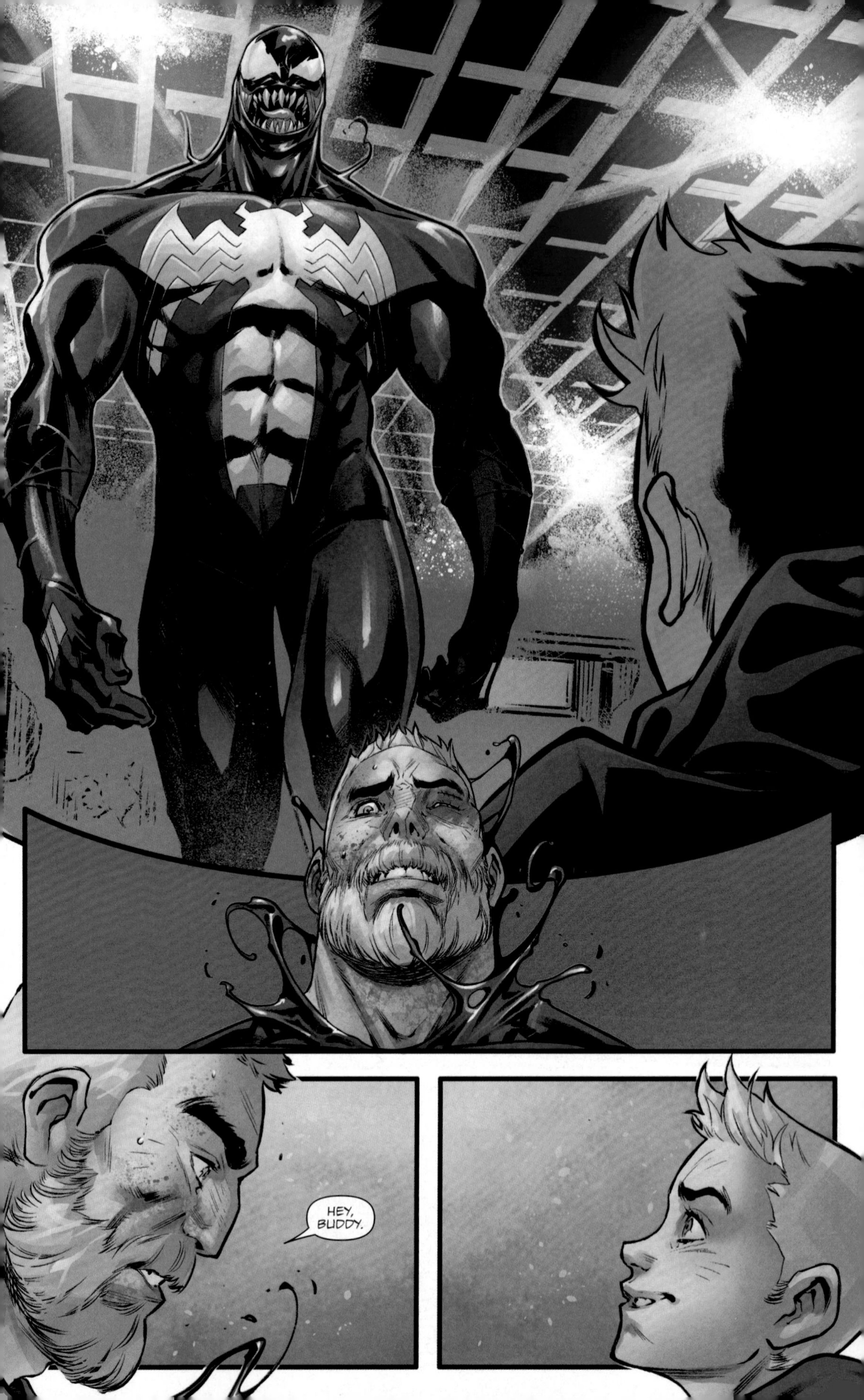
HEY, BUDDY.

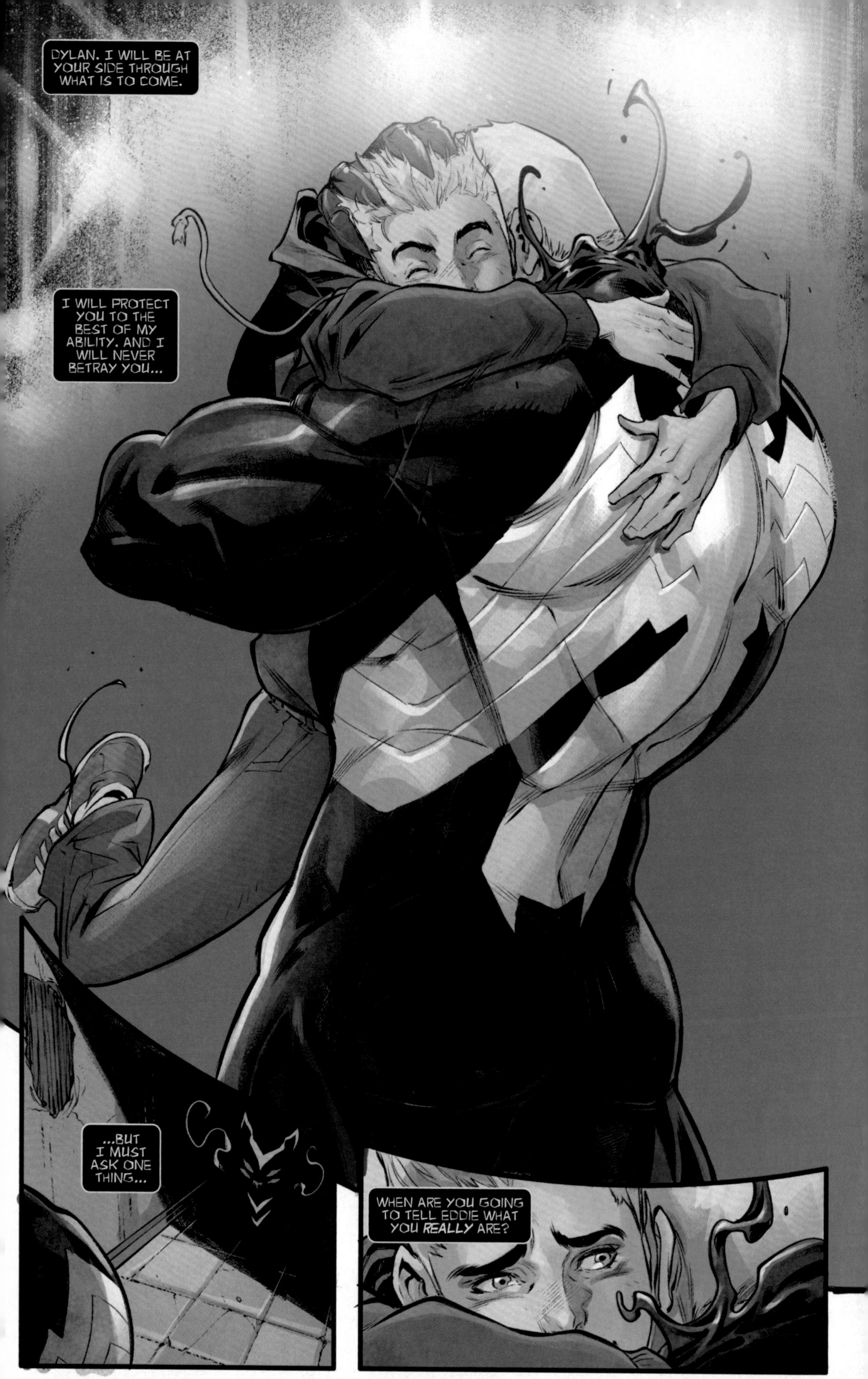
DYLAN. I WILL BE AT YOUR SIDE THROUGH WHAT IS TO COME.
I WILL PROTECT YOU TO THE BEST OF MY ABILITY. AND I WILL NEVER BETRAY YOU...
...BUT I MUST ASK ONE THING...
WHEN ARE YOU GOING TO TELL EDDIE WHAT YOU *REALLY* ARE?

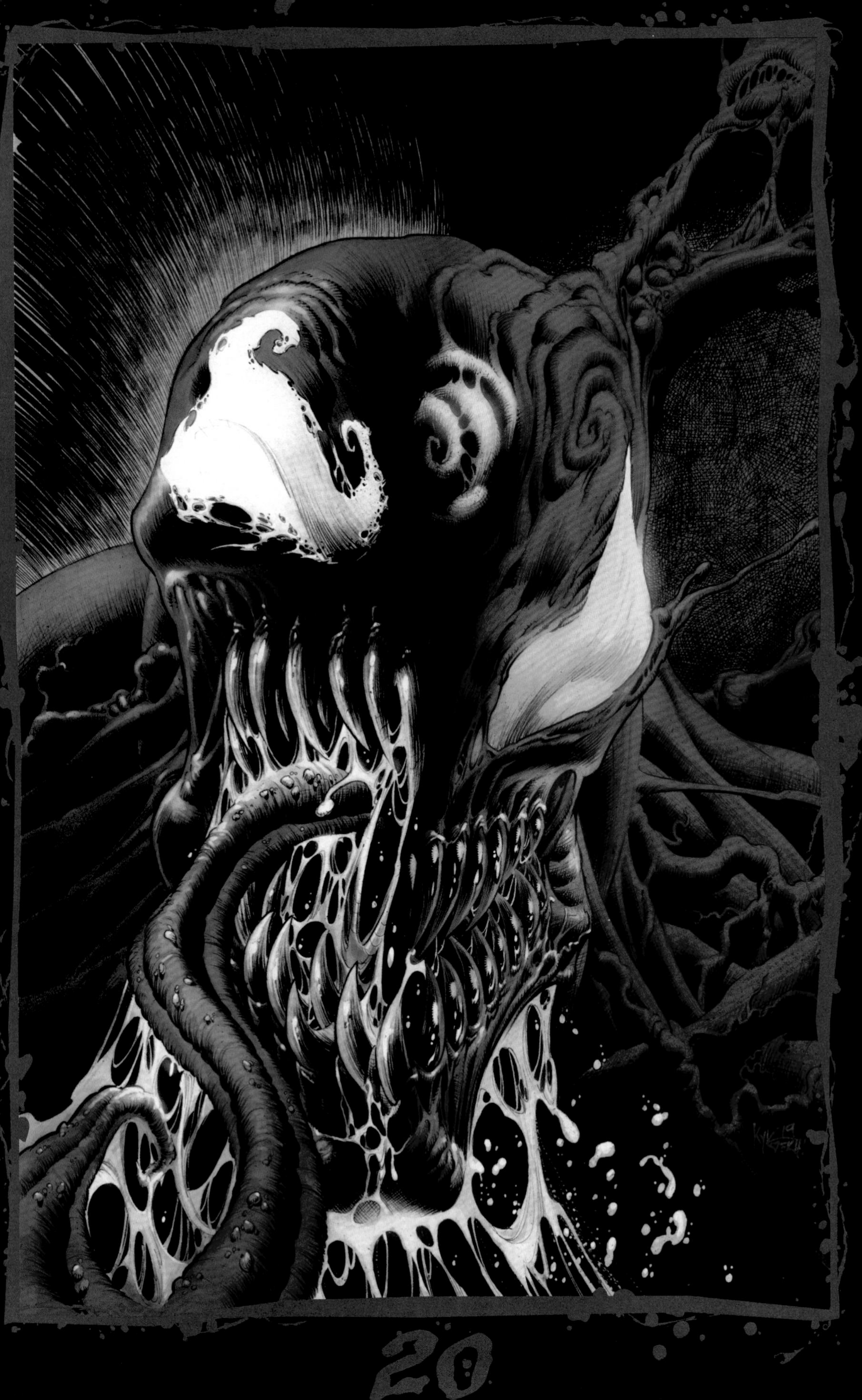
20

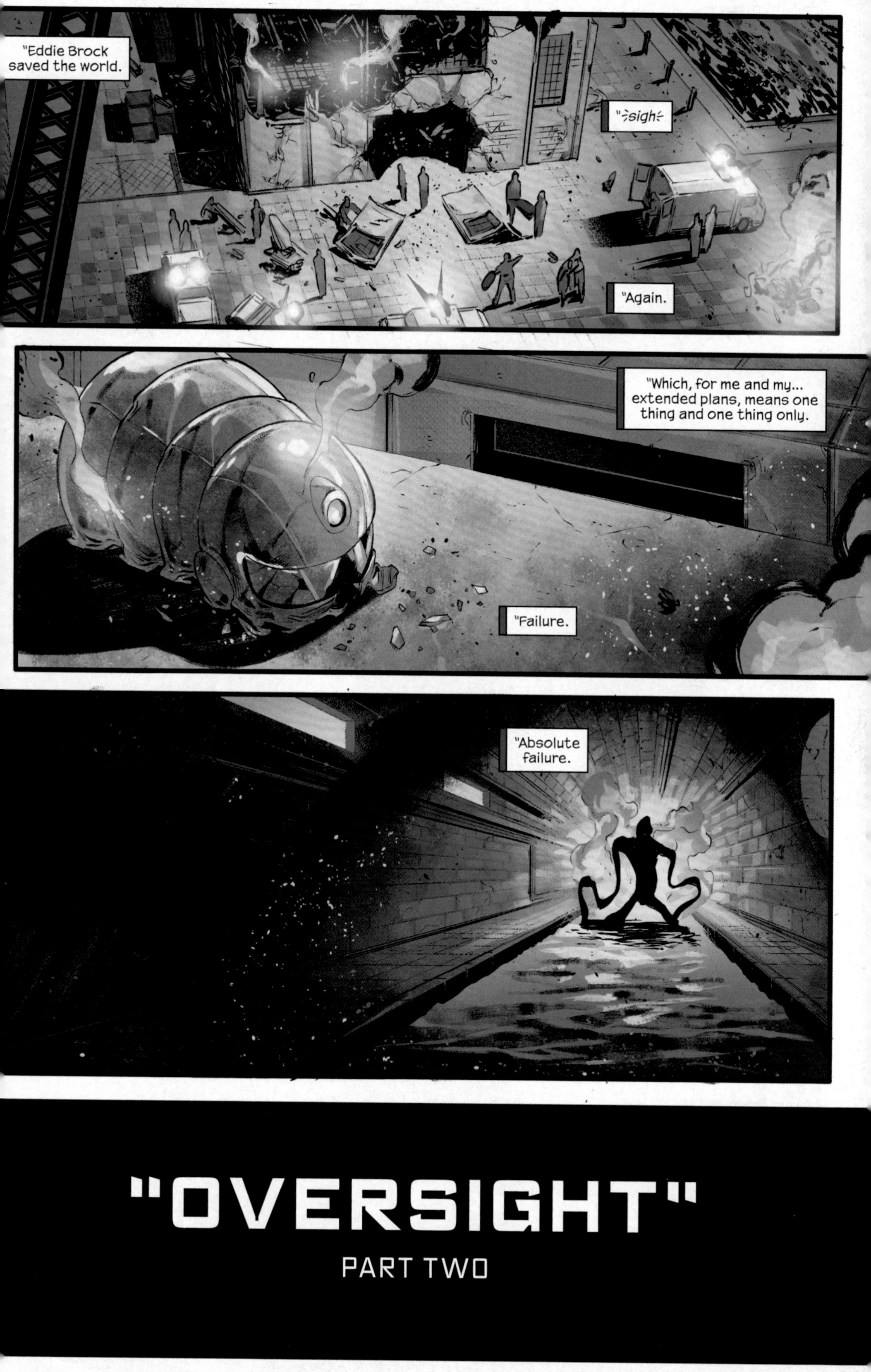
"Eddie Brock saved the world.
"⸗sigh⸗
"Again.
"Which, for me and my... extended plans, means one thing and one thing only.
"Failure.
"Absolute failure.

"OVERSIGHT"

PART TWO

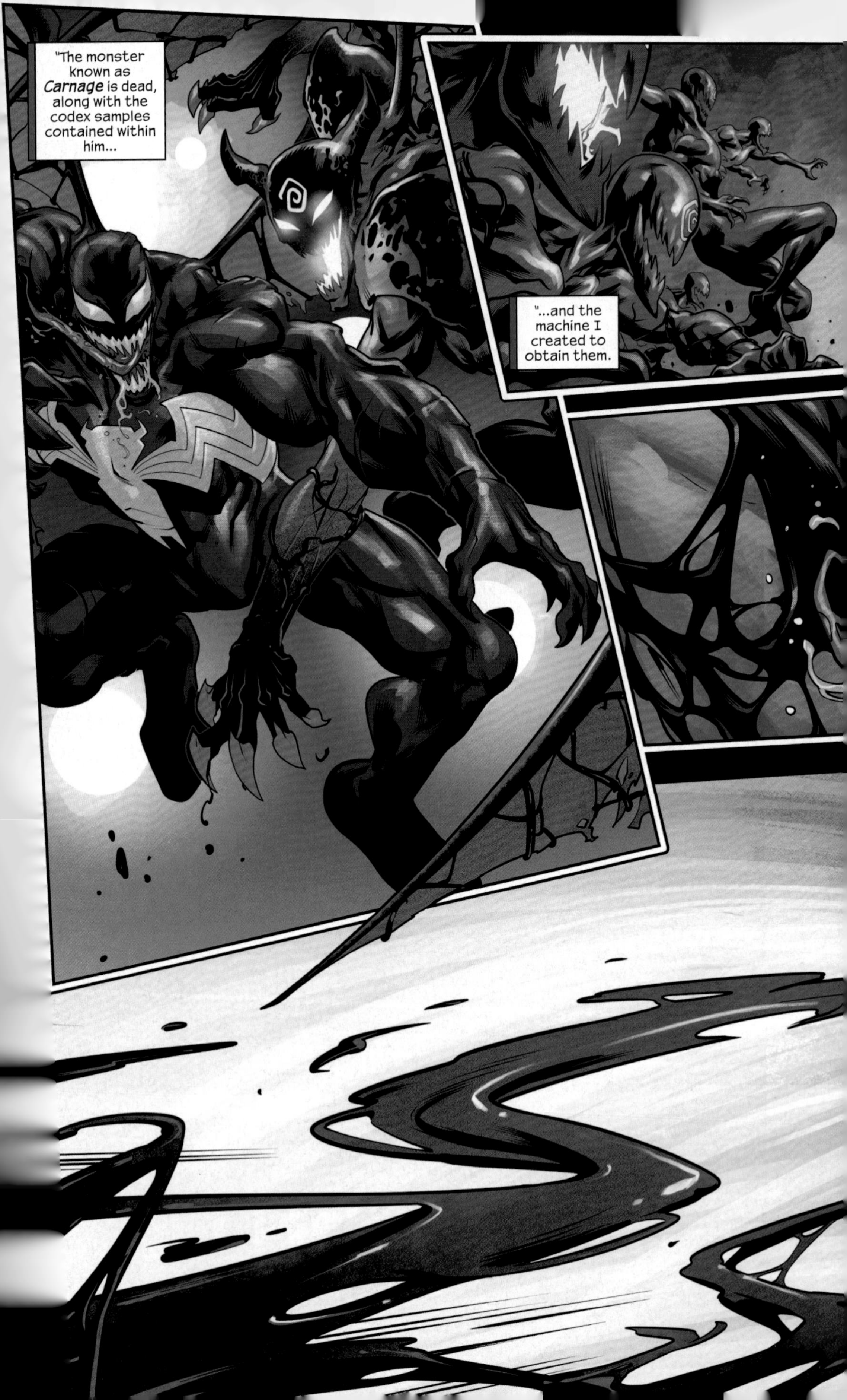
"The monster known as Carnage is dead, along with the codex samples contained within him...
"...and the machine I created to obtain them.

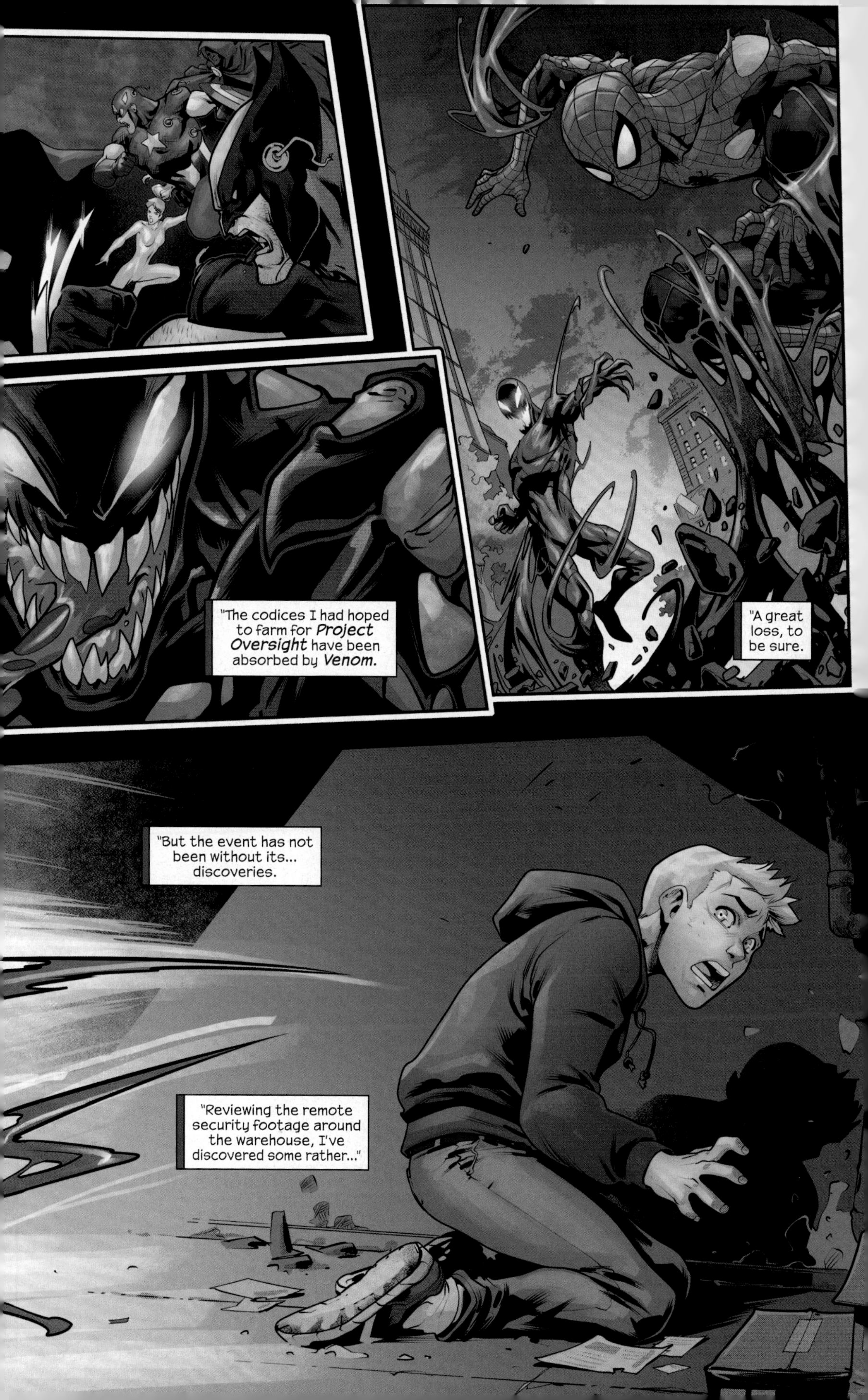
"The codices I had hoped to farm for *Project Oversight* have been absorbed by *Venom.*
"A great loss, to be sure.
"But the event has not been without its... discoveries.
"Reviewing the remote security footage around the warehouse, I've discovered some rather..."

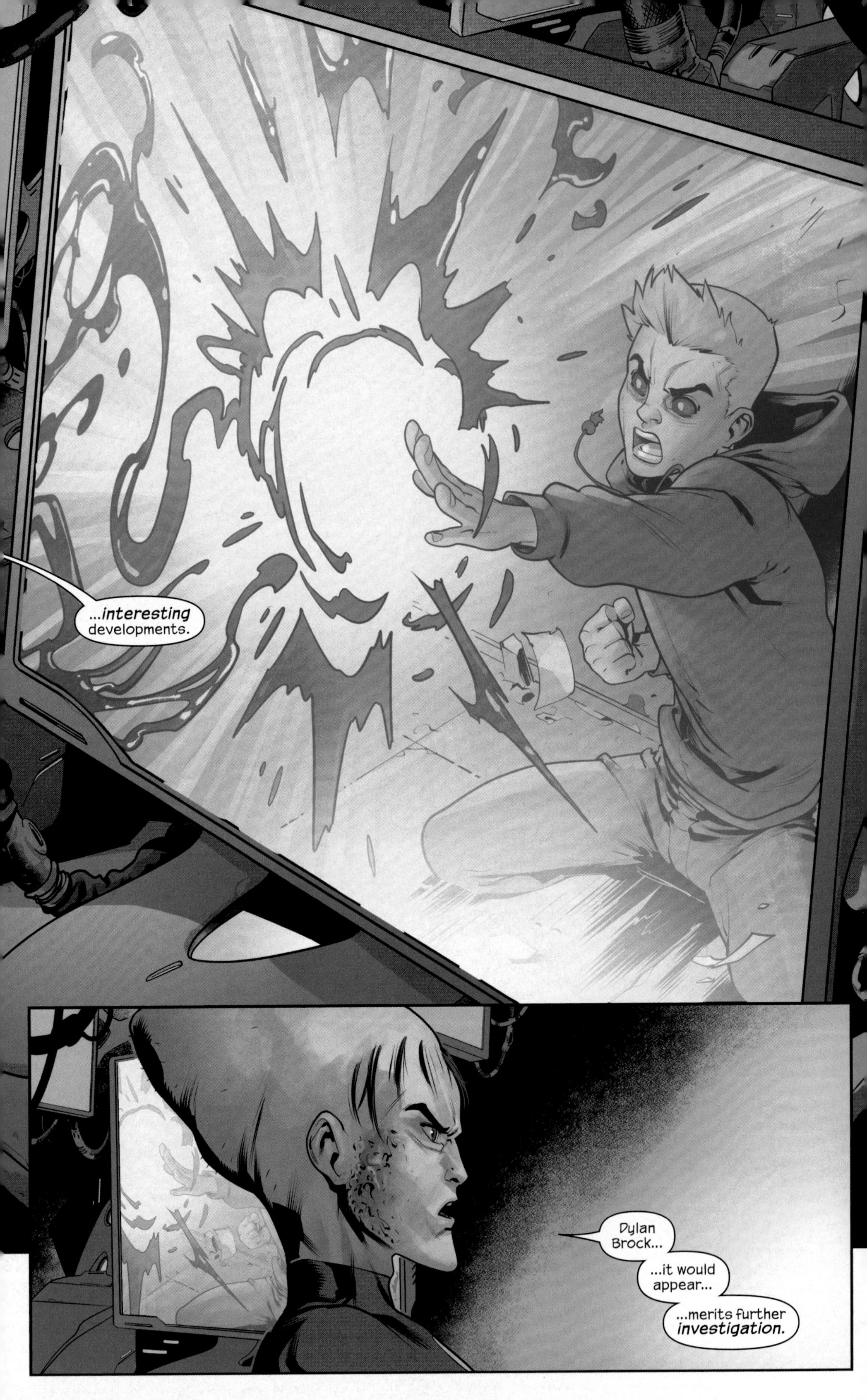
...*interesting* developments.
Dylan Brock...
...it would appear...
...merits further *investigation.*

INTERESTING. DO WE KNOW WHAT THE CHILD IS? BIOLOGICALLY?

In theory, yes.

"From a blood sample I acquired some time ago, I've surmised that the child is a kind of...living codex."*

*BACK IN VENOM #10, VENOMANIACS! --DEVIN

Essentially, a piece of the original alien combined with a living human fetus.

Though the child's power set seems to be...greater than anything I expected.

HYPOTHESES?

Yes. In the past, it was generally accepted that the symbiote species reproduced asexually and free of any apparent pattern.

That they spawned almost...at random.

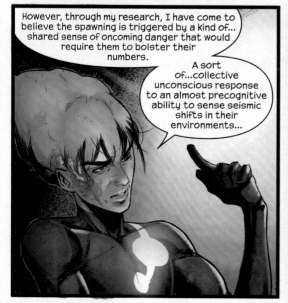

However, through my research, I have come to believe the spawning is triggered by a kind of... shared sense of oncoming danger that would require them to bolster their numbers.

A sort of...collective unconscious response to an almost precognitive ability to sense seismic shifts in their environments...

...or, perhaps more worrying, of impending danger to the hive.

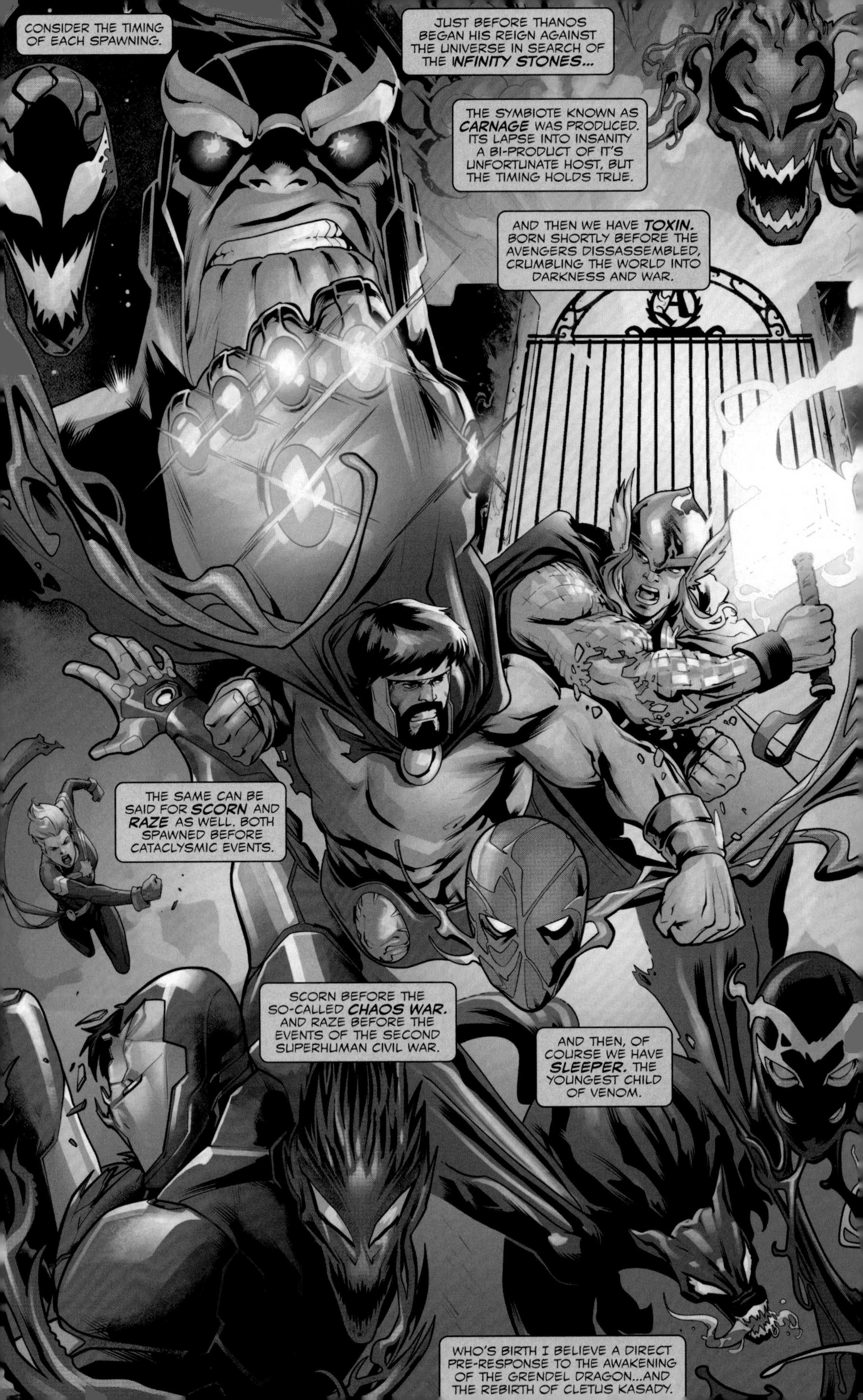
CONSIDER THE TIMING OF EACH SPAWNING.
JUST BEFORE THANOS BEGAN HIS REIGN AGAINST THE UNIVERSE IN SEARCH OF THE INFINITY STONES...
THE SYMBIOTE KNOWN AS CARNAGE WAS PRODUCED. ITS LAPSE INTO INSANITY A BI-PRODUCT OF IT'S UNFORTUNATE HOST, BUT THE TIMING HOLDS TRUE.
AND THEN WE HAVE TOXIN. BORN SHORTLY BEFORE THE AVENGERS DISSASSEMBLED, CRUMBLING THE WORLD INTO DARKNESS AND WAR.
THE SAME CAN BE SAID FOR SCORN AND RAZE AS WELL. BOTH SPAWNED BEFORE CATACLYSMIC EVENTS.
SCORN BEFORE THE SO-CALLED CHAOS WAR. AND RAZE BEFORE THE EVENTS OF THE SECOND SUPERHUMAN CIVIL WAR.
AND THEN, OF COURSE WE HAVE SLEEPER. THE YOUNGEST CHILD OF VENOM.
WHO'S BIRTH I BELIEVE A DIRECT PRE-RESPONSE TO THE AWAKENING OF THE GRENDEL DRAGON...AND THE REBIRTH OF CLETUS KASADY.

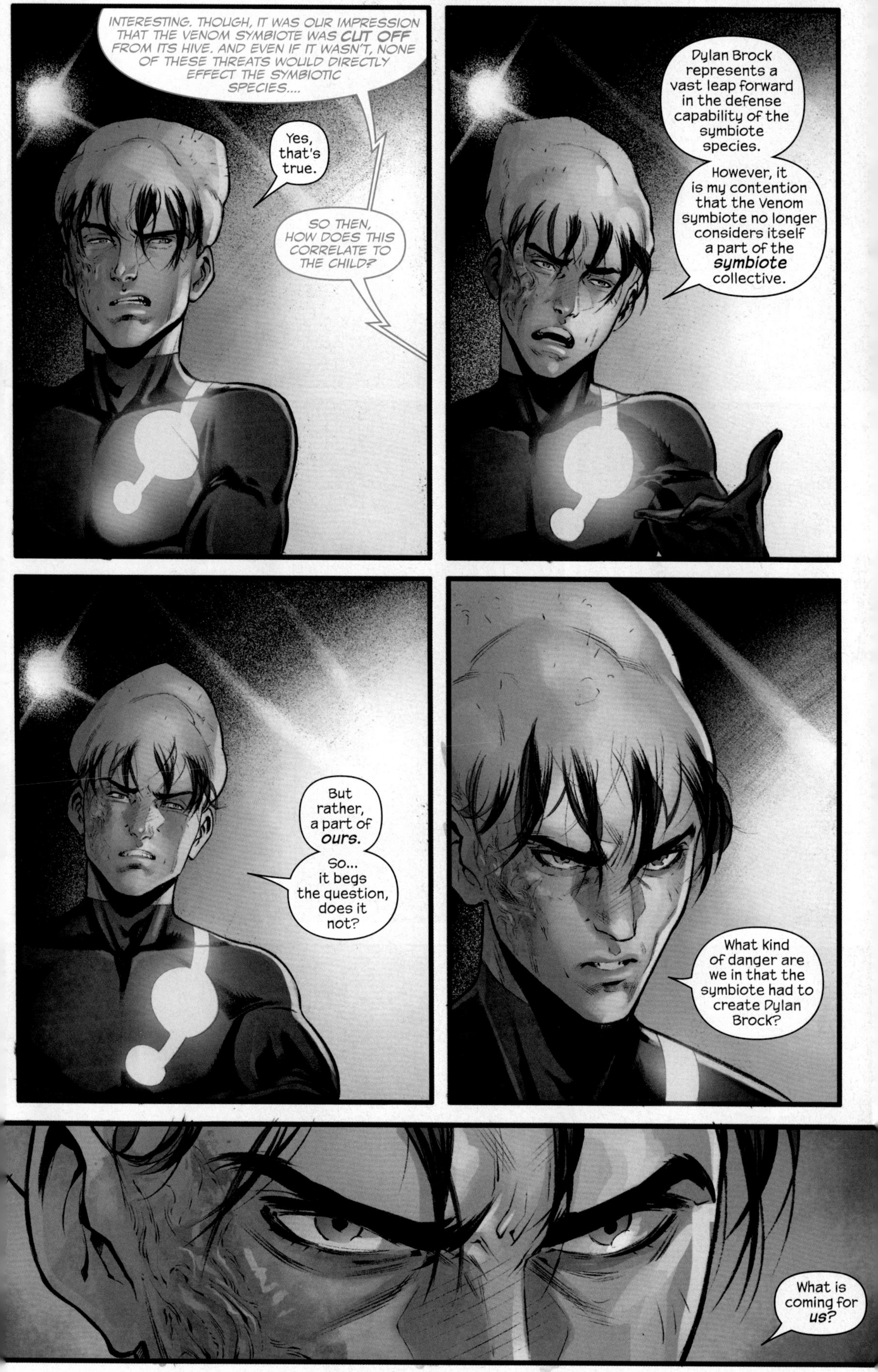
INTERESTING. THOUGH, IT WAS OUR IMPRESSION THAT THE VENOM SYMBIOTE WAS CUT OFF FROM ITS HIVE. AND EVEN IF IT WASN'T, NONE OF THESE THREATS WOULD DIRECTLY EFFECT THE SYMBIOTIC SPECIES....
Yes, that's true.
SO THEN, HOW DOES THIS CORRELATE TO THE CHILD?
Dylan Brock represents a vast leap forward in the defense capability of the symbiote species.
However, it is my contention that the Venom symbiote no longer considers itself a part of the symbiote collective.
But rather, a part of ours.
So... it begs the question, does it not?
What kind of danger are we in that the symbiote had to create Dylan Brock?
What is coming for us?

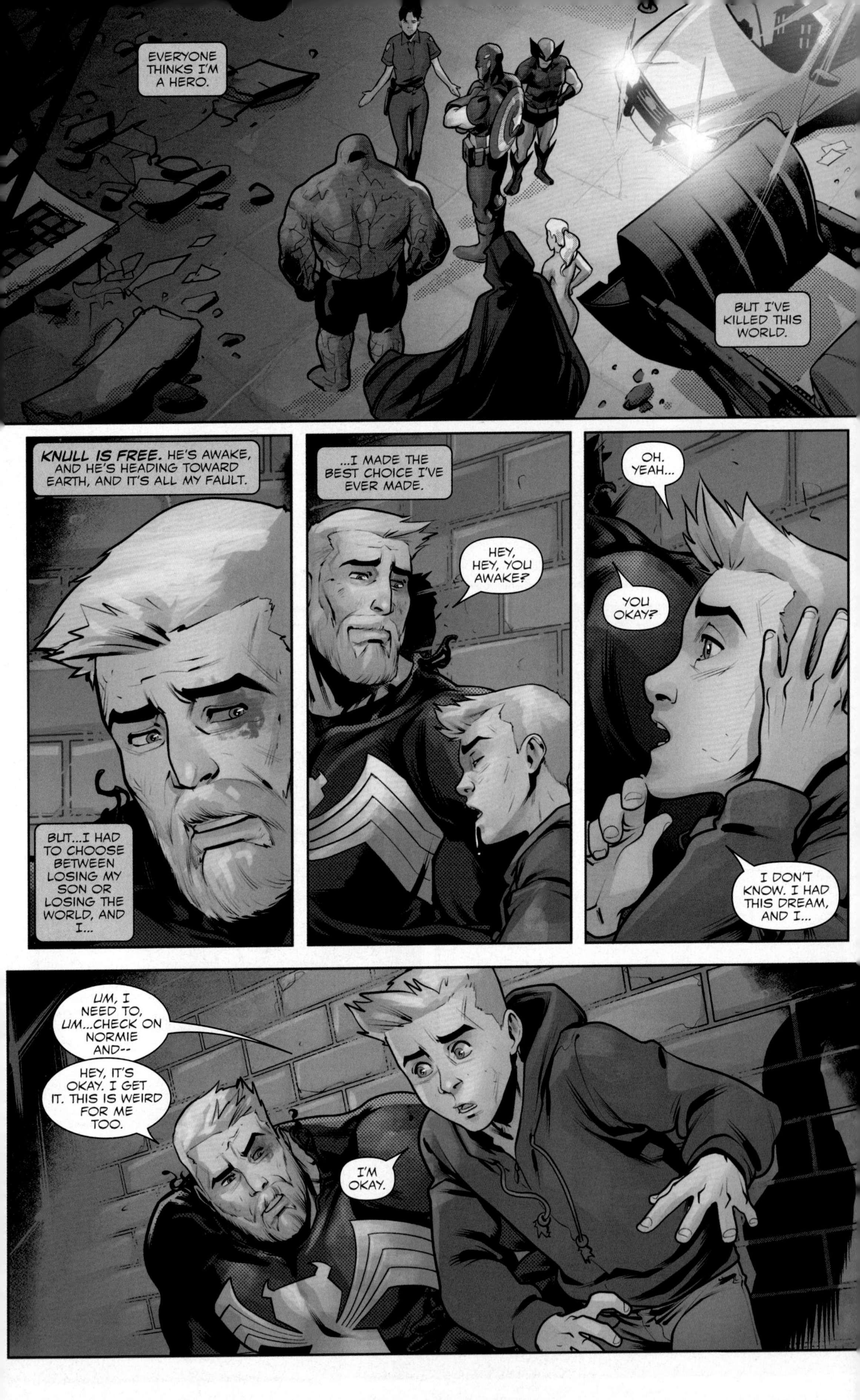
EVERYONE THINKS I'M A HERO.
BUT I'VE KILLED THIS WORLD.
KNULL IS FREE. HE'S AWAKE, AND HE'S HEADING TOWARD EARTH, AND IT'S ALL MY FAULT.
BUT...I HAD TO CHOOSE BETWEEN LOSING MY SON OR LOSING THE WORLD, AND I...
...I MADE THE BEST CHOICE I'VE EVER MADE.
HEY, HEY, YOU AWAKE?
OH. YEAH...
YOU OKAY?
I DON'T KNOW. I HAD THIS DREAM, AND I...
UM, I NEED TO, UM...CHECK ON NORMIE AND--
HEY, IT'S OKAY. I GET IT. THIS IS WEIRD FOR ME TOO.
I'M OKAY.

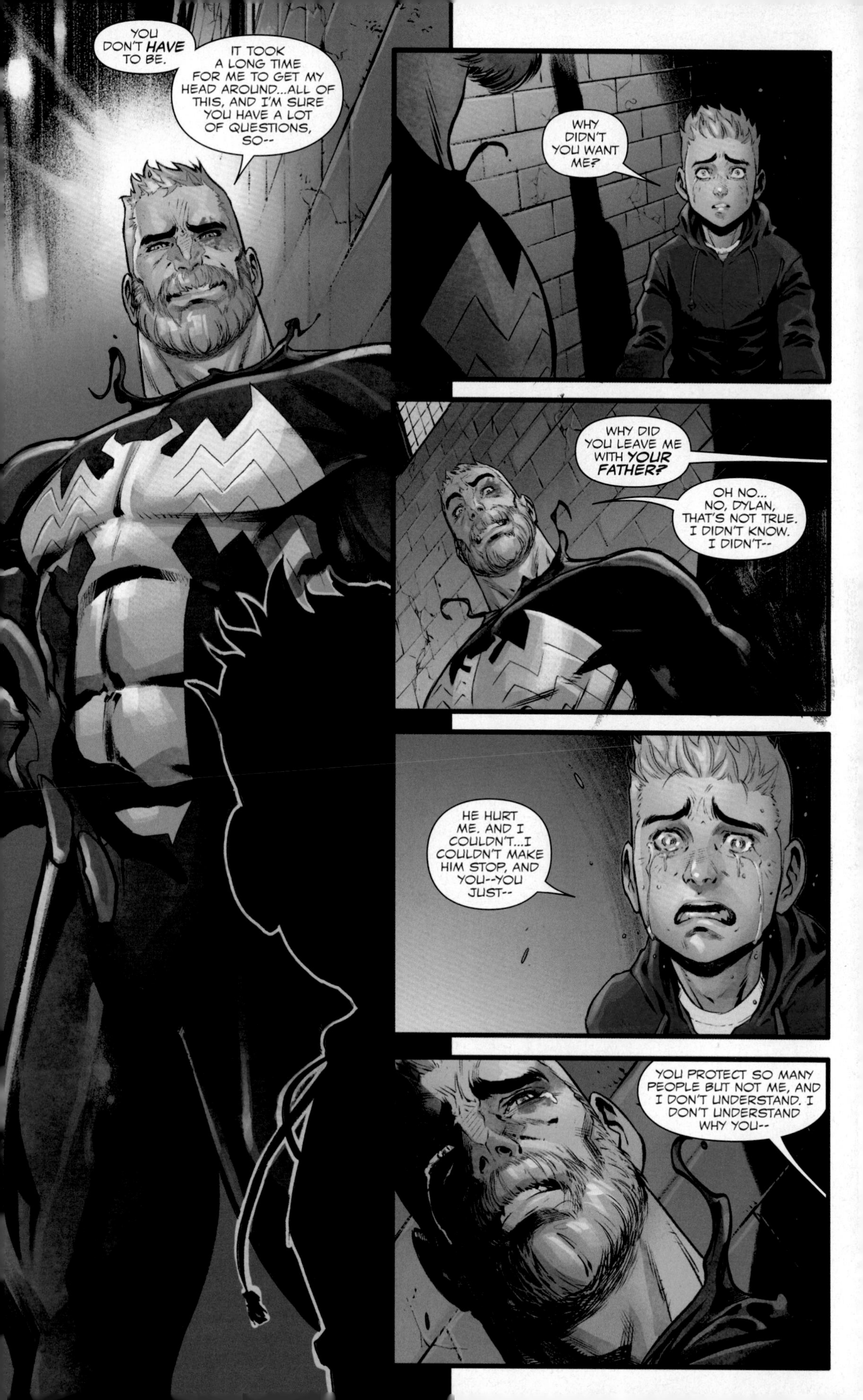
YOU DON'T **HAVE** TO BE.
IT TOOK A LONG TIME FOR ME TO GET MY HEAD AROUND...ALL OF THIS, AND I'M SURE YOU HAVE A LOT OF QUESTIONS, SO--
WHY DIDN'T YOU WANT ME?
WHY DID YOU LEAVE ME WITH **YOUR FATHER?**
OH NO... NO, DYLAN, THAT'S NOT TRUE. I DIDN'T KNOW. I DIDN'T--
HE HURT ME. AND I COULDN'T...I COULDN'T MAKE HIM STOP, AND YOU--YOU JUST--
YOU PROTECT SO MANY PEOPLE BUT NOT ME, AND I DON'T UNDERSTAND. I DON'T UNDERSTAND WHY YOU--

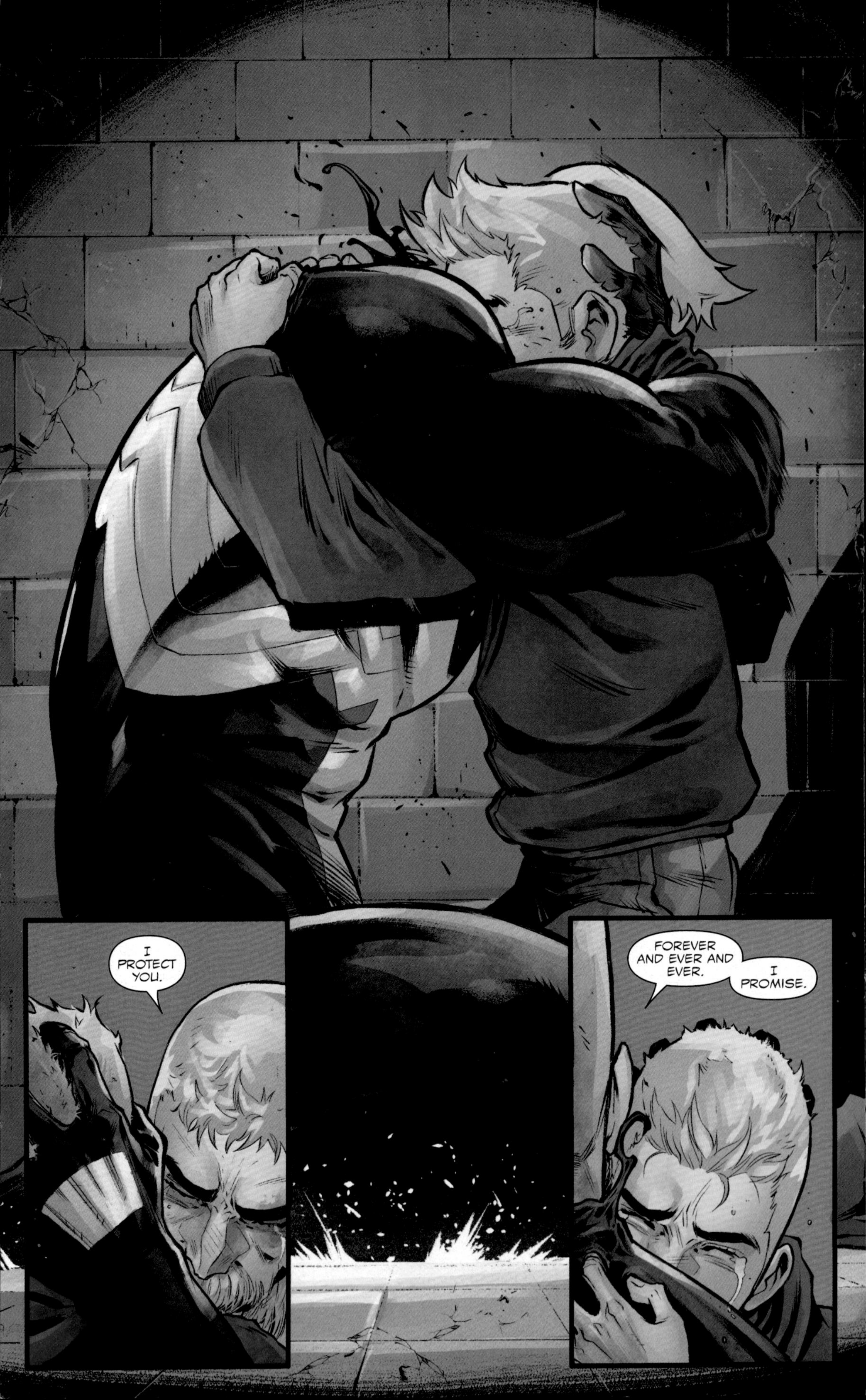
I PROTECT YOU.
FOREVER AND EVER AND EVER.
I PROMISE.

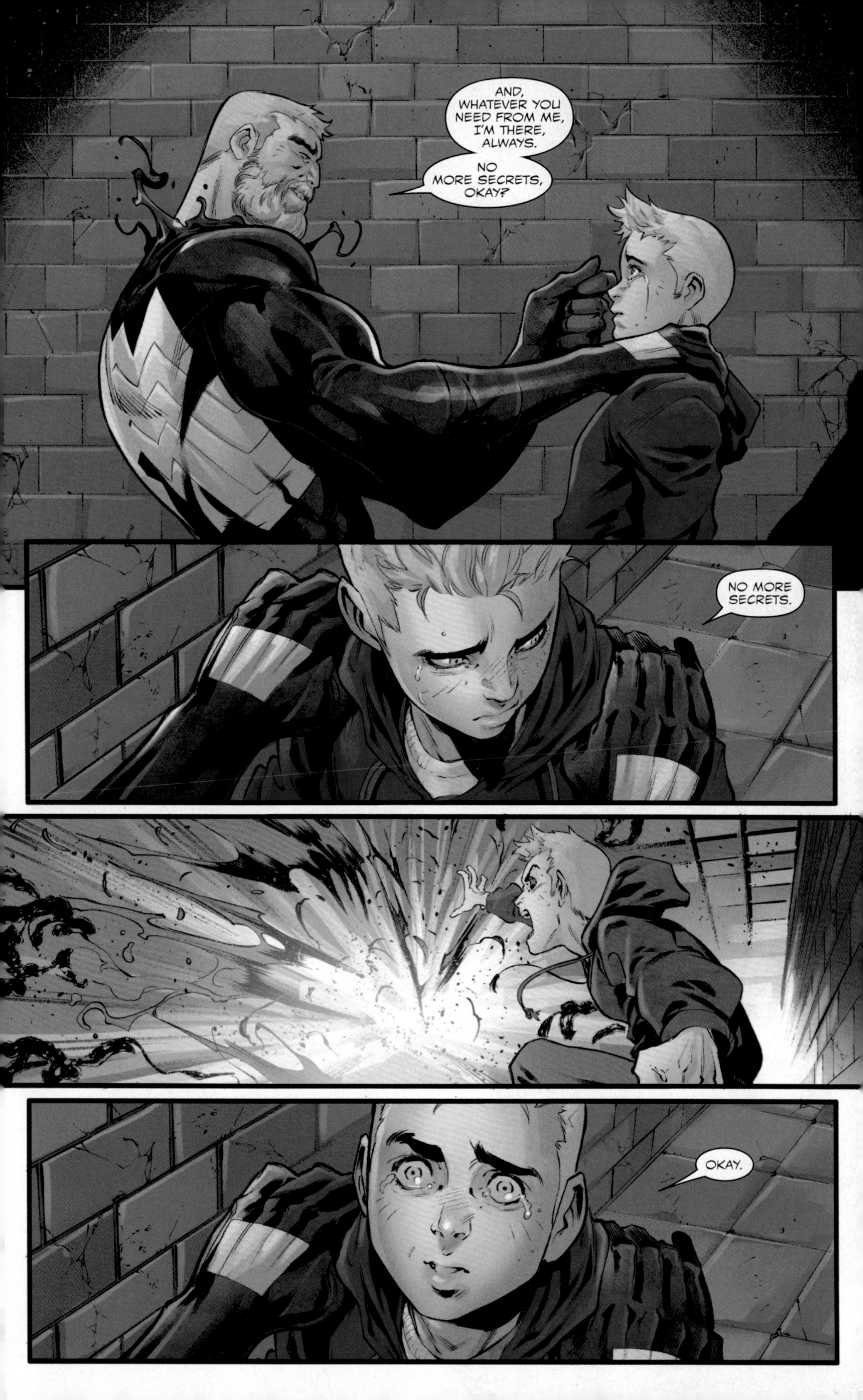
AND, WHATEVER YOU NEED FROM ME, I'M THERE, ALWAYS.
NO MORE SECRETS, OKAY?
NO MORE SECRETS.
OKAY.

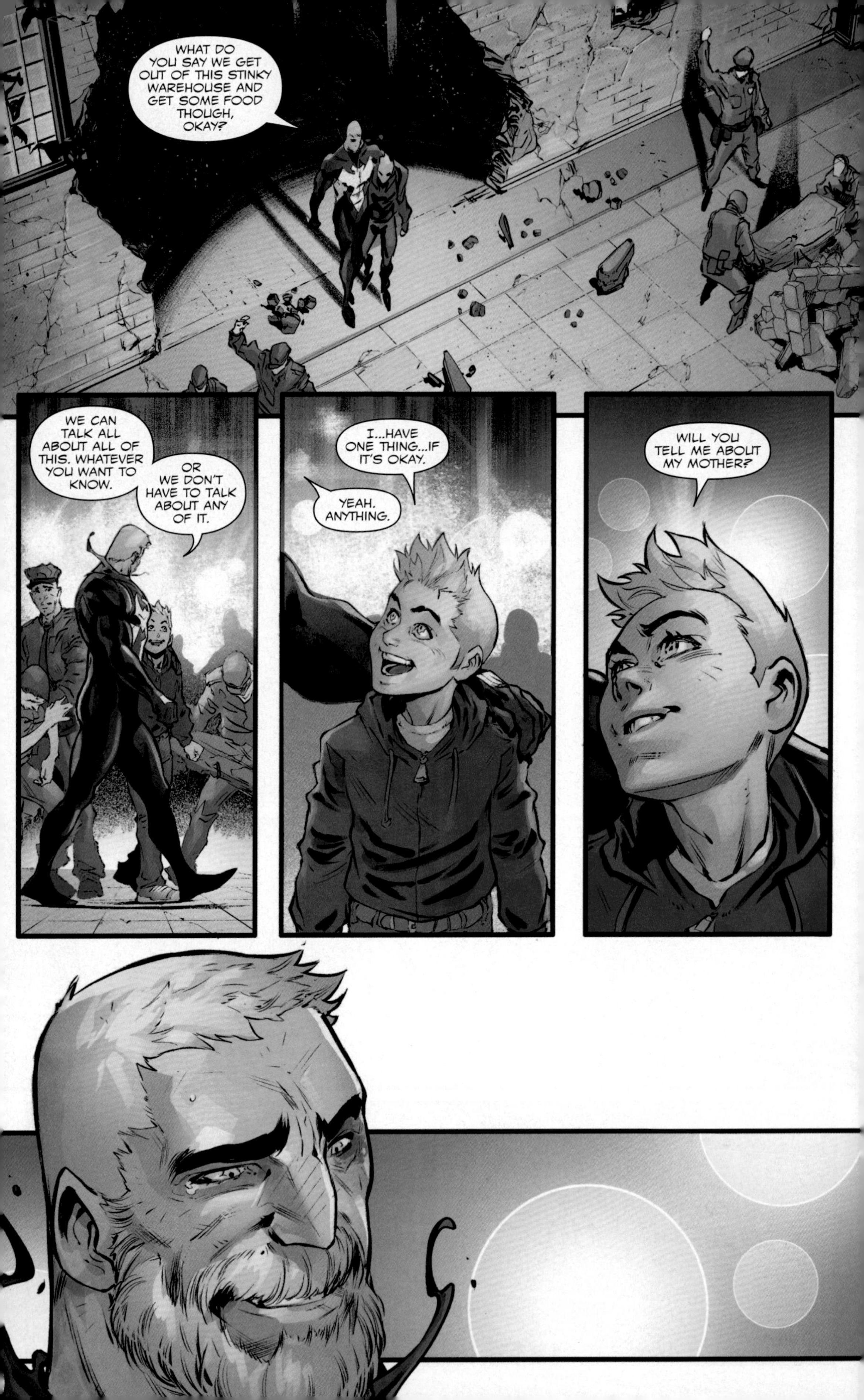
WHAT DO YOU SAY WE GET OUT OF THIS STINKY WAREHOUSE AND GET SOME FOOD THOUGH, OKAY?
WE CAN TALK ALL ABOUT ALL OF THIS. WHATEVER YOU WANT TO KNOW.
OR WE DON'T HAVE TO TALK ABOUT ANY OF IT.
I...HAVE ONE THING...IF IT'S OKAY.
YEAH. ANYTHING.
WILL YOU TELL ME ABOUT MY MOTHER?

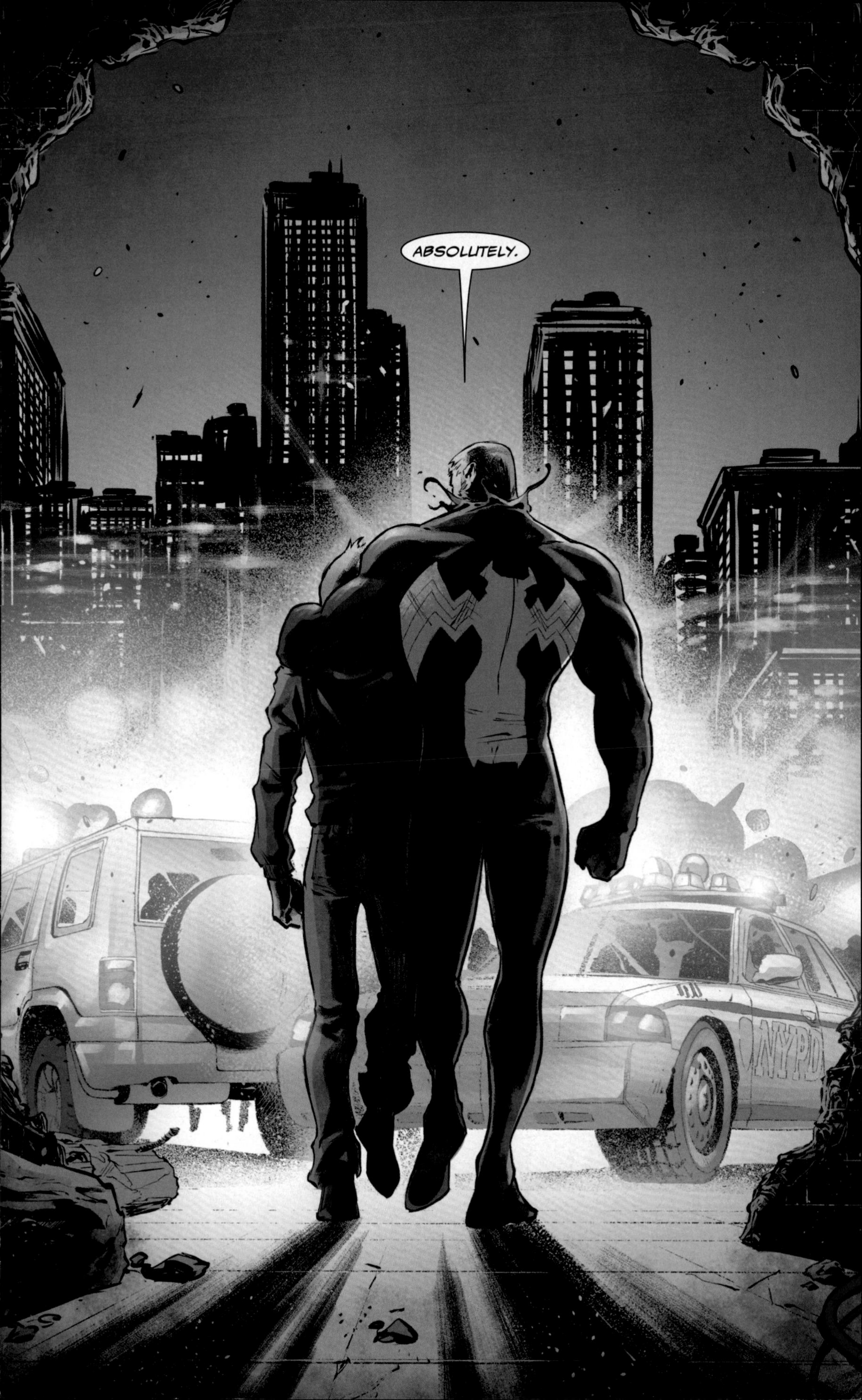
ABSOLUTELY.

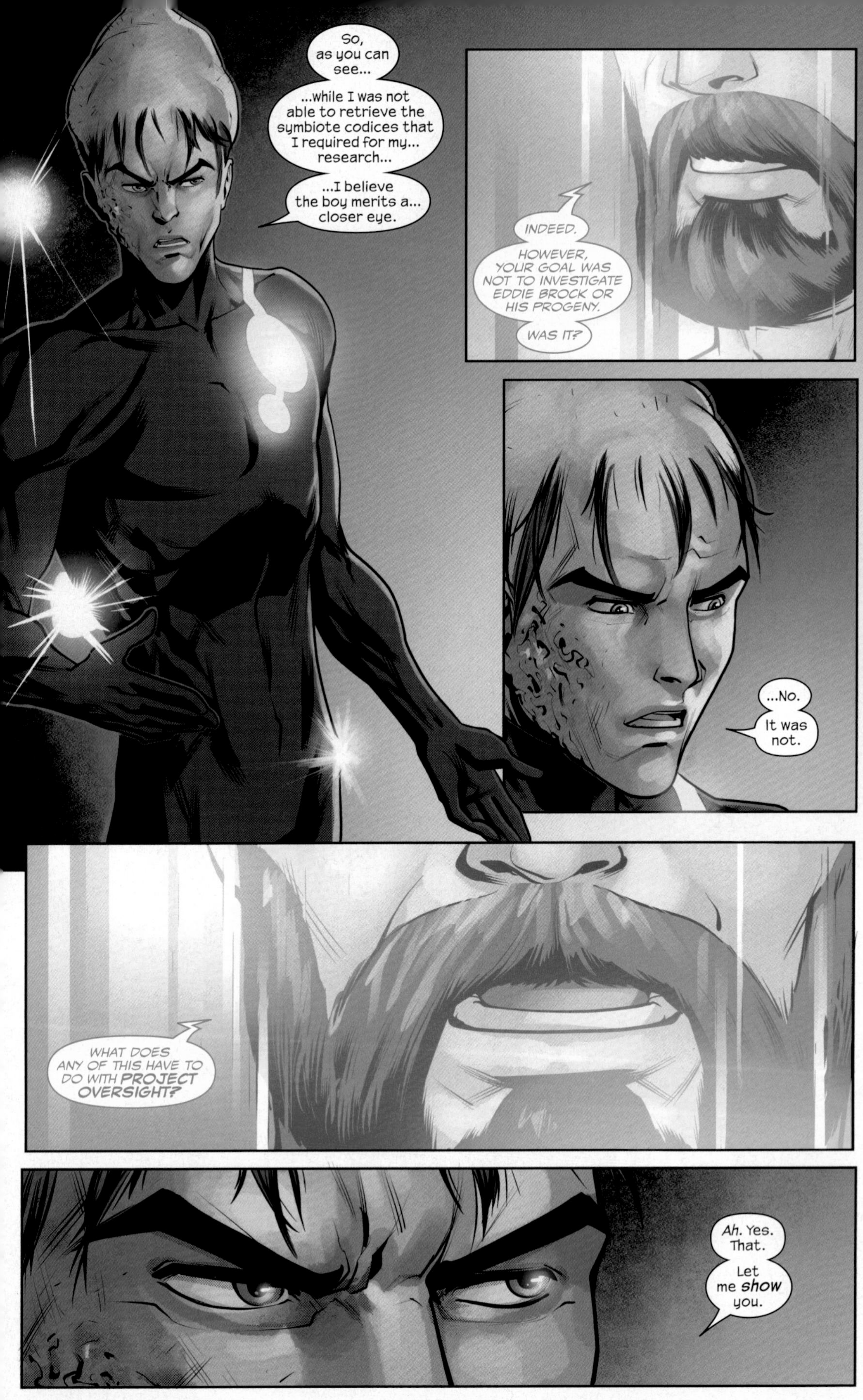
So, as you can see...
...while I was not able to retrieve the symbiote codices that I required for my... research...
...I believe the boy merits a... closer eye.
INDEED.
HOWEVER, YOUR GOAL WAS NOT TO INVESTIGATE EDDIE BROCK OR HIS PROGENY.
WAS IT?
...No.
It was not.
WHAT DOES ANY OF THIS HAVE TO DO WITH PROJECT OVERSIGHT?
Ah. Yes. That.
Let me show you.

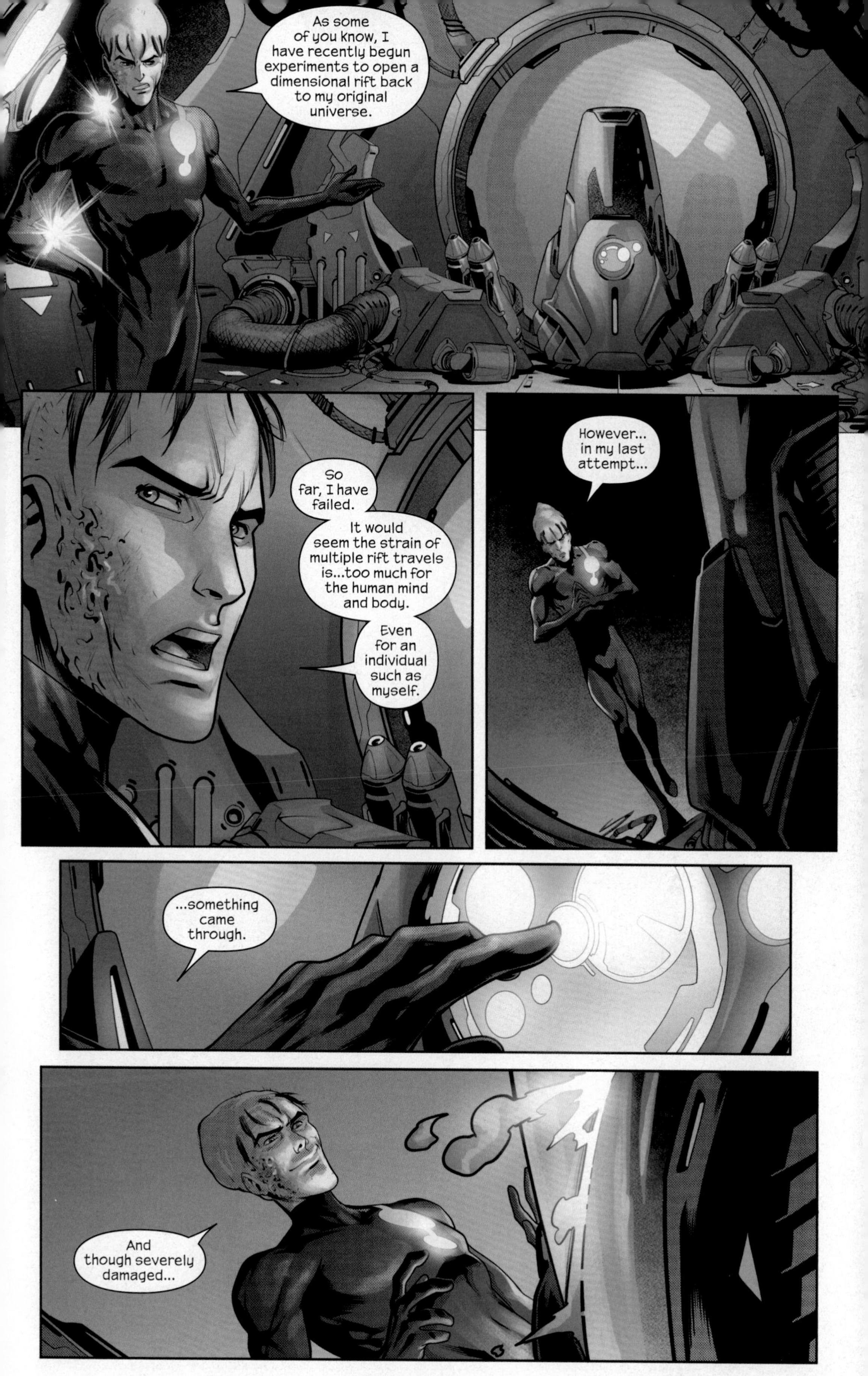
As some of you know, I have recently begun experiments to open a dimensional rift back to my original universe.
So far, I have failed.
It would seem the strain of multiple rift travels is...too much for the human mind and body.
Even for an individual such as myself.
However... in my last attempt...
...something came through.
And though severely damaged...

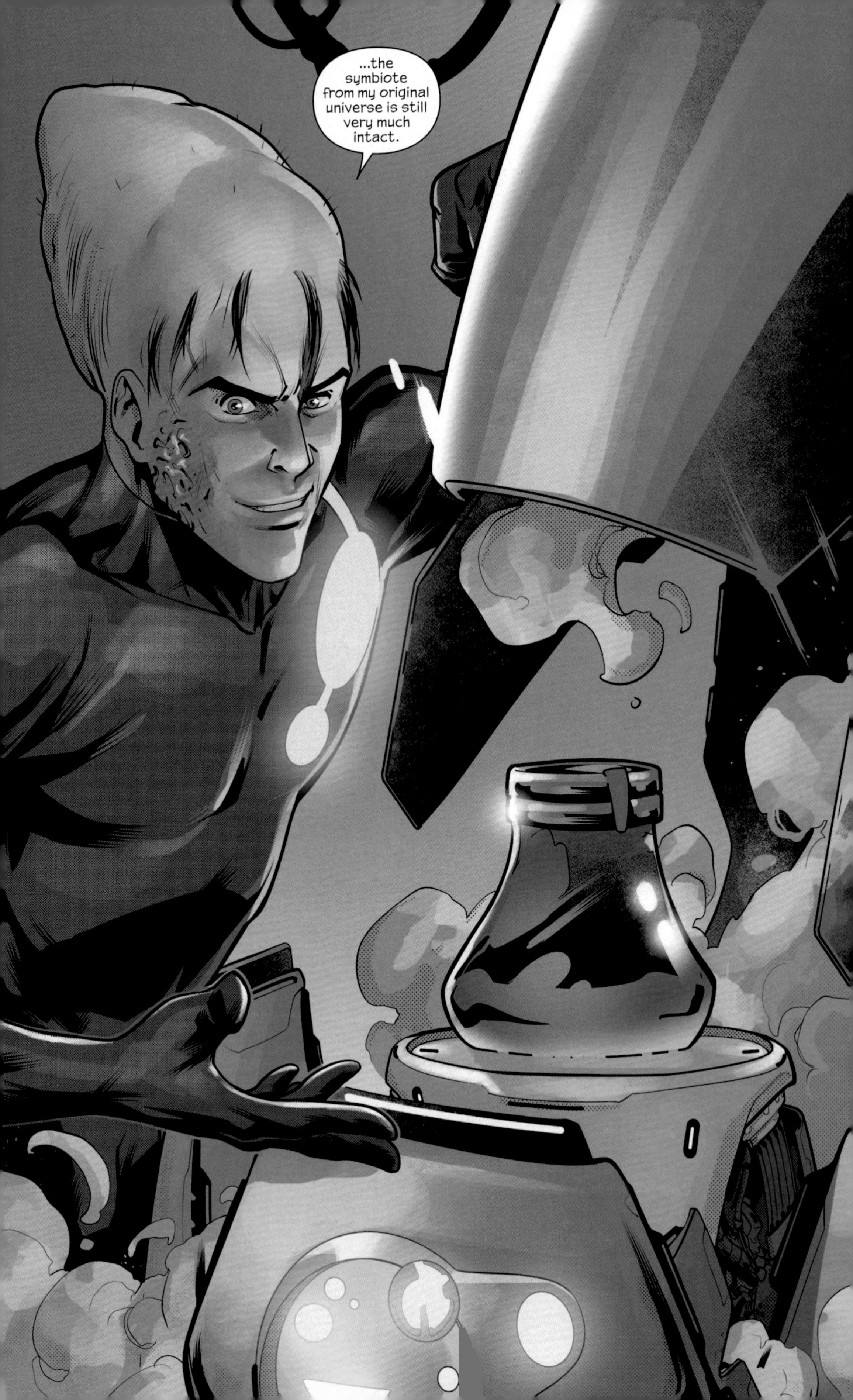
...the symbiote from my original universe is still very much intact.

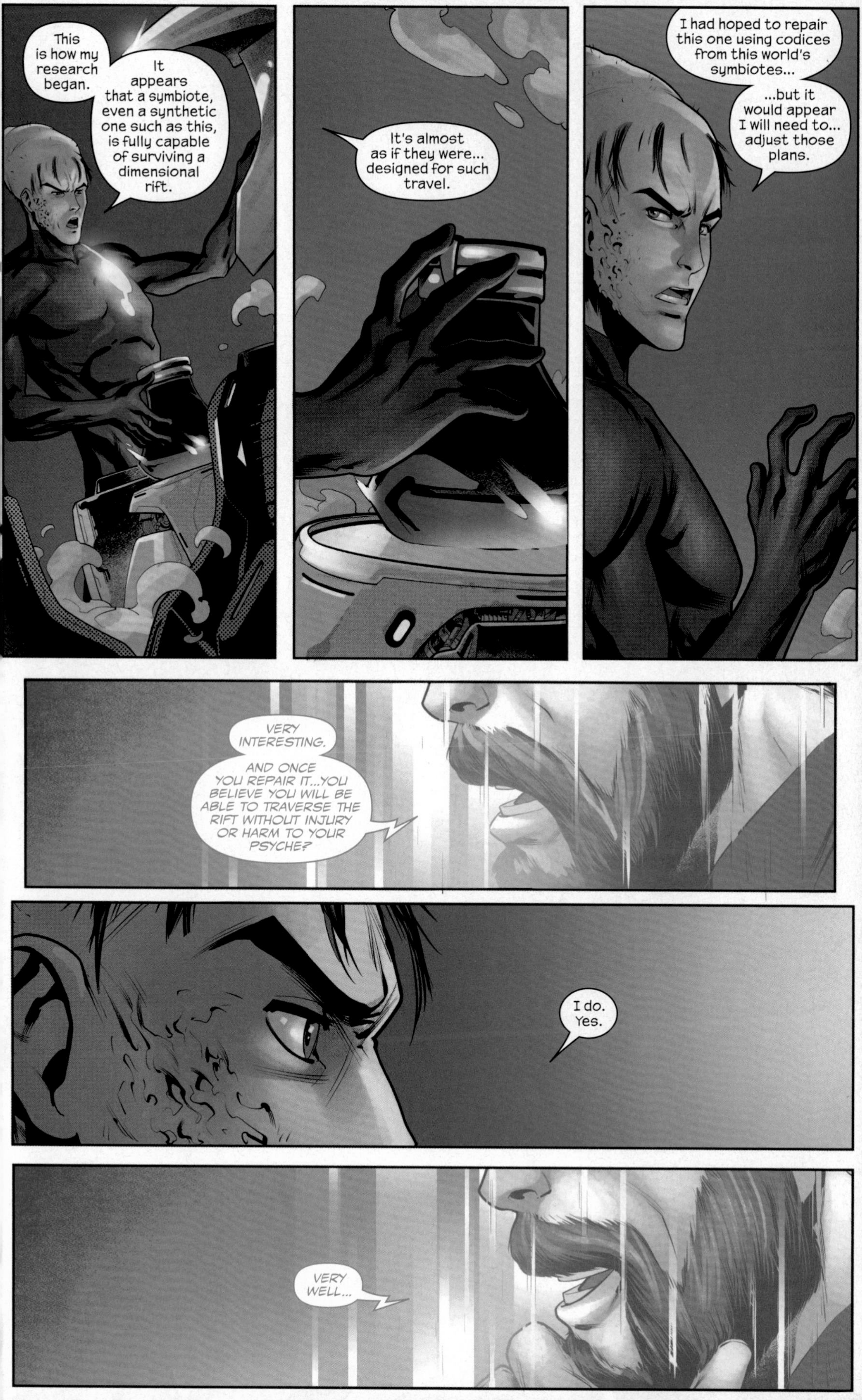
This is how my research began.
It appears that a symbiote, even a synthetic one such as this, is fully capable of surviving a dimensional rift.
It's almost as if they were... designed for such travel.
I had hoped to repair this one using codices from this world's symbiotes...
...but it would appear I will need to... adjust those plans.
VERY INTERESTING.
AND ONCE YOU REPAIR IT...YOU BELIEVE YOU WILL BE ABLE TO TRAVERSE THE RIFT WITHOUT INJURY OR HARM TO YOUR PSYCHE?
I do. Yes.
VERY WELL...

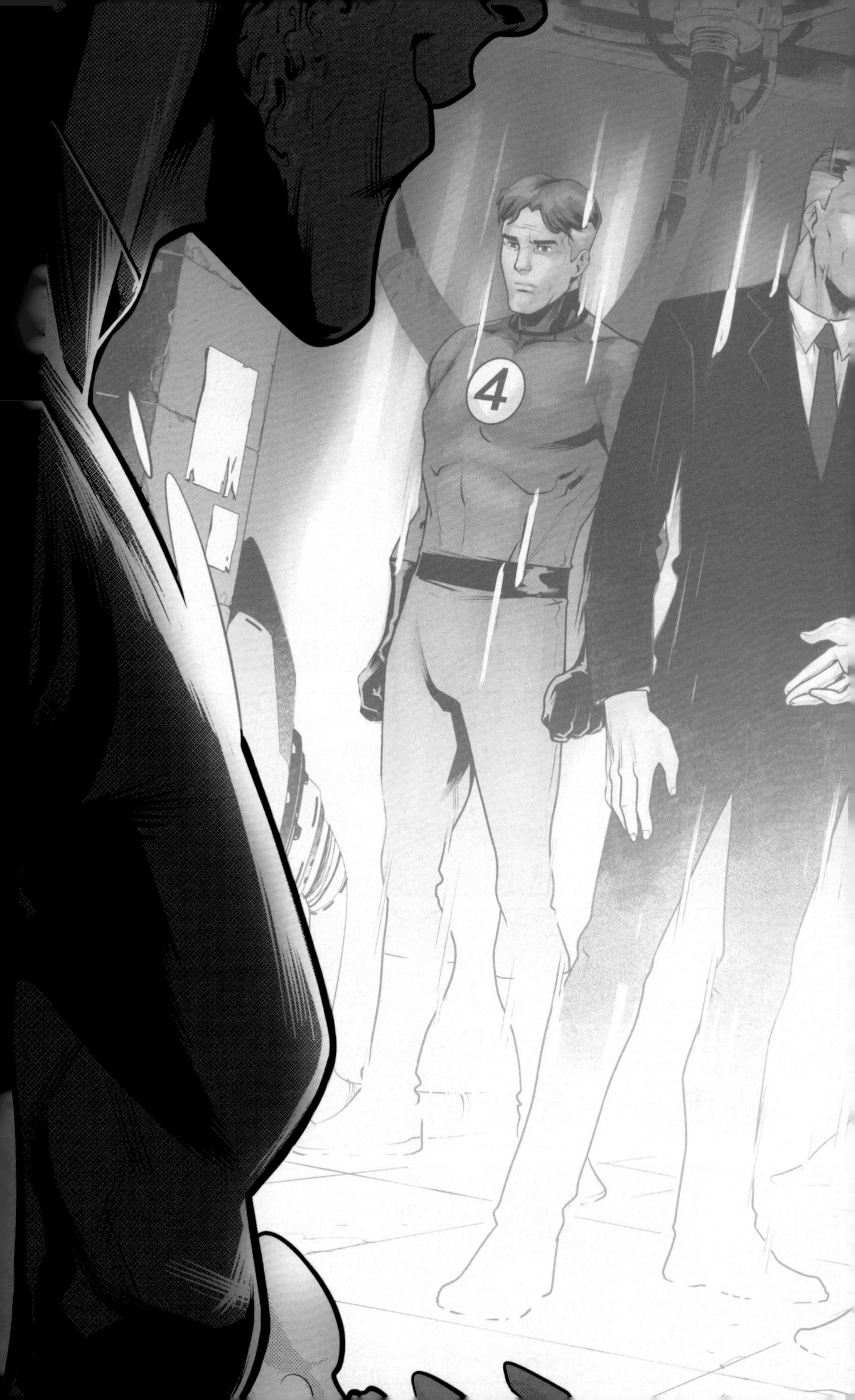

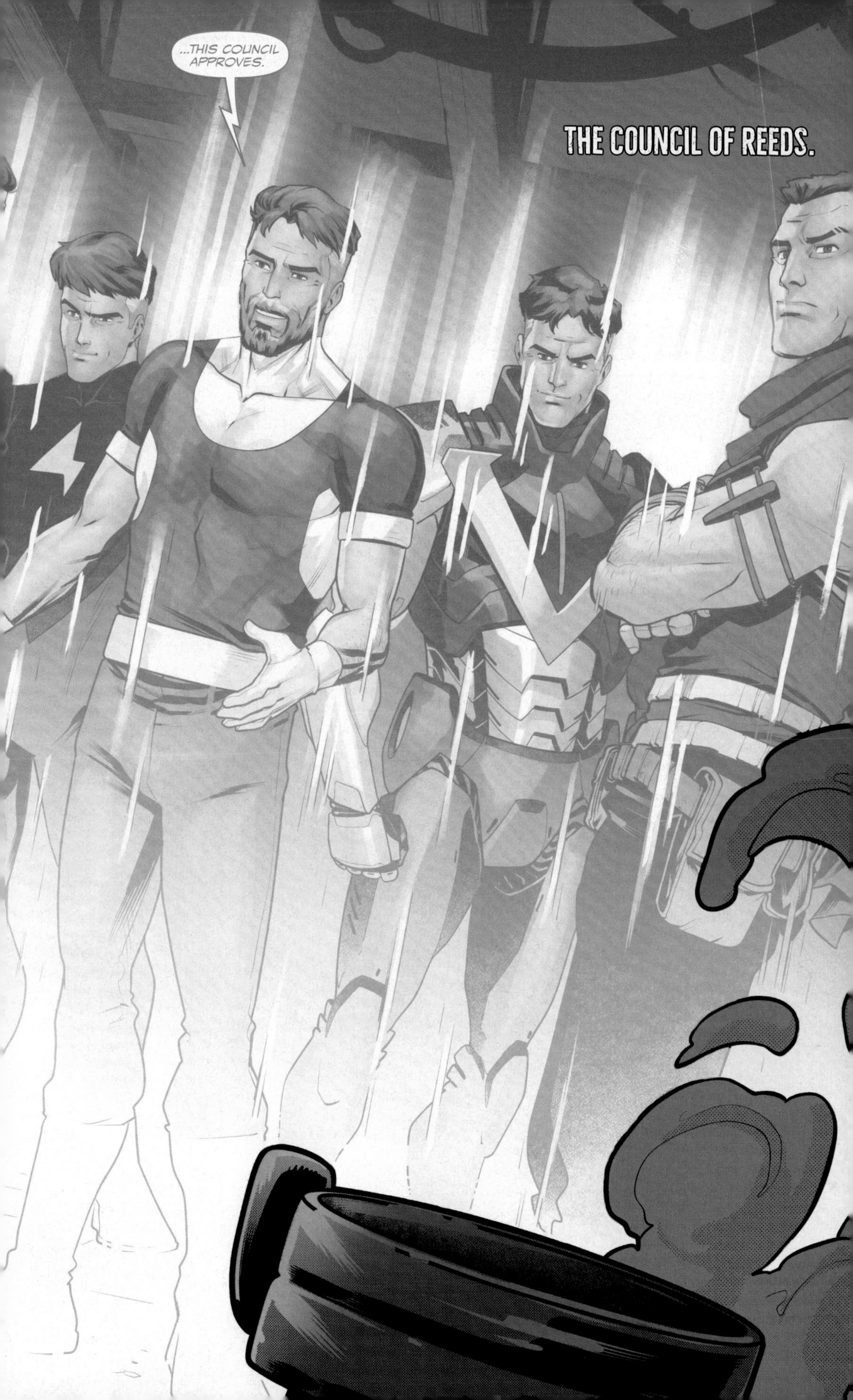
...THIS COUNCIL APPROVES.
THE COUNCIL OF REEDS.

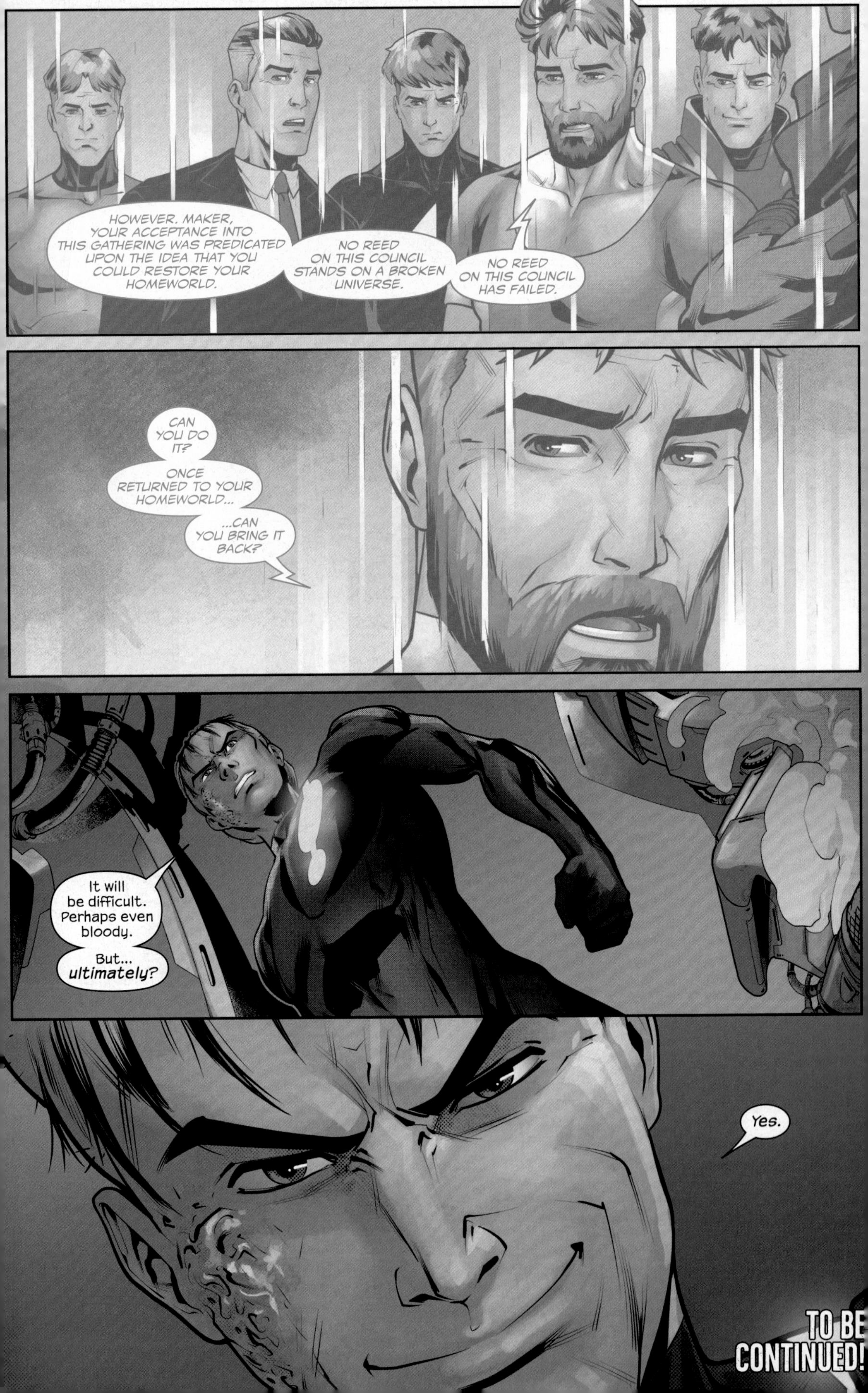
HOWEVER. MAKER, YOUR ACCEPTANCE INTO THIS GATHERING WAS PREDICATED UPON THE IDEA THAT YOU COULD RESTORE YOUR HOMEWORLD.
NO REED ON THIS COUNCIL STANDS ON A BROKEN UNIVERSE.
NO REED ON THIS COUNCIL HAS FAILED.
CAN YOU DO IT?
ONCE RETURNED TO YOUR HOMEWORLD...
...CAN YOU BRING IT BACK?
It will be difficult. Perhaps even bloody.
But... ultimately?
Yes.
TO BE CONTINUED!

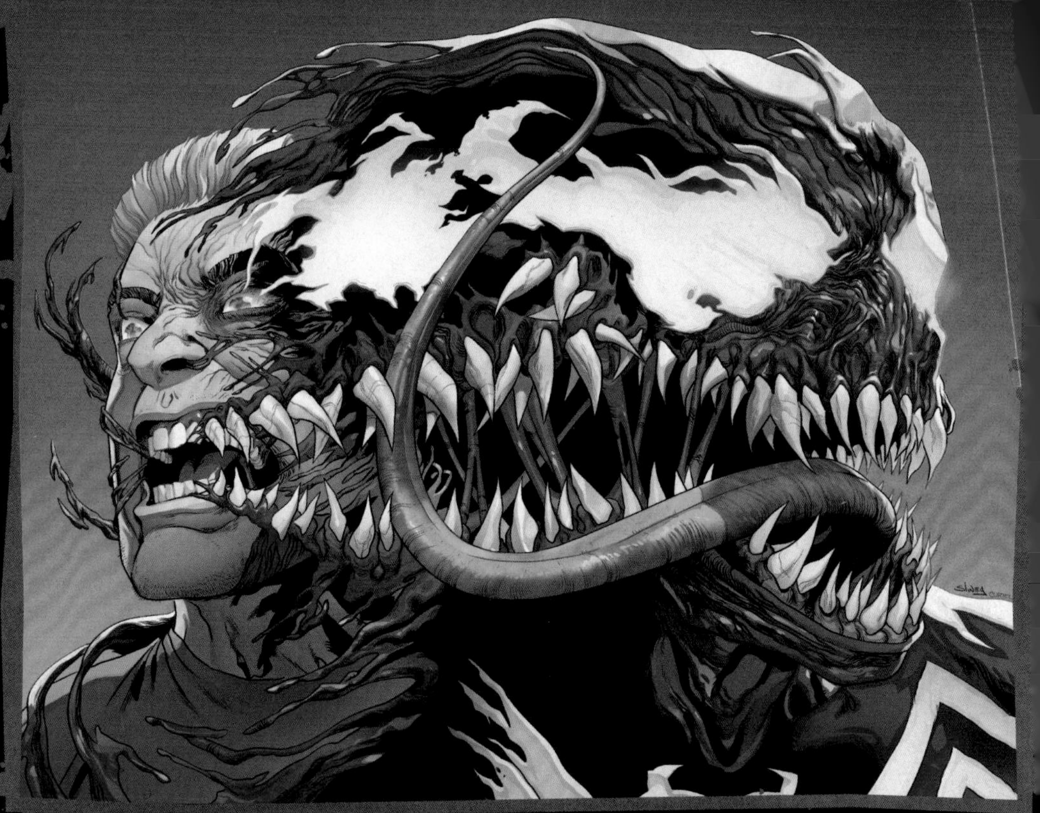

#18 IMMORTAL VARIANT
BY **WILL SLINEY** & **DAVID CURIEL**

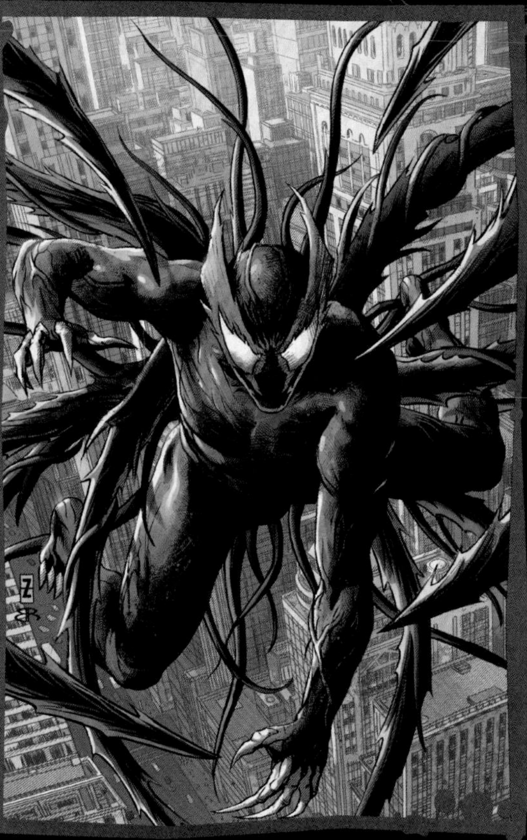

#18 CODEX VARIANT

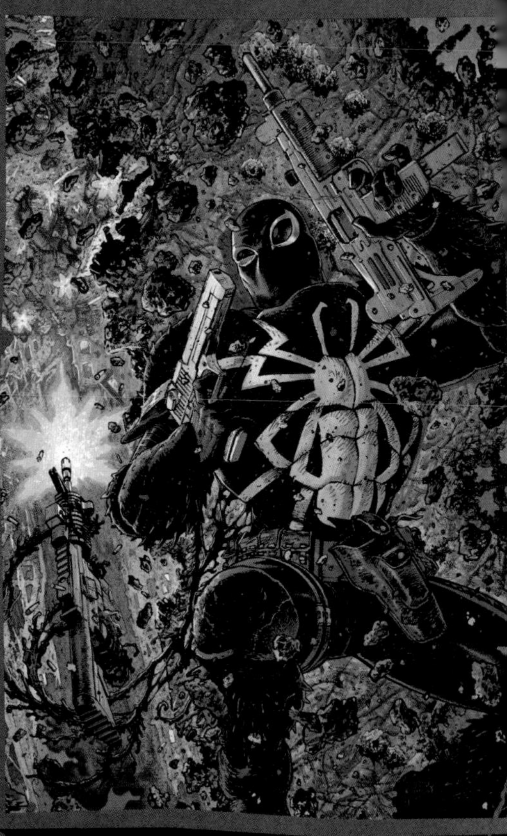

#19 CODEX VARIANT

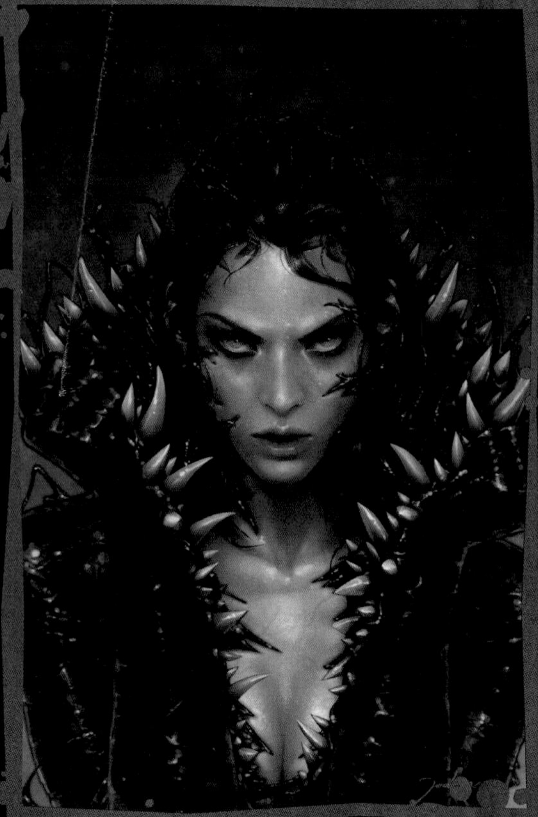

#19 MARY JANE VARIANT
BY **JEEHYUNG LEE**

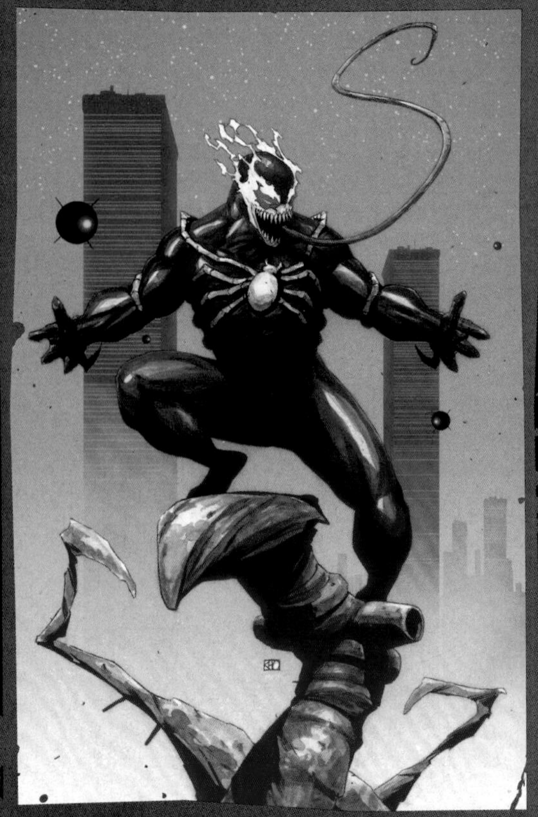

#20 2099 VARIANT
BY **KHOI PHAM** & **MORRY HOLLOWELL**

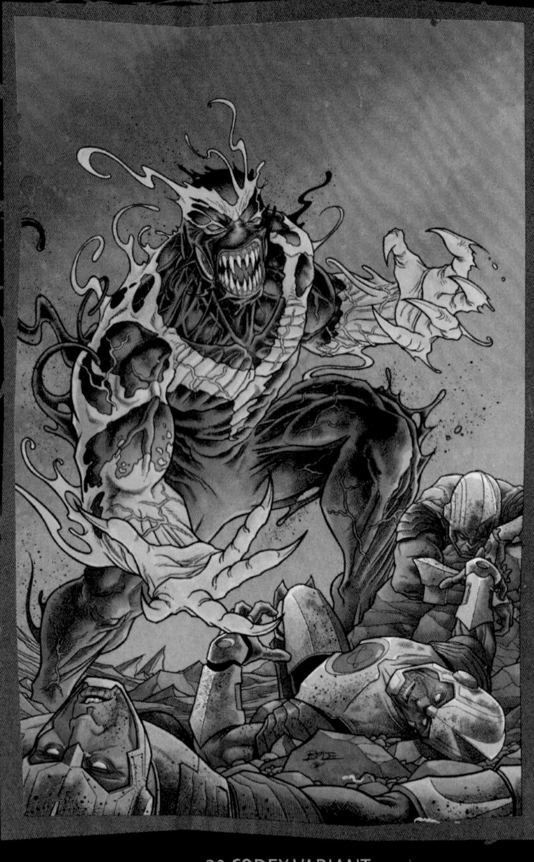

#20 CODEX VARIANT
BY **RYAN BODENHEIM** & **MICHAEL GARLAND**